T5-BQA-823

Alter Orient und Altes Testament
Veröffentlichungen zur Kultur und Geschichte
des Alten Orients und des Alten Testaments

Band 236

Ronald H. Sack

Neriglissar – King of Babylon

Alter Orient und Altes Testament

Veröffentlichungen zur Kultur und Geschichte des Alten Orients
und des Alten Testaments

Herausgeber

Manfried Dietrich · Oswald Loretz

1994

Verlag Butzon & Bercker Kevelaer

Neukirchener Verlag Neukirchen-Vluyn

Neriglissar – King of Babylon

Ronald H. Sack

1994

Verlag Butzon & Bercker Kevelaer

Neukirchener Verlag Neukirchen-Vluyn

Die Deutsche Bibliothek – CIP-Einheitsaufnahme

Sack, Ronald Herbert:
Neriglissar – king of Babylon / Ronald H. Sack. – Kevelaer: Butzon und Bercker; Neukirchen-Vluyn: Neukirchener Verl., 1994
(Alter Orient und Altes Testament; Bd. 236)
ISBN 3-7666-9894-X (Butzon und Bercker)
ISBN 3-7887-1480-8 (Neukirchener Verl.)
NE: GT

Herstellung: Weihert-Druck GmbH, Darmstadt
Printed in Germany
ISBN 3-7887-1480-8 Neukirchener Verlag
ISBN 3-7666-9894-X Verlag Butzon & Bercker

Preface

In recent years, the Chaldean, or Neo-Babylonian, Period has received as much attention as virtually any other area within the field of Assyriology. Thanks to the noble efforts of Dandamaev, Joannes and many others, great strides have been made in the way of piecing together the varied sources surviving the ages for the purpose of writing a detailed, analytical history of the period. Several worthwhile efforts have been made to fathom the personal letters and economic documents of the entire age to gain a knowledge of how the "system" functioned. While corpora of letters and contracts in transliteration, translation and copy have appeared with only occasional paragraphs or pages of commentary, they, nevertheless, have added a great deal to our knowledge of the period and have further illustrated the fact that there is, literally, a mountain of material with which to deal. To subject every letter or published contract to the utmost scrutiny would perhaps require a lifetime. Nevertheless, worthwhile attempts have been made to synthesize and analyze the increasing quantity of evidence with an eye to revising standard studies such as those of San Nicolò, which were based only on a limited quantity of material available half a century ago. While San Nicolò's studies were significant, at times detailed in the extreme and, consequently, of great value to the student of the period, they were, unfortunately, narrow in their scope and tended to focus on only one or two sites. While an examination of documents from one city may yield interesting conclusions, they are not necessarily applicable to all sites at all times. Work presently being done recognizes the fact that each area from which cuneiform documents can be obtained must be studied in order to gain a more complete perspective.

While the writing of a "political" history of the Chaldean period has proved to be somewhat difficult, sources that might enable such a survey to be done are available to a much greater extent than they were even twenty years ago. Not only has the work of A.K.Grayson and Erle Leichty resulted in the publication of collections of Chronicles and a massive Catalogue of British Museum tablets available for analysis, but studies of the reigns of Nebuchadnezzar by Wiseman and Nabonidus by Beaulieu have proved to be very valuable. While the problems with writing a history of the period are, in many respects, the same as before (i.e, too many sources in one place, too few in others), much progress has been made. There is still much to be done, of course, but our knowledge of the period is certainly much more complete today.

What is contained in the following pages is, certainly, not a solution to any or all of the problems that remain to be solved. It does not pretend to be either an "economic" analysis of the entire period or a "political" history of it. It is, however, an attempt to analyze the sources for the reign of Neriglissar, king of Babylon (560-556 BC). Included in this analysis are the Greek, Latin and Hebrew sources, as well as material from the Middle Ages. In addition, available cuneiform documents are discussed; among these are over twenty that have never appeared in photograph, transliteration or translation before. Some of these texts provide us with valuable information concerning the king's reign itself, while others elaborate on the activities of prominent "families" in Babylonia in the sixth century, BC. It is for them and the privileges connected with their use that I owe my heartfelt thanks to Dr. John Curtis and Mr. Christopher Walker, Keeper and Assistant Keeper, respectively, of the Department of Western Asiatic Antiquities of the British Museum.

At the rear of this volume, the reader will find an edition of over one hundred contract tablets dated in the reign of Neriglissar, which includes commentary where pertinent. Since over one hundred and ninety tablets are known to have been dated in the king's reign, one might legitimately brand the included text edition as incomplete. There are, however, several reasons for this. First, many of the previously-published tablets are fragmentary or are too short to enable meaningful translation. Second, while the approximately twenty Neriglissar texts copied by Pinches in the nineteenth century were published in *CT* 55, 56 and 57, most were in pitiful condition when Pinches copied them; they are in even poorer condition now. In fact, only two (*CT* 55:669 and *CT* 57:329) are long enough or well preserved enough to enable translation or analysis. Finally, although texts discussed in Chapter 3 include many not found in the text edition, they have fairly recently appeared in transliteration and translation in articles in professional journals. In addition, considering the length of the texts published by Evetts, Winckler and Pinches (*VR* 67, 1-4) and the names of the persons contained therein, it was essential to provide collated transliterations and translations of these important British Museum documents. Reviews of BT 6-B written by Peiser and Tallqvist in the nineteenth century point to the necessity for collations of these important texts. A list of the personal names included in the documents will be found at the rear of the volume as well.

In conclusion, I should like to extend my thanks to the Department of Western Asiatic Antiquities for enabling me to collate the documents (published previously by Evetts) while I was in London in May of 1990. I should also like to thank North Carolina State University for providing me with the funds allowing me to photograph, transliterate and translate the previously-unpublished Sippar tablets for inclusion in this volume.

Raleigh, North Carolina
April 30, 1993

Table of Contents

Abbreviations

AfO	*Archiv für Orientforschung*
AnOr	*Analecta Orientalia*
AOATS	*Alter Orient und Altes Testament -- Sonderreihe*
ArOr	*Archiv Orientalní*
BIN	*Babylonian Inscriptions in the Collection of James B. Nies*
BiOr	*Bibliotheca Orientalis*
BM	*Babylonian Tablets in the Collection of the British Museum*
BR	M. San Nicolò, *Babylonische Rechtsurkunden aus dem 6 Jahrhundert v. Chr.*
BRM	*Babylonian Records in the Library of J. Pierpont Morgan*
Camb.	J. N. Strassmaier, *Die Inschriften von Cambyses*
CT	*Cuneiform Texts from Babylonian Tablets in the British Museum*
Cyr.	J. N. Strassmaier, *Die Inschriften von Kyros, König von Babylon*
EvM	B. T. A. Evetts, *Inscriptions of Evil-Merodach*
GCCI	R. P. Dougherty, *Goucher College Cuneiform Inscriptions*
JCS	*Journal of Cuneiform Studies*

JNES	*Journal of Near Eastern Studies*
Langdon, *Kish*	*Oxford University Joint Expedition to Mesopotamia, Excavations at Kish:* III
Liverpool	J. N. Strassmaier, *Die babylonischen Inschriften im Museum su Liverpool, Actes du 6ᵉ Congrès International des Orientalistes,* II, Section Sémitique I (1985)
Lutz, *UCP*	*University of California Publications in Semitic Philology*, Vol. 9
NBC	Nies Babylonian Collection
Nbk	J. N. Strassmaier, *Inschriften von Nabuchodonosor, König von Babylon*
Nbn	J. N. Strassmaier, *Die Inschriften von Nabonidus, König von Babylon*
NCBT	Newell Collection of Babylonian Tablets
Ner	B. T. A. Evetts, *Inscriptions of Neriglissar*
Peiser, *Rechtsleben*	F. E. Peiser, *Aus dem babylonischen Rechtsleben*
PTS	Princeton Theological Seminary
R	H. C. Rawlinson, *The Cuneiform Inscriptions of Western Asia*
San Nicolò, *Prosopographie*	M. San Nicolò, *Beiträge zu einer Prosopographie neubabylonischer Beamten der Zivil-und Tempelverwaltung*
Speleers, *Recuel*	L. Speleers, *Recueil des inscriptions de l'Asie antérieure des Museés Royaux du Cinquantenaire à Bruxelles*
TCL	*Textes cunéiformes, Musée du Louvre*

TEBR	F. Joannes, *Textes Économiques de la Babylonie Récente*
TLB	*Tabulae Cuneiformes à F. M. Th. de Laigre Bohl Collectae*
TMH	*Texte und Materialen der Frau Professor Hilprecht Collection of Babylonian Antiquities im Eigentum der Universität Jena*
VAB	*Vorderasiatische Bibliothek*
VAS	*Vorderasiatische Schriftdenkmäler*
YNER	*Yale Near Eastern Researches*
YOS	*Yale Oriental Series*
YOS. Res.	*Yale Oriental Series, Researches*
ZA	*Zeitschrift für Assyrologie*

Neriglissar, King of Babylon

Chapter One
The Sources

Before an attempt at writing the biography of Neriglissar can be made, it is essential that the available source material be noted and discussed. Unfortunately, what one might call "primary" source material (i.e., cuneiform documentation) for the political history of the reign is almost entirely lacking. One is therefore forced to use the numerous secondary works which have survived the ages. These, as their contents show, are interesting not only in the varied amounts of information they contain, but also because of the striking similarities or differences among them. Included in this group are the writings of the classical authors, as well as material from the Middle Ages. Some of these contain items not found elsewhere; others merely repeat what earlier writers had to say. Although the topic of the sources for the Neo-Babylonian period as a whole has already been treated by Assyriologists in several places, in this case it is worthwhile to attempt a reexamination.

The Cuneiform Sources

The reigns of a number of the monarchs of the Neo-Babylonian period are copiously attested either through the *Babylonian Chronicle* or numerous building inscriptions. Neriglissar, Amēl-Marduk and Labaši-Marduk are clearly exceptions. To date, no chronicle detailing any military campaign Amēl-Marduk or Labaši-Marduk may have conducted has ever been published. Likewise, only a small number of economic texts datable to the reign of Labaši-Marduk have been published and, in the case of Amēl-Marduk, the few vase fragments which do survive serve no useful purpose other than that of confirming the fact that Amēl-Marduk was the son of Nebuchadnezzar. Fortunately, several cylinder inscriptions and a short chronicle survive from Neriglissar's reign. While the language of the cylinders is quite formulaic, it nevertheless details building activity in Babylon and elsewhere during the king's reign. In attending to needed repairs in Esagila and Ezida, as well as to necessary work on his palace and the walls around Babylon, he was fulfilling a traditional responsibility of Babylonian monarchs.[1] His accounts provide us with a beautiful description of a royal attitude toward his responsibilities and his god that was, centuries later, to find its way (in different form) into the secondary literature of other peoples.

The Chaldean kings, like monarchs of earlier periods, left us accounts of military campaigns conducted during their reigns. For Neriglissar, only one such account survives. Although very brief, it details a campaign against a certain Appuašu, king of Pirindu, in Neriglissar's third year (557 BC). While greater attention to the contents of this chronicle will be reserved for a later chapter, it nevertheless suggests that the king may have conducted other campaigns elsewhere in earlier years.[2] Perhaps future discoveries will provide us with needed information regarding his first and second years.

In addition to the surviving cylinder inscriptions and chronicle, there are numerous economic texts that comment on Neriglissar's personal activities. In this regard, they are truly unique in that they comment on his personal activities prior to becoming king. The earliest of these are datable to Nebuchadnezzar's ninth and thirty-fourth years;[3] they suggest that he was already well advanced in age when he ascended the throne in 560 BC. Documentation from the reign of Amēl-Marduk reveals that Neriglissar had rather extensive business dealings with members of the Nūr-Sin and Egibi families, especially in regard to the affairs of the scribe[4] Nabû-apla-iddina, son of Balāṭu, who was faced with a number of obligations that he could not satisfy.[5] While the details of this activity are still incomplete (see below, Chapter 2), what does survive suggests that his business ties may have at least facilitated his succession to the throne. More detail will be provided on this topic later.

The economic texts are of considerable value for yet another reason. Their date formulae enable the historian to determine fairly accurately the length of the reign of not only Neriglissar, but also of the other members of his dynasty.

---

1 See Stephen Langdon, *Die neubabylonischen Königsinschriften* (= *Vorderasiatische Bibliothek* 4) Leipzig, 1912, 209 ff. (Neriglissar, Cylinders 1-4).

2 See A. Kirk Grayson, *Assyrian and Babylonian Chronicles* (= *Texts From Cuneiform Sources* Vol. 5) Locust Valley, 1975, 103 ff. (Chronicle 6).

3 J. Strassmaier, *Die Inschriften von Nabuchadonosor, König von Babylon* (= *Babylonische texte* Heft V-VI) Leipzig, 1889, Nbk 13, 266, etc.

4 BM30333 (= R. Sack, *Amēl-Marduk - 562-560 B.C.*, *Alter Orient und Altes Testament Sonderreche* 4) Neukirchen-Vluyn, 1972, 55 ff.

5 *Ibid.*, 35 ff.

It was with these tablets in hand that Parker and Dubberstein[6] devised the following chronology:

Nabopolassar	May 17(?), 626	-	Aug. 15, 605
Nebuchadnezzar	Sept. 7, 605	-	Oct. 8, 562
Amēl-Marduk	Oct. 8, 562	-	Aug. 7, 560
Neriglissar	Aug. 13, 560	-	Apr. 16, 556
Labaši-Marduk	May 3, 556	-	June 20, 556
Nabonidus	May 25, 556	-	Oct. 13, 539

While there are indications (though, admittedly, meager) that a coregency may have existed prior to Nebuchadnezzar's death,[7] texts published to date suggest that Neriglissar succeeded his predecessor sometime in early August of 560 BC. However, recent discoveries indicate that this may not have been the case. Whether his succession was the result of a *coup d'état* is still open to debate. More will be said on this subject later.

In addition to the vase fragments and contract tablets already mentioned, a Neo-Babylonian king list was discovered during the course of the excavations at Uruk.[8] This list is also interesting, particularly because of the inaccuracy of the lengths of the reigns and the fact that no figure is given for Nebuchadnezzar.

Nebuchadnezzar	
Amēl-Marduk	2 years
Neriglissar	2 years, 8 months
Labaši-Marduk	3 months
Nabonidus	5 years

6 Richard Parker and Waldo Dubberstein, *Babylonian Chronology, 626 B.C. - A.D. 75* Providence, 1956, 10-14.

7 See AOATS 4, 3 ff. for further commentary on this subject, see Donald Wiseman, *Nebuchadnezzar and Babylon* (Oxford, 1985) and H. Hunger and S. Kaufman, "A New Akkadian Prophecy Text" in *The Journal of the American Oriental Society*, Vol. 95, No. 3, 1975, 371 ff. It should be noted that not everyone agrees with this interpretation. See Weisberg (JNES 1974) and Dandamaev (BiOr 1974).

8 See Heinrich Lenzen, ed., *Vorläufiger Bericht über die Ausgrabungen von Uruk-Warka* (Berlin, 1956) vol. XVIII, p. 53. For a discussion of this list, see R. Borger, "Der Aufstieg des neubabylonischen Reiches" (*Journal of Cuneiform Studies*, XIX [1965]), p. 60.

Unfortunately, there is no way of knowing precisely who was responsible for this text or what sources its composer (or composers) utilized.[9]

The Classical Sources

In addition to the cuneiform documents, numerous secondary sources in Greek from the Classical, Hellenistic and Roman periods have survived. These deal with the Neo-Babylonian period as a whole, but nevertheless (in one or two instances) they contain information regarding Neriglissar specifically that is not mentioned elsewhere. Megasthenes, the earliest of these writers chronologically,[10] flourished at the time of Seleucus I Nicator (312-280 BC). He was an Ionian, who wrote primarily on the geography and people of India. He participated in several embassies to that country between 302-291 BC dispatched to the court of the Indian king Sandrocottus.[11] His *History of India*, as Josephus tells us[12], included in its fourth book a discussion of the Babylonian kings of the sixth century, BC, with particular attention, as might be expected, paid to Nebuchadnezzar. Unfortunately, his work has not survived. However, a fragment of it, including a dynastic list, has fortunately been preserved by a certain Abydenus (whose work will be discussed later) and this was in turn preserved by Eusebius. It reads in part as follows:

---

9 Mention should be made here of the large octagonal prism (found by Koldewey during the course of his excavations at Babylon) from the reign of Nebuchadnezzar. Unger refers to it as "der älteste Hof- und Staatskalender der Welt." See Eckhard Unger, *Babylon, die heilige Stadt nach der Beschreibung der Babylonier* (Berlin, Walter de Gruyter u. Co., 1931), p. 35. Although Amēl-Marduk is not specifically mentioned by name, the reference in Col. IV of the prism to "the crown prince" (pp. 290-91) is obviously intended to refer to him.

10 It is perhaps worth mentioning while both Herodotus and Xenophon deal with the Neo-Babylonian period in their works, both focus their attention on the reign of Nabonidus (whom Herodotus calls Labynetus), the fall of Babylon, and the takeover of Cyrus. Neither author mentions by name or discusses the reign of Amēl-Marduk. See George Rawlinson, *The History of Herodotus of Halicarnassus* (London, 1935) Bk. I, 188-191 and Xenophon, *Cyropaedia*, trans. by T.E. Page and W.H.D. Rouse (London, William Heinemann, 1912) Bk. IV, 6 and Bk. VII, 5.

11 Cary and Denniston, *The Oxford Classical Dictionary* (Oxford, The Clarendon Press, 1949), p. 553.

12 Flavius Josephus, *Contra Apionem in The Works of Flavius Josephus* with an English translation by H. St. John Thackeray (London, William Heinemann, 1926) Bk. I, 20.

> Abydenus, in his history of the Assyrians, has preserved the following fragment of Megasthenes, who says: That Nabuchodrosorus (Nebuchadnezzar), having become more powerful than Hercules, invaded Libya and Iberia, (Spain), and when he had rendered them tributary, he extended his conquests over the inhabitants of the shores upon the right of the sea ... he expired, and was succeeded by his son Evilmaruchus (Evil Merodach), who was slain by his kinsman, Neriglisares (Neriglissor), and Neriglisares left a son, Labassoarascus (Labarosoarchod), and when he also has suffered death by violence, they made Nabannidochus king, being of no relation to the royal race.[13]

It is impossible, of course, to determine exactly what sources Megasthenes used in the writing of this account. The length of the reign of each king is not designated in number of years, even though the list in what it covers is correct. However, it is possible that Megasthenes had access to cuneiform documents which were still being composed in the Hellenistic period and that he could read the script himself, or had someone available who could read it for him. The relationship of one king to another in his list, in addition to his mention of the fact that Nabonidus was not related to any of his predecessors, seems to confirm this assertion.

Following closely after Megasthenes is Berossus, a Babylonian priest of the third century, BC, who wrote in Greek on Babylonian history. He was, as Josephus remarks, "a Chaldean by birth, but familiar in learned circles through his publication for Greek readers of works on Chaldean astronomy and philosophy." He also says that he followed "the most ancient records"[14] in the preparation of his history, known either as

---

13 The English translation here employed is to be found in Isaac Cory, *Ancient Fragments of the Phoenician, Chaldean, Egyptian, Tyrian, Carthaginian, Indian, Persian and Other Writers* (London, 1832), pp. 71-72. This fragment is preserved by Eusebius in Greek in his *Preparatio Evangelica*, Caput IX, 41 and in Latin (Jerome's translation) in the *Chronicorum*, Lib. I, Caput X, 3. See J.P. Migne, *Patrologia Cursus Completus, Series Graecae* (Paris, 1857), vol. 19, 125-126.

14 Josephus, *Contra Apionem*, Bk. I, 19.

χαλδαικά or βαβυλωνικά; this was "dedicated to Antiochus Seleucus I (281-260 BC); apparently it was composed to provide the Macedonian king with the history of the land he ruled".[15]. Like the history of Megasthenes, Berossus' χαλδαικα has perished, but an important fragment of it has been preserved both by Josephus and Eusebius. It reads as follows:

> Nabuchodonosor, after he had begun to build the above-mentioned wall, fell sick, and departed this life, when he had reigned forty-three years; whereupon his son Evilmerodachus obtained the kingdom. He governed public affairs in an illegal and improper manner; and, by means of a plot laid against him by Neriglissoorus, his sister's husband, he was slain when he had reigned only two years. After his death, Neriglissor, who had conspired against him, succeeded him in the kingdom, and reigned four years. His son, Laborosoarchodus, obtained the kingdom, although a mere child, and reigned nine months. But, on account of the evil practices which he manifested, a plot being made against him by his friends, he was tortured to death.
>
> After his death, the conspirators having assembled, by common consent, put the crown on the head of Nabonnedus, a man of Babylon, one of the leaders of that insurrection ... In the seventeenth year of his reign, Cyrus came out of Persia.[16]

---

15 James Westfall Thompson, *A History of Historical Writing* (New York, MacMillan and Co., 1942), p. 12.

16 Cory, p. 67. See Josephus, *Contra Apionem*, Bk. I, 12-21 and Eusebius, *Chronicorum*, Lib. I, Caput XI. Both the Greek text of Josephus and the Latin version of Eusebius can be found in Migne, vol. 19, 126-131. See also Joanne Richter, *Berosi Chaldaeorum Historiae* (Lipsiae, 1825), pp. 64-68 and Müller, *Fragmenta Historicorum Graecorum* (Paris, 1848) vol. II, p. 504-505.

See also Stanley Burstein, *The Babyloniaca of Berossus* (= *Sources from the Ancient Near East*, 1/5) Malibu, 1978, 4 ff. and the discussion in Paul Schnabel, *Berossus und die babylonisch-hellenistirche Literatur*_(Hildesheim, 1968), 273-75.

Of all the lists of Neo-Babylonian monarchs which have survived and are contained in secondary works, the arrangement of Berossus most closely corresponds to that of the cuneiform documents.[17] Only in one instance, that of Labaši-Marduk, is there any discrepancy. It is obvious, I think, that, if Berossus himself could not read the cuneiform script, at least someone must have been at hand who could read it for him. As for Labaši-Marduk, it is hardly likely (in view of his overall accuracy) that Berossus could have been incorrect in his figures for the reign of this latter monarch. However, one is forced, then, into explaining why (at least according to the dated economic texts) the reigns of Labaši-Marduk and his successor Nabonidus overlap by almost one month, and why cuneiform tablets are known which document only about two months of his reign. It is possible, of course, that errors arising from manuscript transmission could have resulted in the nine month figure given by Josephus. It was this theory that prompted Parker and Dubberstein to propose a quite plausible alternative hypothesis (i.e., that the Greek *θ* could have been mistaken for a *β*).[18] This position seems all the more sensible since the earliest text from the reign of Nabonidus (May 25, 556 BC) is clearly dated nearly a full month prior to the latest document bearing the name of Labaši-Marduk (June 20, 556 BC).

There is an interesting piece of information contained in this list regarding Amēl-Marduk and his successor Neriglissar that is not mentioned in any other source. It is here stated that Neriglissar was the brother-in-

---

If the conclusions of Drews concerning the real nature of the *Babyloniaca* are accepted, then we are indeed fortunate to possess this information. It is the only source to assert that Neriglissar was the brother-in-law of Amēl-Marduk. Furthermore, it reflects what must have been an unstable political situation since it states that he ascended the throne of Babylon after assassinating his predecessor. See Robert Drews, "The Babylonian Chronicles and Berossus" in *Iraq* 37 (1975), 52-5.

17 This includes the reign of Nabopolassar, the founder of the dynasty. Berossus says he ruled twenty-one years, which is likewise corroborated by cuneiform sources. See Josephus, *Contra Apionem*, Bk. I, 19, and Eusebius, *Chronicorum*, Lib. I, Caput XI, 2. His commentary on Labaši-Marduk is also at least partially substantiated by cuneiform evidence. See Langdon, Nabonidus Cylinder VIII, Col. 5.

18 See Parker and Duberstein, p. 13 who suggest that confusion may have been the result of the transmission of Berossus' manuscript (if, indeed, that manuscript originally contained numerals designating the reigns of each king). A misreading of the numerals, then, might have occurred. However, their suggestion that a *theta* (θ) could have been mistaken for a *beta* (β) does not necessarily follow, since two years are designated for Amēl-Marduk, for which a *beta* would have been used. Perhaps Berossus himself used a source that was in error.

law of Amēl-Marduk. Thus far, no cuneiform evidence has been uncovered to lend support to this assertion, and no other writer before or after his time mentions it, though it is vaguely hinted at in Megasthenes.[19]

Alexander Polyhistor, our next source, was probably born about 105 BC in Miletus or Caria. He was carried off as a prisoner of war to Rome during an age when feuds between Marian and Sullan factions were all too prevalent. It is said that he was once the pedagogue of a certain Cornelius Lentulus and that he taught C. Julius Hyginus. He received the name Polyhistor because of his "voluminous historical writings" which covered a number of countries and peoples, including the Jews.[20] It seems that his works contained mostly material borrowed from other sources which no longer exist.[21] Like Megasthenes' *History of India*, Polyhistor's works have perished, but, again as with Megasthenes, portions are preserved in Eusebius. Included in these fragments is another dynastic list, which reads as follows:

> Then Nabupalsar (Nabopollassar), reigned 20 years; and after him Nabucodrossorus (Nebuchadnezzar), reigned 43 years ... And after Nabucodrossorus, his son, Amil-marudochus (Evil Merodach), reigned 12 years.
>
> And after him, Neglisarus (Neriglissor), reigned over the Chaldeans 4 years; and then Nabodenus (Nabonidus) reigned 17 years.[22]

---

19 See the discussion in Paul Schnabel, *Berossus und die babylonisch-hellenistische Literatur* (Hildesheim, Georg Olms, 1968), pp. 273-275.

20 Cary and Denniston, p. 35. For a commentary on Alexander Polyhistor and his value as an historian, see Felix Jacoby, *Fragmenta der griechischen Historiker* (Leiden, E.J. Brill, 1964), Dritter Teil A., p. 259 ff. Thompson, p. 13.

21 Thompson, p. 13.

22 The English translation of the Armenian version of Eusebius' *Chronicle* is from Cory, pp. 87-88. Cory employed Auchers' edition of the *Chronicle* published in Venice in 1818, pp. 44-45. A more readily available translation of the Armenian version of the *Chronicle* (in German) has been done by J. Karst, *Eusebius' Werke V. Die Chronik aus dem Armenischen übersetzt* (Leipzig, 1911). For the Latin version of Polyhistor, see Migne, vol. 19, 119 (Eusebius' *Chronicorum*, Lib. I, Caput VI, 5). See also Eusebius Pamphili, *Eusebii Chronicorum Libri Duo*, ed. by A. Schöne, 2 vols. (Berlin, 1866) and

The list is interesting for two reasons. First, Labaši-Marduk is omitted, for what reasons we do not know. Secondly, and more important, is the fact that the figures given in all cases are correct save one -- the assignment of twelve years to Amēl-Marduk. There does not seem to be any reason whatever to dispute Olmstead's conclusion that Alexander Polyhistor "borrowed from Berossus direct"[23], but why, then, are we presented with a twelve year reign for Amēl-Marduk? Two solutions seem plausible. Either the manuscript of Polyhistor which Eusebius used (or some previous one, of which his was a copy) registered an *iota* (ι) or < (ἔτος) before the *beta* (β) (assuming, of course, that numerical values were contained in it), or Eusebius himself was guilty of a misreading of the text.

Another writer who has left us varied information concerning the Neo-Babylonian period and, particularly, Neriglissar, is Josephus, a Jewish historian of the first century AD. He went to Rome during the reign of Vespasian, and later became a friend of the emperor's son Titus, in whose company he made a second trip to Rome after the fall of Jerusalem (70 AD).[24] In addition to his *Autobiography* and the *Jewish War*, he composed two works which, in part at least, cover the conquest of the Jews and the fall of Jerusalem in the time of Nebuchadnezzar as well as the release of Jehoiachin in the accession year of Amēl-Marduk. These works are the *Contra Apionem* and *Jewish Antiquities* (Ἰουδαικὴ Ἀρχαιολογία).

As we have already seen, the information contained in his *Contra Apionem* is largely derived from Berossus[25], and thus no further comments are necessary. However, the *Jewish Antiquities* presents a multitude of problems which are not so easily solved. Some of what Josephus included concerning the Jew Jehoiachin, Amēl-Marduk and the other members of the eleventh Babylonian dynasty is not to be found in any other source. Furthermore, due to the varied character of this information, it is almost impossible to dismiss the discrepancies because of difficulties encountered through transmission of manuscript. To begin with, Josephus (like all the writers we have dealt with thus far) preserves a Neo-Babylonian king list, which is totally unlike any we have heretofore encountered. After stating

---

particularly S. Hieronymus, Hieronymi Chronicon," 2 ed., in R. Helm, ed., *Die griechischen christlichen Schriftsteller der ersten Jahrhunderte, Eusebius' Werke*, vol. VII (Berlin, 1956).

23 A.T.E. Olmstead, *Assyrian Historiography* (University of Missouri Studies, 1916), p. 63.

24 Thompson, p. 105.

25 See note 14.

that Nebuchadnezzar lived "twenty-five years after the overthrow of Jerusalem" he continues as follows:

> After the death of Nebuchadnezzar his son Abilmathadachos, who took over the royal power, at once released Jechonias, the king of Jerusalem, from his chains and kept him as one of his closest friends, giving him many gifts and setting him above the kings in Babylonia. For his father had not kept faith with Jechonias when he voluntarily surrendered himself with his wives and children and all his relatives for the sake of his native city, that it might not be taken by siege and razed, as we have said before. When Abilmathadachos died after reigning eighteen years, his son Eglisaros took over the royal power and held it for forty years until the end of his life. After him the succession to the throne fell to his son Labosordachos and, after holding it nine months in all, he died.[26]

Josephus continues on to say that Babylon was taken by Cyrus after Labaši-Marduk's successor, Nabonidus, who was also called Belshazzar, had reigned eighteen years.

There is no difficulty in determining the source of the information contained in Josephus' first statement concerning the release of Jehoiachin. It is clearly taken from II Kings 25:27-30 and Jeremiah 52:31-2 where almost the exact same words occur. But what about the king list, and what about the statement that Neriglissar was the son of Amēl-Marduk? With the exception of the *Chronicle* of the Venerable Bede (who says he borrowed his material from the *Jewish Antiquities)* this list has no equal anywhere.[27] Josephus states several times that he never supplemented

---

26 Flavius Josephus, "Antiquities of the Jews" in *The Works of Flavius Josephus*, trans. by H. St. John Thackeray (London, William Heinemann, 1926-37), Bk. X, 11, 2.

27 See Bedae, "Chronicorum" in *Chronica Minora*, vol. III in Theodor Mommsen, *Monumenta Germaniae Historica* (Berlin, Apud Weidmannof, 1898), vol. IX, pp. 269, 146 and pp. 270, 149. The exact same words occur here.

material from the Scriptures with information gathered from other places[28], yet here is clearly an instance where that has been done.[29]

Unfortunately, as Feldman has pointed out[30], a few people have attempted to determine the sources Josephus employed in the compilation of his *Jewish Antiquities*. Nevertheless, it seems that one or two conclusions can be drawn. First, Josephus probably obtained his nine-month figure for the reign of Labaši-Marduk from Berossus' χαλδαικά (from his list preserved in the *Contra Apionem*). Secondly, the only sources containing any information which even approximates what is in the rest of the list are the rabbinical works (to be discussed more fully later), composed long after his time, and the *Book of Baruch* forming part of the *Apocrypha*. The *Talmud* states that Nebuchadnezzar reigned forty-five years[31], which at least partially parallels Josephus' statement. However, both the *Talmud* and the midrashim forming what is known as the *Midrash Rabbah*[32] declare that Belshazzar was the successor of Amēl-Marduk (perhaps because of the similarity in the names Bel-sharra-uṣur and Nergal-sharra-uṣur), leaving Labaši-Marduk and (what is more important) Neriglissar, who is not mentioned in any of the midrashim or in the Apocrypha and who is given a forty year reign in the *Jewish Antiquities*, completely out of the sequence. Also, the *Book of Baruch*[33] fails to mention Amēl-Marduk, but instead declares Belshazzar to be the direct successor of Nebuchadnezzar (as does Daniel 5). Indeed, Amēl-Marduk is not even mentioned in the Apocrypha. Furthermore, the *Talmud* assigns a twenty-three year reign to Amēl-Marduk (based, it is said, on Jewish tradition), a figure which finds no previous parallel elsewhere, including

---

28 μήτε προστιθεὶς πράγμασιν αὐτὸς ἰδία (*Antiquities of the Jews*, Bk. I, 17).

29 See the treatment of Harold W. Attridge, *The Interpretation of Biblical History in the Antiquitates Judaicae of Flavius Josephus (= Harvard Dissertations in Religion*, 7) Missoula, 1976, 1 ff.

30 Louis Feldman, "Scholarship on Philo and Josephus 1937-1959" in *The Classical World* (vol. 55, no. 8-9 May, 1962 and June, 1962), p. 236 ff. and 278 ff. Unfortunately, this is only a bibliographical essay rather than an attempt to deal with the problem itself.

31 Dr. I. Epstein, ed., *The Babylonian Talmud* (London, Soncino Press, 1938), *Megillah* 11b.

32 Rabbi Dr. H. Freedman, *Midrash Rabbah* (London, Soncino Press, 1901). See in particular II *Targum Esther* 1. 1 (vol. IX, p. 44), *Bereshit Rabbah* XLIV, 15 (vol. I, p. 370) and especially Esther Rabbah III, 1, 8 (Vol. IX, p. 51) and *Esther Rabbah*, *Proem*, 12 (vol. IX, p. 17) where it is implied that Belshazzar was the son of Amel-Marduk.

33 See Alfred Rahlfs, *Septuaginta* (Stuttgart, Privilegierte Württembergische Bibelanstalt) *Baruch* I, 1-15. This account is probably based on Daniel 5-6 where only Nabonidus and Belshazzar are mentioned.

the works of Josephus. Finally, Josephus' comment that Nabonidus and Belshazzar are one and the same person cannot be found in any source (save Bede's *Chronicle*) either before or after his time. In view of the fact that the author of the *Jewish Antiquities* was well acquainted with Berossus, and since neither his figures nor relationships are in accord with even existing rabbinical works, several analysts, Schaff and Wace included, have been led to the assumption that he was either possessed of a superficial knowledge of Jewish tradition, or else, for some unexplained reason, he altered it.[34] However, his obvious unwillingness to tamper with the account given in the Old Testament seems to point more in the direction of still another source employed by Josephus that is no longer extant.[35]

The second century AD produced another writer, noted for his versatility and meticulousness, whose work contains mention of our period. This is Claudius Ptolemy, whose studies in the field of geography, astronomy and mathematics are well known to the student of Ancient History. His famous κανῶν βασιλέων or *Ptolemaic Canon*, preserves (with but one exception) in order the names of the Chaldean monarchs from Nabopolassar through Nabonidus and includes the lengths of their reigns. It reads as follows:

Ναβοπολλασσάρου ἔτη κά	(21 years)
Ναβοκολασσάρου ἔτη μγ́	(43 years)
'Ιλλοαρουδάμου ἔτη β'	(2 years)
Νεϱικασολασσάρου ἔτη δ'	(4 years)
Ναβοναδίου ἔτη ιή	(17 years)[36]

34 Thackeray seems to be in accord with this judgment, but goes a step further: "Anyhow, he has to attract his Greek readers, diversified the record with a mass of legendary matter, which is of considerable interest to us. He has called from all quarters ... But a large proportion find parallels, or partial parallels, in the Rabbinic works, which were not compiled until a century or more later, and these, with other traditions for which no parallel can be traced, may be regarded as a valuable collection of the first century Midrash." See H. St. John Thackeray *Josephus, the Man and the Historian* (New York, Jewish Institute of Religion Press, 1929), p. 91.

35 The subject of Jehoiachin's release from prison and the relationship of Josephus account of it to the Bible and rabbinical sources will be treated more fully in Chapter 2.

36 See Κλαυδίοου πτολεμαίου μαθηματικὴ συντάξις, *Composition Mathematique de Claude Ptolemée*, ed. by M. Halma (Paris, Chez Henri Grande, Librairie, 1813), vol. I, p. LXXI. See also the work by E.J. Bickerman, *Chronology of the Ancient World* (Ithaca, Cornell University Press, 1968), p. 108. His precision suggests that he either had access to the documents themselves, or

Although the list is correct in the number of regnal years it lacks mention of Labaši-Marduk. Such was also the case with Polyhistor's list, as we have seen.[37] But did Ptolemy leave him out of the list because he used Polyhistor (who was dependent upon Berossus) as a source, or because he thought him too insignificant to include in his canon? The second conclusion is certainly possible, since a discrepancy exists between Polyhistor and the *Ptolemaic Canon* in the number of years assigned to Amēl-Marduk, although this may be due to an error on the part of Eusebius. One, of course, will never know, but if he derived his information direct from Berossus, one wonders why his list is incomplete.

The last of the writers normally included in this group requires only one or two sentences. This is Abydenus, whom we have already encountered. Writing in the second or third century, AD, he was largely a preserver of information contained in the older works composed before his time. His great work was περὶ 'Ασσυρίων, in which segments of Alexander Polyhistor and Megasthenes were included. The work has perished, but, thanks to Eusebius, the fragment of Megasthenes which he included in his book dealing with the Neo-Babylonian period has survived.[38]

Late Roman and Medieval Sources

The third and fourth centuries of the Christian era witnessed the production of numerous chronicles which were intended to be records of important historical events from the time of Adam to the dates of their composition. Perhaps the most famous of these was the *Chronicle* (χρονικοὶ κανόνες) of Eusebius Pamphilius, or Eusebius, Bishop of Caesarea (c.a. 265-340 AD). It commenced with the birth of Abraham and terminated (until Jerome extended it during the course of translating it into Latin) in 324 AD. Eusebius used the previous work of Julius Africanus as a model, and the result was "a comparative chronology of all known people." It "was, above all, apologetic, the author wishing to prove by means of it that the Jewish religion, of which the Christian was the

---

perhaps utilized an intermediary source (now lost) based on the dates given in the documents.

37 See note 20.

38 "Abydenos" in Georg Wissowa, *Realencyclopaedie der classischen Altertumswissenschaft* (Stuttgart, J.B. Metzherscher Verlag, 1894), vol. I, p. 130. See also note 14. Beyond this, nothing relevant to this period from περὶ 'Ασσυρίων has survived.

legitimate continuation, was older than the oldest of heathen cults, and thus deprive pagan opponents of their taunt of novelty, so commonly hurled against Christianity.[39] It was divided into two books, with the first continuing in narrative form to 329 AD, and the second consisting of chronological tables (Olympiads, consular fasti, Egyptian, Assyrian and Babylonian king lists, etc.). In all cases Eusebius considered Jewish history as "the point of departure of all peoples. Every date in the end is calculated according to the chronology of the Bible, even the succession of Roman emperors."[40] The Greek version of the text is lost, but Greek fragments survive, as well as Armenian, Syriac, and Latin (Jerome) translations.

The importance of the *Chronicle* lies not in the fact that it sheds new light on Neriglissar's reign or the reigns of any Neo-Babylonian monarchs, for there is nothing in it (save one short comment in Book II)[41] that is not to be found elsewhere. It is noteworthy, however, because it preserves not only Berossus (through Josephus) but also those fragments of Megasthenes (via Abydenus) and Polyhistor which would have been otherwise been totally lost to us. While the information may be partially inaccurate, nevertheless Eusebius has performed a service which surely merits commendation.

Eusebius Sophronius Hieronymus, more often referred to as St. Jerome (340-420 AD) is yet another writer who dealt with Mesopotamian and Jewish history in the sixth century, BC. Although he is better known for his Latin Vulgate Bible and his translation of Eusebius' *Chronicle*, he was also responsible for composing commentaries on several books of the Old Testament, including Daniel and Isaiah. These are important for our purposes, because some of the information he includes is not to be found in any source, including the rabbinical works.

---

39 Philip Schaff and Henry Wace, *A Select Library of the Nicene and Post Nicene Fathers of the Christian Church* (Grand Rapids, William Beerdman's Publishing Co., 1961), vol. I, p. 31.

40 Thompson, p. 129.

41 See notes 11, 14, 15, and 20. Eusebius also mentions (though only briefly) Amēl-Marduk in Book II of his *Chronicle*. See Migne, vol. XIX, 465-466. Another edition of Eusebius' *Chronicle*, Book II, was published by John Knight Fotheringham, *Eusebii Pamphili Chronici* (London, Humphrey Milford, 1923), pp. 178, 22. Here the following interesting words appear: "*Mortuo Nabuchodonosor Babyloniorum rege suscepit imperium Evilmerodach. Cui successit frater eius Baltasar.*" This statement of Eusebius (that Amel-Marduk was the brother of Belshazzar) is thus not in agreement with either the Book of Daniel, the Apocryphal *Book of Baruch*, or the Midrash *Esther Rabbah* (a source composed much later) where it is implied that Belshazzar was Amēl-Marduk's son. See note 33.

To begin with, his commentary on Daniel, Chapter 5:1, includes a king list, commencing with Nebuchadnezzar and ending with Belshazzar.[42] His list is an unbroken succession from father to son. What is interesting is that Nebuchadnezzar is the only king to whom a definite number of years is assigned. Also, Belshazzar is mentioned as having been the son of Labaši-Marduk; this cannot be found in any other source. Jerome himself says that he got his information from Josephus (his exact words are *refert indem Iosephus*), probably from his *Jewish Antiquities*, Book X, 11, 2. Yet Jerome does not mention the lengths of the reigns of the kings, nor does he equate the name Nabonidus with Belshazzar, as we have seen Josephus does. Since there is no mention in the *Jewish Antiquities* of the relationship of Labaši-Marduk to Belshazzar, perhaps Jerome simply implied what he thought was obvious.

Further information regarding Amēl-Marduk specifically lies in Jerome's commentary on the Book of Isaiah. It concern his accession to the throne following Nebuchadnezzar's death. According to this source, the "magnates of the state" objected to his ascending the throne because they feared Nebuchadnezzar might somehow return. Hence, they prevented him from doing so. Jerome describes this incident as "a fable told by the Hebrews" (*narrant Hebraei huius modi fabulam*).[43] Yet this "fable" is not found in any rabbinical source, nor is it mentioned elsewhere.

The *Liber Genealogus*, or *Liber Generationis*, like the several chronicles before it, deals with Jewish and Mesopotamian history in the time of Amēl-Marduk and Neriglissar. Composed probably in the fifth century of the Christian era[44], this work included the earlier composition of Hippolytus of Porta, a contemporary of Clement of Alexandria and

---

42 See S. Hieronymi, *Presbyteri Opera Commentarium in Danielem II*, Visio V, 1 in *Corpus Christianorum Series Latina* (Turnholti, Typographi Brepobs Editores Pontifici, 1964), vol. 75A, p. 820. Here the following words appear: *post Nabuchodonosor, qui regnavit annis quadraginta tribus, successisse in regnum eius filium qui vocabatur Evchil-marodach – de quo scribit et Ieremias: quod in primo anno regni sui levaverit caput regis Iudae et eduxerit eum de domo carceris in regno patris successerit filius eius Neglissar, post rursum filius eius Labor-sordech, quo mortuo, Baltasar filius eius regnum tenuerit quem nunc scriptura commemorat.*

43 S. Hieronymi, *Presbyteri Opera Commentarium in Esaiam V*, Visio XIV, 19 in *Ibid.*, vol. 75, pp. 169-170. See also Louis Ginsberg, *The Legends of the Jews* (Philadelphia, The Jewish Publication Society of America, 1946), vol. VI, pp. 427-428.

44 For a discussion of the composition of the Liber Genealogus, see Theodor Mommsen, "Auctores Antiquissimi" in *Monumenta Germaniae Historica* (Berlin, Apud Weidmannof, 1892), vol. IX, p. 78.

Tertullian (which in turn was based on that of Julius Africanus) and it probably served as a source for the later *Chronicle of Fredegar*.[45] In mentioning Amēl-Marduk (called Ulemadar) and the release of the Jew Jehoiachin (Iechonias) it gives no new information, but merely reiterates what is contained in the Bible (Jeremiah 52:31-3) and II Kings 25:27-30) and in Josephus (*Jewish Antiquities* X, 11, 2).[46]

The seventh, eighth and ninth centuries produced yet three other chroniclers in whose works references to Amēl-Marduk and Neriglissar occur. The first of these, the Venerable Bede, (672-735) probably composed his *Chronicle* around 730 AD. In it he utilized not only the Old Testament (Jeremiah and II Chronicles) and the writings of St. Augustine and Ambrose, but also those of Eusebius, Jerome (his commentary on Daniel is often quoted) and especially Josephus.[47] In fact, as has already been pointed out, it is from the tenth book of the *Jewish Antiquities* (which Bede mentions by name) that his Neo-Babylonian list comes. Furthermore, his stories of the beginning of the Captivity and the final release of Jehoiachin are lifted directly from the Book of Jeremiah, which he also mentions by name.[48]

---

45 "Liber Genealogus" in Georg Wissowa, *Realencyclopaedie der classischen Altertumswissenschaft* (Stuttgart, J.B. Metzherscher Verlag, 1913), vol. VIII, p. 1878. For a discussion of the relationship of the *Liber Genealogus* to the *Chronicle of Fredegar*, see J.M. Wallace-Hadrill, *The Fourth Book of the Chronicle of Fredegar and its Continuations* (London, Thomas Nelson and Sons, Ltd., 1960), p. XI where the sources of the Chronicle are discussed. See also the prologue to the Chronicle itself (p. 1) where the author(s) states, "I have most carefully read the chronicles of St. Jerome, of Hydatius, of a certain wise man, of Isidore and of Gregory, from the beginning of the world to the decline of Guntramm's reign." The "certain wise man," says Walter Goffart in "The Fredegar Problem Reconsidered" in *Speculum* (April, 1963), p. 210, "is almost certainly the anonymous author of the *Liber Generationis*." Further comments may be found in Wattenbach and Levison's *Deutschlands Geschichtsquellen im Mittelalter bis zur Mitte des dreizehnten Jahrhunderts* (Weimar, Herman Bohlaus Nachfolger, 1952), vol. I, p. 54, and an excellent review of the possible sources used by the composer of the *Liber Generationis* can be found in Martin Schanz, *Geschichte der römischen Literatur* (München, C.H. Becksche Verlagsbuchhandlung, 1914), IV. Teil, I. Band, pp. 64-65 and 516-517.

46 See "Liber Generationis" in *Chronica Minora*, Volumen I in Theodor Mommsen, *Monumenta Germaniae Historica* (Berlin, Apud Weidmannof, 1892), vol. IX, p. 181. It should be noted, however, that an interval of thirty years is mentioned separating the beginning of the Captivity and the release of Jehoiachin, whereas in the Bible it is thirty-seven years.

47 See notes 13-14.

48 For the precise location of these references in Bede's *Chronicle* see note 14. For an English translation, see Josephus Stevenson, "The Historical Works of

Georgius Syncellus, the last of what I have called the "Medieval sources," was a Byzantine chronicler of the late eighth and early ninth centuries. As his name implies, he was the "confidential companion" of the patriarch of Constantinople and from 784-806 he was in the service of Tarausius. He finally retired from service, at which time he completed his *Chronographia*, which included events from Adam to Diocletian. He is extremely important because he not only preserves information contained in Eusebius' *Chronicle*, but also includes segments of the *Ptolemaic Canon* and Josephus.

To say that Syncellus poses problems is an understatement. His *Chrongraphia* has king lists everywhere, with each one being different from the one that precedes or follows it. Part of the problem lies in the fact that he had so many sources with which to deal. Consequently, his attempt to give "equal time" to all resulted in a confusion that in several instances is beyond belief. To begin with, Syncellus' version of the *Ptolemaic Canon* gives the following information regarding the period Nabopolassar through Nabonidus:

Ναβοπολασάρου πατρὸς Ναβουχοδόνοσωρ ἔτη κά	(21 years)
Ναβοπολασάρου τοῦ καὶ Ναβουχοδόνοσωρ ἔτη μγ΄	(43 years)
᾿Ιλλοαρουδάμου ἔτη γ΄	(3 years)
Νιριγασολασάρου ἔτη ε΄	(5 years)
Ναβοναδίου τοῦ καὶ ᾿Αστυάγους ἔτη λδ΄	(34 years)[49]

One can immediately notice striking differences between the list and the section of the κανῶν Βασιλέων previously quoted.[50] Although both copies leave Labaši-Marduk out of the list, the years assigned to Amēl-Marduk, Neriglissar and especially Nabonidus by Syncellus are strikingly different from those cited before. In addition, Nabonidus is equated with Astyages. This does not occur in any source, although it is reminiscent of Josephus' relationship of Nabonidus to Belshazzar.

To complicate matters further, a second king list is included, which Syncellus states is derived from "ecclesiastical computations" (ἔτη κατὰ

the Venerable Beda" in *Church Historians of England*, I, Part 2 (London, Seeleys, 1853).

49 Georgius Syncellus, "Chronographia" in B.G. Niebuhr, *Corpus Scriptorum Historiae Byzantinae* (Bonnae, Impensis Ed. Weberi, 1829), vol. 12, p. 390-391.

50 See Bickerman, p. 108 to compare the figures Syncellus cites with those in the κανων Βασιλεων as it has come down to us through other channels.

τὴν ἐκκλησιαστικὴν στοιχείωσιν). The section relevant to our period reads as follows:

Ναβοπαλάσαρος ἔτη κά (21 years)
Ναβουχοδόνοσωρ ὑιὸς ἔτη μγ' (43 years)
'Ευειλὰδ Μάροδαχ ἔτη ε' (5 years)
Νιριγλήσαρος ὁ καὶ Βαλτασάρ ἔτη γ' (3 years)
Ναβονάδιος ὁ καὶ 'Αστυάγης Δαρεῖος 'Ασουήρου
Καὶ 'Αρταξέρξης ἔτη ιη' (17 years)[51]

The list is the total antithesis of the one cited previously. Not only are the figures for Amēl-Marduk and Neriglissar reversed, but not Neriglissar is for the first time equated with Belshazzar and Astyages, Darius, Xerxes and Artaxerxes are all declared to be one and the same person, namely Nabonidus, who is said to have ruled seventeen years. This list is repeated elsewhere in his *Chronographia*[52], as is the fragment of Berossus quoted in Josephus' *Contra Apionem*[53].

The blame for the confusion of both names and years which one finds in Syncellus' *Chronographia* can probably be laid at his doorstep. His work contains mention of every Greek source, from Megasthenes to Claudius Ptolemy, but he probably knew most of them only through Eusebius' *Chronicle*[54]. He perhaps had copies of Josephus' *Contra Apionem* (where Berossus' chronology is preserved) and the *Jewish Antiquities*[55], as well as the Scriptures. His attempt to incorporate all of this material into his work, however, resulted in erroneous quotation and the attribution of information to the wrong author[56]. While part of the fault probably lies in the manuscripts he used, nevertheless there is much contained in the *Chronographia* which cannot be dismissed on these grounds alone. His own carelessness seems a more likely cause of these discrepancies.

Finally, the end of the fifteenth century witnessed the publication of the so-called *Antiquitatum Variarum Volumina* XVII. It first appeared in

51 Syncellus, "Chronographia" in Niebuhr, p. 393.

52 *Ibid.*, p. 421-422.

53 *Ibid.*, p. 427.

54 See *Ibid.*, pp. 426-428.

55 See *Ibid.*, pp. 426-427.

56 See particularly *Ibid.*, pp. 427-428, where he distorts Berossus and Josephus while adding the equation Nabonidus = Astyages = Xerxes = Darius.

Venice in 1498 and was commented on by the "notorious monk" Annius Viterbensis. Its importance for our purposes lies in the fact that it includes a Neo-Babylonian king list supposedly lifted from the writings of Megasthenes. However, as J.W. Bosanquet pointed out long ago, "it has been copied unfortunately by some illiterate interpreter of history, who has largely interpolated his own imperfect ideas concerning the Babylonian kings, and owing to these interpolations, the passage has generally been rejected as spurious and worthless[57]. The list reads as follows:

Nabugodonosor, annis 45;
Amilinus Evilmerodach, annis 30;
Filius hujus primus Ragassar, annis 3;
Secundus Lab-Assardoch, annis 6;
Tertius Baltassar, annis 5.[58]

When compared to the fragment of Megasthenes (preserved by Eusebius through Abydenus) previously cited,[59] one immediately notices a number of striking differences. First, while it is true that no numerical figures appear in the preceding list, nevertheless the *Antiquitatum Variarum Volumina* XVII asserts that Neriglissar, Labaši-Marduk and Belshazzar were all sons of Amēl-Marduk. Secondly, the numbers of years given are not in accord with any list, not even those contained in Syncellus' *Chronographia*. What source (our sources) did the author use? Probably the Hebrew works, namely the *Talmud* and the *Chronicle* of Jerachmeel[60]. The figure of forty-five years assigned to Nebuchadnezzar is found only in the *Talmud*, while the assertion that Amēl-Marduk's three "successors" were all his sons has no parallel except in the Hebrew Chronicle of Jerachmeel. Annius therefore must have been acquainted with the Hebrew language and falsely attributed information taken from these works to Megasthenes.

---

57 J. W. Bosanquet, "Cyrus the Second" (*Transactions of the Society of Biblical Archaeology*, 1872), vol. I, p. 247.

58 See *Ibid.*, p. 262 and Dougherty, pp. 13-14.

59 See note 13.

60 See discussions of the Talmud and the *Chronicle of Jerachmeel*, as well as notes 64 and 66-67.

The Hebrew, Secondary Sources

Although the Hebrew sources comment extensively on the reign of Amēl-Marduk, only two contain mention of his successor. Of these, the Book of Jeremiah of the Old Testament seemingly associates Nergal-šarra-uṣur with the Babylonian Captivity, for in Chapter 39:3 we read:

> And all the princes of the king of Babylon came in, and sat in the middle gate, even Nergal-sharezer, Samgar-Nebo, Sarse-chim, Rab-saris, Nergal-sharezer, Rab-mag, with all the residue of the princes of the king of Babylon.

Although this passage has received much attention[61] and questions are still being raised as to the identification of the persons mentioned here, there seems little doubt, as Bright has already pointed out,[62] that Nergal-sharezer is to be identified with our Nergal-šarra-usur of the cuneiform tablets. This passage, more than likely, served as a source for Josephus' commentary on the capture of Jerusalem in his *Jewish Antiquities*, where he asserts that Nergal-šarra-usur was one of the several commanders taking part in the siege.[63] This information, coupled with the contents of the contract tablets discussed above, suggests that he was already advanced in both age and experience long before he ever ascended the throne.

---

61 "The names, however, are confused in Hebrew: 'Nergalsharezer, Samgarnebo, Sar-sekim the Rab-saris, Nergalsharezer the Rab-mag' We construct with the aid of vs. 13 ('...Nebushazban the Rab-saris, Nergal-sharezer the Rabmag') ... 'Samgar' conceals the name Sin-magir, a district of which Nergalsharezer is known from a contemporary inscription to have been governor (read sar simmagir). The two Nergalsharezers are the same person. This is almost certainly the Nergal-šarri-uṣur (Neriglissar) who succeeded Nebuchadnezzar's son on the Babylonian throne in 560." See John Bright, "Jeremiah" in *The Anchor Bible* (New York, Doubleday and Co., 1965), vol. 21, p. 243. See also von Soden, ZA 62, p. 86.

62 Flavius Josephus, "Antiquities of the Jews" in *The Works of Flavius Josephus*, trans. by H. St. John Thackeray (London, William Heinemann, 1926-37) Bk. X, 135. "As for the names of the commanders to whom the sack of Jerusalem was assigned, if anyone should desire to know them, they were Neregalsaros, Aremantos, Semegaros, Nabosaris, and Acharanpsaris."

63 All of the other Greek and Latin commentaries are either I) elaborations of scripture and, as such, say little about Nergal-šarra-uṣur or 2) are king lists which, ultimately, can be traced back to Berossus.

The last remaining Hebrew source to be accounted for is the work of a certain Jerachmeel ben Solomon (or Yerachmeel). Living in Southern Italy in the twelfth century, he was the author of a *Chronicle* which, like that of Syncellus before him, paid special attention to the Neo-Babylonian period. He employed numerous sources, including the works of Strabo, Nicolaus of Damascus, Josippon (Yosippon, or Pseudo-Josephus), Philo, the rabbinical works (II *Abot de Rabbi Nathan, Seder 'Olam Zuta* and *Wayikra Rabbah*) and especially those of Josephus and Jerome.[64] In using these sources, however, he, like Syncellus, confused them. The result was not only a further alteration of what had been written before his time, but the inclusion of material (undoubtedly, the result of his own errors) which is not to be found in any other source.

The section of the *Chronicle* dealing specifically with Amēl-Marduk includes a partial oversimplified king list, which reads as follows:

> Evil Merodach had three sons,
> whose names were Regosar, Lebuzer
> Dukh, and Nabhar, who was Belshazzar,
> with whom the Chaldean kingdom came to
> an end.[65]

The information is undoubtedly taken from Josephus (*Jewish Antiquities* X, 11, 2), although the names are badly distorted. Both Josephus and Jerachmeel equate the name Nabonidus with Belshazzar, yet Jerachmeel has further confused the arrangement by saying that Neriglissar, Labaši-Marduk and Nabonidus were all sons of Amēl-Marduk. Jerome, as will be recalled, also confused Josephus' list, but nowhere in his commentary on Daniel does the equation Nabonidus = Belshazzar appear.

In addition to this, Jerachmeel borrowed from Jeromes' commentary on Isaiah 14:19, where, as has already been noted, the "fable told by Hebrews" dealing with the circumstances surrounding Amel-Marduk's accession to the throne occurs. However, in retelling it, he presents an entirely new picture of the events immediately preceding Nebuchadnezzar's death. After referring to the release of Jehoiachin, he goes on to write the following:

---

64 "Jerachmeel ben Solomon" in Jakob Klatzkin, *Encyclopaedia Judaica* (Berlin, Verlad Esckol, 1931), vol. VIII, p. 1083.

65 Moses Gaster, *The Chronicle of Jerachmeel* (London, Royal Asiatic Society, 1899), p. 207.

> He did this because Nebuchadnezzar the Great did not keep faith with him, for the Evil-Merodach was really his eldest son; but he made Nebuchadnezzar the Younger king, because he had humbled the wicked. They slandered him to his father, who placed him (Evil-Merodach) in prison together with Jehoiachin, where they remained together until the death of Nebuchadnezzar, his brother after whom he reigned.[66]

These statements of Jerachmeel, especially the second relating the imprisonment of Amēl-Marduk together with Jehoiachin, find only a partial parallel in the *Wayikra Rabbah* (18, 2) and no parallel whatsoever in any Greek or Latin source. It is likely that they are the result of his own reading of additional words into the *Wayikra Rabbah* and the "fable" told by Jerome[67].

These, then, are the sources with which one has to deal. Obviously, most of them are repetitions, and there is much in them that is not based on historical fact. Nevertheless they are quite interesting and, when taken together, paint a fascinating picture of a king about whom his own contemporary cuneiform documents have been thus far strangely silent.

---

66 *Ibid.*, pp. 206-207. It should also be noted that Jerachmeel's tale about Amēl-Marduk regarding his removal of Nebuchadnezzar's corpse from the grave (mentioned in this section of the *Chronicle*) probably came from either the *Wayikra Rabbah* or II *Abot de-Rabbi Nathan*. He adds, however, that it was Jehoiachin who told Amēl-Marduk to remove the corpse. This is not found in any other source.

67 For a summary of theories developed by historians over the past century concerning the Neo-Babylonian and Persian Periods, see Dougherty, pp. 13-14 and particularly H.H. Rowley, *Darius the Mede* (New York, 1964). For a further examination of rabbinical sources, see H. Strack, *Einleitung zum Talmud und Midrash* (1921). See also William Adler, *Time Immemorial: Archaic History and Its Sources in Christian Chronography from Julius Africanus to Georgius Syncellus*. Washington, 1989, 1 ff. and John van Seters, *In Search of History*, New Haven, 1983, 8-54 and 60-99.

Neriglissar, King of Babylon

Chapter Two
Biography

It is, perhaps, somewhat of an overstatement to label what is contained in the following pages a "biography" of Neriglissar. We noted earlier that much of our information regarding the king comes from sources well removed from the Chaldean period chronologically. Furthermore, much of what the Greek and Latin sources say cannot be corroborated in any contemporary cuneiform evidence. It is, nevertheless, worthy of note that what survives provides us with more information concerning the "private life" of Neriglissar than about any other king of the Chaldean "dynasty." Also, unlike Nebuchadnezzar, Amēl-Marduk and especially Nabonidus, strongly positive or negative characterizations of the king are almost entirely lacking. Instead, the sources for Neriglissar's reign are very dry and straightforward. As such, they are probably more reliable, thus making an analysis of their contents considerably less difficult. As we shall see, what they tell us about Neriglissar's activities during the years prior to and after 560 B.C. is interesting in itself, and deserving of examination.

The earliest known mention of Neriglissar occurs in a contract dated in the ninth year of Nebuchadnezzar[1]. Our present evidence suggests not only that he was well advanced in age when he became king, but that he was a member of a prominent family known for its business activities in northern Babylonia.[2] Contracts dated in the reign of his predecessor,

---

1 See Strassmaier, *Nbk* 83. Translations and/or discussions of this text can be found in Koschaker, *Bürgschaftrecht*, p. 49, Peiser, KB 4, p. 186ff, and Kohler and Peiser, *Rechtsleben*, 1, p. 12ff.

2 *Nbk*. 266 (translated by Peiser, KB 4, p. 194ff.) This text is also discussed in an article by Vitali A. Beljawski, "Der politische Kampf in Babylon in den Jahren 562-556 v. Chr." in Manfred Lurker, ed., *In Memoriam Eckhard Unger. Beiträge zur Geschichte, Kultur und Religion des Alten Orients*, pp. 200. This text, dated to the second of Ululu of Nebuchadnezzar's thirty-fourth year, includes mention of the famous Nabû-aḫḫē-iddina, son of Šulâ of the Egibi house, with whom Neriglissar would have a seemingly profitable relationship for several years.

Although none of the contracts from this period contains mention of his family name, it is certainly possible that he came from the Nūr-Sin "house" that produced such businessmen as Iddina-Marduk (that is, if one attaches

Amēl-Marduk, indicate that he was active in dealings with members of the prestigious Egibi house, especially the famous Nabû-aḫḫē-iddina. One fascinating group of tablets commenting on these activities concerns the scribe[3] Nabû-apla-iddina, son of Balāṭu, who was faced with a number of obligations that he could not satisfy.4 Thus far, no text has been discovered or published that would solve the problem of the origin(s) of his financial predicament. It is known, however, that his creditors, anxious to recover their loans, laid claim to the scribe's property[5] and turned to Neriglissar (who undoubtedly already possessed considerable wealth) for satisfaction. Probably coming from a prestigious banking family,[6] he can be found buying property and loaning money in the reign of Amēl-Marduk. A number of contract tablets indicate that he purchased the house of Nabû-apla-iddina for the price of one mina of silver.[7] Subsequently, through his agent Nabû-aḫḫē-iddina of the Egibi house, he proceeded to pay off the numerous creditors (either in full or in part) awaiting reimbursement. As a consequence, he returned the eleven minas of silver loaned by the brothers Nabû-mukīn-apli and Zababa-uṣur. In yet another text, a certain Nabû-bāni-aḫi receives the (twenty-five and three-fourths) shekels of silver he

---

more than merely "coincidental" significance to the appearance of a Bēl-šuma-iškun as a witnesses in BM 30492 (=AOATS 4, p. 52, l. 13). It may be that we have here mention of Neriglissar's father, who is described elsewhere as a "wise prince" (*rub emqa*). See Langdon, VAB 4, p. 214.

See also D.J.Wiseman, *Nebuchadrezzar* and *Babylon* (Oxford, 1985), p. 9ff for further discussion of this matter.

3 See BM 30333, lines 1, 16-17 (=AOATS 4, no. 10, p. 55) for this information.

4 For treatments of this corpus of texts, see Herbert Petschow, *Neubabylonisches Pfandrecht* (Berlin, 1956), pp. 41ff. and 129ff. and J. Kohler and F.E.Peiser, *Aus dem babylonischen Rechtsleben* (Leipzig, Eduard Pfeiffer, 1894), vol. 3, p. 27ff.

5 See B.T.A Evetts, "Inscriptions of the reigns of Evil-Merodach, Neriglissar and Laborosoarchod" in *Babylonische Texte* (Leipzig, Eduard Pfeiffer, 1892), vol. 6-B, no. 19,3-6 and no. 16,2 (=AOATS 4 9 and 4, respectively). For a discussion of the phrase *pàni šudgulu rašutānu* ("to place at one's disposal) see Petschow, *Pfandrecht*, pp. 42 and 139ff, as well as notes 422 and 428 as well as Mariano San Nicolò, "Eine kleine Gefängnismeuterei in Eanna" in *Festschrift für Leopold Wenger*, Bd. II (München, C.H.Beck'sche Verlagsbuchhandlung, 1944), p. 31.

6 See above, note 2.

7 For a discussion of *ana šimi gamrutu*, see Herbert Petschow, *Die neubabylonischen Kaufformulare* (Leipzig, 1939), p. 45ff and *Pfandrecht*, pp. 35,118,120,126,129,135. After the accession of Neriglissar, the property of Nabû-apla-iddina is referred to as having gone "to the palace" (*ana ekalli*) in *Ner.9*.

loaned to Nabû-apla-iddina. Also, the three sons of one creditor, Bēl-ēṭir, namely, Bēl-iddina, Bēl-kāṣir and Ina-qībi-Bēl, receive fifteen shekels of silver "according to the rate set by the creditor",[8] silver with which Nabû-apla-iddina had been debited. This is confirmed by the copy of the agreement given to the older brother Bēl-iddina.[9] However, yet another trxt indicates that a certain Marduk-apla-uṣur, the son of the deceased creditor Bēl-zēra-ibni, was not as fortunate. He received only half of the money loaned Nabû-apla-iddina by his father.[10] In each case it was the responsibility of those receiving payments to inform the "royal scribes"[11] and to turn over their contract tablets to Neriglissar. An examination of the evidence[12] reveals that, periodically, tablets were drawn up recording the exact amounts of silver he paid out through Nabû-aḫḫē-iddina.[13] It is not known exactly how much money was owed by Nabû-apla-iddina or how many creditors he had. However, in view of the large amounts recorded in these tablets,[14] it is quite obvious that much of this story still remains to be written.

Earlier we noted that the dated contract tablets heretofore published offered no suggestion of any irregularity in Neriglissar's succession to the throne. All the evidence pointed to mid August of 560 B.C. as the probable date of Amēl-Marduk's death.[15] Furthermore, the earliest

---

8 *akī eṭēru ša rašutānu innetru*. From these documents, it cannot be said how much was actually loaned by Bēl-ēṭir and, consequently, what percentage of the loan the three surviving sons received. It also cannot be said whether or not Nabû-apla-iddina had put up his house as security (*maškānu*) when he received his loans.

9 *BM* 32853 (=AOATS 4 7).

10 See Petschow, *Pfandrecht*, pp. 41-42 and Peiser, *Rechtsleben* 3, p. 27ff. Lines 16-18 of BM 30302(=*EvM* 19 and AOATS 4 9) refet to a certain Nabû-aḫḫē-bulliṭ, who bore the responsibility of paying the remianing one-third mina of silver owed. In view of this, it is more likely that either he himself was indebted to Nabû-apla-iddina or that he owed money to Neriglissar and, through payment, the debt was cancelled.

11 See *Ibid.*, p. 42 and Mariano San Nicolò, "Zum *atru* und anderen Nebenleistungen im neubabylonischen Immobiliarkauf" in Orientalia(N.S.) 16 (1947), p. 286.

12 See texts BM 30302 and BM 30850 (=AOATS 4 9 and 11 respectively).

13 Text BM 30850 contains the phrase ina *šīmi bītišu* referring to the house of Nabû-apla-iddina which Neriglissar had purchased.

14 See AOATS 4 texts 10 and 11 (=BM 30333 and BM 30850). The former text(l. 3-6) records payments of forty-two shekels of silver to a certain Iddina-⌜ahu⌝ and five shekels to a Kurbanni-Marduk.

15 See Richard A. Parker and Waldo H. Dubberstein, *Babylonian Chronology, 626 B.C.-A.D. 75 (=Brown University Studies XIX)* Providence, Brown University Press, 1956, p. 12-13.

previously-published contract mentioning Neriglissar as "king of Babylon" can be dated to the twenty-third of Abu, 560 B.C., just six days after the latest document datable to Amēl-Marduk's reign.[16] However, new evidence suggests that this "orderly succession" may not have taken place. In fact, thanks to the contents of BM 75489(= text no.91--- a Sippar document published here for the first time)[17] we can now definitely establish the fact that texts were being dated to Neriglissar's accession year as early as late May of 560 B.C. The information contained in this document (although, admittedly, scanty) is significant for at least two reasons. First, the overlap of at least three months in the documents datable to the reigns of Neriglissar and his predecessor, Amēl-Marduk, has, to my knowledge, no parallel in the Chaldean period, and it is particularly intriguing in this instance, given the proximity of Sippar to Babylon. Secondly, although texts dated to the months of Ajaru, Simanu and Du'uzu of Amēl-Marduk's second year have been known for more than a century,[18] recently-catalogued contracts indicate that they continued to be dated in the same manner in Sippar as well![19] One would be foolhardy, of course, to jump to sweeping conclusions based on the contents of only one short text. However, it should really not be surprising to find a Sippar document identifying Neriglissar as "king of Babylon" earlier than was formerly thought. It will be remembered that the Babylonian priest Berossus asserted in his *Babyloniaca* that Amēl-Marduk's reign ended through assassination and that Neriglissar thus seized the throne through a *coup d'état*.[20] Furthermore, Wiseman noted years ago that Neriglissar appears to have been given some official responsibility in connection with the Ebabbar temple in Sippar by Nebuchadnezzar.[21] As will be seen shortly, information contained in sources from southern Babylonia has

---

16 *Ibid.*, p. 12 (=VAS 3 40).

17 This text was catalogued by Erle Leichty and appeared by number in vol. VIII of the *Catalogue of the Babylonian Tablets in the British Museum--- Tablets from Sippar 3* (London, The British Museum, 1988). I am indebted to Dr. John Curtis and Christopher Walker for being granted the privilege of including this and other Sippar texts in this volume.

18 See Evetts, *EvM* 21 and 24 (=AOATS 4 24 and 60, respectively), etc.

19 BM 74709 (receipt for wool dated to the fifteenth of Du'uzu, 560 BC); BM 74831 (receipt for a garment and bracelet-- ninth of Abu, 560) and BM 75106 (receipt for lambs delivered to Ebabbar-- month of Du'uzu, second year of Amēl-Marduk). All of these documents form a part of the British Museum Sippar collection.

20 See above, Chapter 1 discussion of Berossus' *Babyloniaca*.

21 See Donald J. Wiseman, *Chronicles of Chaldean Kings* (London, the British Museum, 1961), p.38.

suggested for years that Berossus was correct in asserting that Neriglissar was a usurper.

Once safely on the throne, Neriglissar appears to have 1) removed temple administrators from their positions of authority in areas where support for his rule would be minimal at best, or 2) established ties with prominent personnel in other temples. In the second instance, he seemingly formed an alliance with a certain Nabû-šuma-ukīn, the priest of Nabû and *šatammu* of the Ezida temple in Borsippa. He is the same person mentioned in two "real estate sale" documents dated in Amēl-Marduk's accession and first years (17 and 6 Tašritu, respectively).[22] They are important because the other individuals involved are Ina-qībi-Bēl, Bēl-iddina and Bēl-kāṣir, the same three sons of Bēl-ēṭir who received a portion of their deceased father's loan to Nabû-apla-iddina.[23] Although only a portion of BM 32210 survives, it is clear that a certain Širikti-Marduk, son of Nabû-udammiq, purchased a parcel of land[24] located in the city of Itbarratu from these men. However, it appears that the buyer died shortly after the deal was concluded and before the full price of the field was paid. As a result, the sale of the property was voided and his son, the same Nabû-šuma-ukīn, set about to recover the money that had been paid to the original owners.[25] This he subsequently did.[26] What is extremely fascinating, however, is that the three sons of Bēl-ēṭir returned the money to both Nabû-šuma-ukīn and the daughter of Amēl-Marduk, Indû. The relationship between these two persons remains a mystery, as does the role Indû played in the recovery of the money. However, what is known is that Berossus, in his *Babyloniaca*, states that Neriglissar had been married to Amēl-Marduk's sister prior to his ascending the throne (although this is not corroborated in the cuneiform sources), that Nabû-šuma-ukīn was already in the Ezida hierarchy by 560 BC, and that he requested the hand of Neriglissar's daughter, Gigitum, in marriage before the end of the king's accession year.[27] After this he disappears, and nothing more is known of his activities, either from the letters or the contract tablets. Although text

---

22 BM 32210 and BM 32879 (=AOATS 4 13 and 14).

23 See *Ibid.*, texts 7 and 8 (=BM 32853 and BM 30232 respectively).

24 See *Ibid.*, text 14, lines 8-9 (*ana kaspi iddinnu*). For a discussion of the phrase *ana kaspi nadānu*, see Petschow, *Kaufformulare*, p. 45ff and San Nicolò, "Parerga Babyloniaca II-III" in *Archiv Orientalní* 5, p. 61ff.

25 See *Ibid.*, text 14, line 13 (1/2 *ana šimi iddinana*).

26 *Ibid.*, text 14, lines 13-16.

27 In text 13, lines 1-2 (=Evetts, *Ner. 13*) he is both the priest of Nabû and *šatammu* of Ezida. For further discussion, see below, Chapter 3.

13 confirms that the marriage took place[28], it is, nevertheless, truly unfortunate that we possess no additional texts that might clarify the relationship between Nabû-šuma-ukīn, Amēl-Marduk's family, and Neriglissar himself. One can only hope that future discoveries will provide the "missing links."

With regard to the Ebabbar (temple of Šamaš) in Sippar, a somewhat different relationship appears to have existed. We have already noted meager indications of Neriglissar's "official responsibilities" during the reign of Nebuchadnezzar. In addition, if one accepts Wiseman's conclusions concerning the date[29] and contents of the still unpublished BM 55920, then one can say that he was charged with overseeing certain of the affairs of Ebabbar. This conclusion appears to be reinforced by the contents of text 91 (BM 75489) which, in addition to providing us with the earliest date for the beginning of Neriglissar's reign, also refers to the return of the overseer (*qīpu*) from Babylon with a group of artisans. Although the personal name is absent from the text, there can be no doubt that the individual being referred to is Nabû-balāṭu-ēriš, who held the office of "overseer of Ebabbar" from at least the month of Kislimu of Nebuchadnezzar's twenty-seventh year (578 BC).[30] Considering his long tenure in the office, coupled with the fact that his successor, Bēl-šūzibanni, does not appear until Neriglissar's third year[31] one is forced to conclude that the king was probably involved with affairs in Ebabbar before he ascended the throne, that the *qīpu* had long been his associate, and that Nabû-balāṭu-ēriš was replaced in 557 through a "normal" process of succession. Sippar and Borsippa may have constituted a "base of support" for his succession, despite the fact that documents continue to be dated in Amēl-Marduk's second year until at least the month of Abu, 560 BC.[32]

Finally, when one turns to the evidence from Uruk, one is immediately faced with an intriguing situation which may have involved

---

28 See also Peiser, *Rechtsleben* 3, p. 10 and Theophilus G. Pinches, "Babylonian Contracts and Tablets with Historical References" in *Records of the Past, New Series* (London, 1890), vol.4, p. 101ff.

29 See Wiseman, *Chronicles of Chaldean Kings*, p. 38.

30 See Mariano San Nicolò, *Beiträge zu einer Prosopographie neubabylonischer Beamten der Zivil- und Tempelverwaltung (=Sitzungsbeirchte der bayerischen Akademie der Wissenschaften)* München, 1941, p. 33.

31 See David B. Weisberg, *Guild Structure and Political Allegiance in Early Achaemenid Mesopotamia (=Yale Near Eastern Researches 1)* New Haven, 1967, p. 26 (YBC 3544,2—6 Ululu 557) where the first known reference to Bēl-šūzibanni occurs. See also text 47,4— 10.10.2 Neriglissar, where Nabû-balāṭu-ēriš appears as *qipu*.

32 See above, note 19.

forced removal of temple administrative personnel. Previously-published documents indicate not only the probability that administrators or trustees of the great Eanna sanctuary in Uruk originally came from Babylon but also that they may have been members of prominent banking families before assuming their "official" duties through royal appointment. This can be seen in the case of Sin-iddina, who appears as *qīpu* of Eanna as early as the eighth of Abu of Nebuchadnezzar's thirty-fifth year.[33] He is found, among other things, loaning barley and serving as a witness before the accession to the throne of Amēl-Marduk[34] During the period 562-660 BC, he is mentioned in promissory notes and receipts[35] and once, in particular, he is found paying two-thirds of a loan made to him by Bariq-ili-tammeš, the *qīpu* of Esagila in Babylon.[36] In addition, thanks to the interesting contents of NCBT 178, it can be shown that Sin-iddina actually owned property in Babylon at the same time he carried out his official duties in Uruk.[37] Also, it appears that he may have owned other properties outright or was a "partner" in other business ventures involving other temple officials or private citizens; the presence of witnesses to transactions involving Sin-iddina from such prestigious families as Ekur-zākir, Gimil-Nanâ (relatives of the temple accountant), Egibi and Bā'iru (including a future *šatammu* of Eanna) strongly suggest this.[38] Unfortunately, one of the keys to the understanding of this situation is not provided by the contracts. None of the known tablets involving Sin-iddina includes mention of his family name. Such is also the case with other Eanna trustees, both before and after his time. It is not until the reign of Nabonidus and the early Achaemenid period that we are provided with

33 Alfred Pohl, *Neubabylonische Rechtsurkunden aus den Berliner Staatlichen Museen (=Analecta Orientalia* 8, 1933, 15, 9ff.). It is not possible to determine with accuracy exactly when Sin-iddina assumed his responsibilities as overseer of Eanna. A huge gap still exists in the documentation for the years 579 to 570 (i.e., between the earliest mention of Sin-iddina and the latest contract of his predecessor as *qīpu*, Ninurta-šarra-uṣur). As in other instances (to be discussed shortly) it is possible that one or several still unknown individuals held the office during this period.

34 For other texts containing mention of him, see Dougherty, GCCI 1:66, 4ff; 94,3ff. and 251,1ff. as well as Keiser, BIN 1:124 and T.G.Pinches, "Glimpses of Life in Erech," *Expository Times* 25 (1913-14), p. 420ff.

35 See TCL 12:60, 1ff.

36 Anu-šarra-uṣur, the *šākin ṭēmi* of Uruk, is also cited as guarantor (TCL 12:62).

37 See Ronald H. Sack, "Some Remarks on Sin-iddina and Zērija, *qīpu* and *šatammu* of Eanna in Erech" in *Zeitschrift für Assyriologie* 66 (1976), p. 282ff.

38 *Ibid.*, p. 283.

some clue as to the possible background of individuals holding this important office. They do seem to indicate, nevertheless, that the holders of this position of authority in the various temples came from the significant banking firms or "families" noted elsewhere for their business activities throughout northern and southern Mesopotamia. Since it is known that Sin-iddina, in his capacity as overseer of Eanna, had dealings with the palace in Babylon and made trips to the capital,[39] it is likely that he himself came from the north and was a member of one of these prominent families. This is certainly suggested by the repeated occurrence in the contracts of the names of such witnesses as Nabû-bāni-aḫi (see below, Chapter 3), Marduk-šuma-iddina (a future *šākin ṭēmi* of Uruk) and especially Bānija of the Bā'iru family, a future *šatammu* of Eanna. If these conculsions are valid, then certainly Sin-iddina was well-known to Neriglissar before he ascended the throne in 560 BC. This would be important, because still other evidence points to his removal from office by the king early in his reign; documents datable to Neriglissar's first year clearly indicate that two men, Enlil-šarra-uṣur and Mušēzib-Marduk, held the office in quick succession.[40]

Such unusual happenings were not confined to the holders of the office of *qīpu*. In fact, it has been known for years that Zērija, son of Ibnâ of the prestigious Egibi house,[41] held the office of administrator (*šatammu*) at two different times. His first term is documented from the month of Nisanu of Amēl-Marduk's second year beyond the twenty-eighth of Abu of Neriglissar's accession year.[42] He continued to serve in that capacity until at least 559 BC[43]. Then, suddenly, he disappeared, and was replaced by a certain Bānija, son of Tabnēa of the Bā'iru family, a man who was probably more loyal to the king than his predecessor. Appearing in the

39 NCBT 178, lines 8-9(=ZA 66 282ff).

40 NBC 4897 and see San Nicolò, *Prosopographie*, p. 14.

41 For a commentary on the activities of the Egibi "family," see S. Weingort, *Das Haus Egibi in den neubabylonischen Rechtsurkunden* (Berlin, 1938). Another study of the same family by Joachim Krecher has yet to be published.

42 See San Nicolò, *Prosopographie*, p. 16.

43 NBC 4897, 45. Even without the information contained in YBC 4141, other tablets, while not mentioning his name, provide enough evidence to warrant the conclusion that he must also have been *šatammu* during the reign of Amēl-Marduk. Cf. Albrecht Goetze, "Additions to Parker and Dubberstein's Babylonian Chronology" in *Journal of Near Eastern Studies 3* (1944), p. 43. See also ZA 66 (1976), p. 290ff.

Uruk tablets as a witness as early as the accession year of Amēl-Marduk,[44] (fifth of Addaru) Bānija assumed the responsibilities of *šatammu* either at the end of the first or the beginning of the second year of Neriglissar.[45] Zērija does not reappear in the contracts until Nabonidus ascended the throne.[46] While the reasons for these changes are not completely known, a seizure of the throne through a *coup d'ètat* would, seemingly, lead to a logical attempt by Neriglissar to build a base of support (where circumstances would permit it) by placing individuals loyal to him in positions of authority. Perhaps, then, Neriglissar removed Sin-iddina and Zērija from their offices in Eanna (replacing them with his own supporters) as one means of further securing his own position. Whatever the case, it is significant that such a situation as this existed; it serves to compliment Neriglissar's efforts to cement ties with prominent personnel in other temples which have been known for so long.

The Royal Inscriptions and Chronicles

We noted earlier (see above, Chapter 1) that the Hebrew sources suggest that Neriglissar had some military experience and, indeed, may have had a hand in the siege of Jerusalem during the reign of Nebuchadnezzar. The relatively few royal inscriptions that survive tell us of at least some military activity after 560 BC. Many of these inscriptions are, by and large, formulaic;[47] and tell us nothing other than that he, (like his predecessors) restored the Esagila and Ezida temples in Babylon and Borsippa.[48] In this light, he refers to himself as the "restorer of the Esagila and Ezida" who carried out the commands of Marduk as a faithful servant.[49] He also repaired a palace on the bank of the Euphrates for his

---

44 See R.H.Sack, "The Scribe Nabû-bāni-aḫi, son of Ibnâ, and the Hierarchy of Eanna as seen in the Erech Contracts" in *Zeitschrift für Assyriologie 67* (1977), p. 43ff (YBC 4038:24. See also ZA 66 (1976), p. 284.

45 Prior to this time, the earliest known mention of Bānija as *šatammu* of Eanna occurred in TCL 12:68, 11ff. (datable to the fifteenth of Simanu of Neriglissar's second year). To this text must now be added YBC 4138, 2, 16 from the fifth of Simanu, 558. See ZA 66, p.290.

46 See San Nicolò, *Prosopographie*, p. 16 (=TCL 12:75, 27).

47 See discussion above, Chapter 1.

48 See Langdon, VAB 4, pp. 212-13 (Ner. Cylinders 1 and 2).

49 See the discussion of these "royal epithets" in Paul-Richard Berger, *Die neubabylonischen Königsinschriften (= Alter Orient und Altes Testament, Band 4/1)* Neukirchen-Vluyn, 1973,. pp. 77-78.

own use,[50] and did some work on some of Babylon's canals, as well as the so-called "chapel of destiny" used in the akitu celebration. Aside from this, the only other significant event of the king's reign mentioned in the primary sources is a campaign into southeast Anatolia during the year 557 BC.[51] BM 25124 deals entirely with a campaign against the state of Pirindu ruled by a certain Appuašu, who conducted a punitive raid into Syria. In it, we read

> The third year:[*On the Nth day of the month...*] Appuašu, the king of Pirindu, mustered his [large] army and set out to plunder and sack Syria. Neriglissar mustered his army and marched to Hume to oppose him.[52]

Although Appuašu prepared for the king's coming, his army was, nevertheless, defeated, and he returned to his capital Ura. Neriglissar's troops proceeded to plunder the city, as well as another city, Kiršu. After several initial successes, Neriglissar returned to Babylon in the month of February-March, 556, having failed to capture his adversary.[53] The purpose of this campaign, as Wiseman long ago pointed out, was "to maintain a hold on East Cilicia which at that time was a buffer state between Lydia and the massing forces of the Medes" since "all too soon the same forces were to be the instrument whereby Babylonia herself was to pass from history as an independent power."[54] Unfortunately, attempts have been made to associate Old Testament prophecy[55] with the king's reign and, by implication, with this[56] and other campaigns the king might

---

50 Wiseman, Chronicles of *Chaldean Kings*, p. 39. It should also be noted that TLB 2, pl. 22 is a (fragmentary) barrel cylinder of Neriglissar.

51 A background sketch for this campaign can be found in *Ibid.*, pp. 39-40. This text, BM 25124, is transliterated and translated on p. 74ff. and in A.K.Grayson, *Assyrian and Babylonian Chronicles (=Texts from Cuneiform Sources, V)* Locust Valley, 1975, Chronicle no. 5.

52 See Grayson, *Assyrian and Babylonian Chronicles*, p. 103.

53 Wiseman, *Chronicles of Chaldean Kings*, pp. 76-7. ("Appuašu fled and his hand did not capture him. In the month of Addaru the king of Akkad returned to his own land.")

54 *Ibid.*,p. 42.

55 Specifically, the contents of Isaiah 21:1-10.

56 See R.H.Sack, "Nergal-šarra-uṣur, King of Babylon as seen in the Cuneiform, Greek, Latin and Hebrew Sources" in *Zeitschrift für Assyriologie 68* (1978), p. 137ff.

have conducted. However, such attempts find no support in either the cuneiform accounts or surviving secondary sources.[57]

Neriglissar died in 556 BC, probably only about two months after he returned home from his campaign against Appuašu.[58] He was succeeded by his son, Labaši-Marduk,[59] who in all likelihood reigned only about two months[60] before being himself succeeded by Nabonidus, a man who, as Megasthenes says, "bore no relation to the royal race."[61] It was Nabonidus who, despite claiming to have had no desire to become king,[62] seized power and ruled for seventeen years (until 539 BC) prior to the conquest of Babylonia by Cyrus II of Persia.

---

57 *Ibid.*, p. 138.

58 See Parker and Dubberstein, p. 12.

59 Langdon, VAB 4 (Nabonidus Cylinder 8, col. 5).

60 Parker and Dubberstein, p. 13.

61 See Sack, ZA 68 (1978), p. 138.

62 See the interesting discussion of A.K.Grayson, *Papyrus and Tablet* (Englewood Cliffs, Prentice Hall, 1973), p. 117ff.

Neriglissar, King of Babylon

Chapter Three
Commentary

It is, of course, not possible to write an economic history of the Chaldean period solely on the basis of information contained in the contract tablets from the time of Neriglissar. The major reason for this is that the number of so-called "economic texts" which could be utilized is very small in comparison with the literally thousands of such documents from the reigns of Nabopolassar, Nebuchadnezzar and Nabonidus. In fact, only about two hundred Neriglissar texts are presently known. This figure includes the approximately twenty-five documents that are published here for the first time. As a consequence, it is very uncertain if these constitute a valid sample of either extant types or geographic distribution. While it would be foolhardy to draw sweeping conclusions from such scanty evidence, nevertheless it is worthwhile to examine and analyze the contents of the tablets, particularly since some of the previously unpublished documents contain new and interesting information.

The People of the Tablets
PART ONE
The Northern Sites

Over one hundred and ninety contract tablets datable to the reign of Neriglissar are presently known. Of these, twenty-seven appear here in transliteration and translation (with photographs) for the first time. These documents represent a wide range of catagories ranging from promissory notes and real estate sales to receipts designating full or partial payment of money or goods. Many of the documents are promissory notes for dates (3,4,22,31, etc), silver (9,16,20,32, etc.), barley (67,77) or other commodities and thus deal with the full or partial payment of "debts". Some texts record payment of tithes (*ešrû*) or commodities to Ebabbar (i.e., the temple of Šamaš in Sippar— 46,70 and 90), while still others deal with the loan of silver (27) for which property serves as surety (24,36,75) or are records of sale of real estate (73,80,87) or are simply rental agreements (29). Still others are either records of rations for personnel (11) or animals (6) or are receipts (91,93,97,102,etc) or slave sale texts

(1,2,7,42). Much of the "idiomatic" phraseology characteristic of these contracts has been exhaustively treated in other publications[1], and thus will not concern us here. Particularly interesting, however, are the people involved in these transactions. Their activities provide an intriguing commentary on business operations and "economic life" in the Chaldean period.

There can be no doubt that one of the most prominent businessmen of this period was Nabû-aḫḫē-iddina, son of Šulâ of the prestigious Egibi house.[2] This firm had already been active in buying, selling and loaning money and commodities long before Neriglissar ascended the throne of Babylon.[3] It developed during the reign of Nabopolassar, and expanded greatly during the reign of Nebuchadnezzar and soon became as prominent as the Nūr-Sin family. Nabû-aḫḫē-iddina was probably the most famous member of the "first generation." He first appears as a scribe in a text dated in Nebuchadnezzar's fifteenth year (4 August 590).[4] Shortly

---

[1]For a complete listing of all published Neriglissar contracts (through 1985) see Muhammad A. Dandamaev, *Slavery in Babylonia*, trans. by Victoria Powell (DeKalb, Northern Illinois University Press, 1984), p. 10.

Several corrections to this list ought to be noted. CIS 2/I 62 is a duplicate of VR 67 no.3; RP (N.S.4) p. 102 is the same text published by Evetts as *Ner.* 13 (text 13 in this volume); CT 57:559 is actually a Nabonidus text.

For more complete discussions of phraseology, see, among other publications, the following: Hugo Lanz, *Die neubabylonischen harranu Geschäftsunternehmen* (1976); Mariano San Nicolò, *Beiträge zur Rechtsgeschichte im Bereiche der keilschriftlichen Rechtsquellen* (Oslo, 1931); Mariano San Nicolò, *Die Schlussklauseln der altbabylonischen Kauf- und Tauschverträge* (München, 1922); Herbert Petschow, *Neubabylonisches Pfandrecht* (Berlin, 1956) as well as *Die neubabylonischen Kaufformulare* (Leipzig, 1939) as well as Mariano San Nicolò, *Der neubabylonische Lehrvertrag in rechtsvergleichender Betrachtung* (München, 1950) and *Beiträge zu einer Prosopographie neubabylonischer Beamten der Zivil-und Tempelverwaltung* (München, 1941).

2 For commentaries on this family, see Kohler and Peiser, *Aus dem babylonischen Rechtsleben* (Leipzig, 1894), 4, p. 21ff, S. Weingort, *Das Haus Egibi in den neubabylonischen Rechtsurkunden* (Berlin, 1938) and A. Ungnad, "Das Haus Egibi" in *Archiv für Orientforschung* (1949) 14, p. 58ff.

3 See Weingort, p. 52. Šulâ appears first in the eighteenth year of Nabopolassar (608-7 BC) and last in *Nbk.* 138 (582-1 BC). His five sons, including Nabû-aḫḫē-iddina, continue to be mentioned in the documents until as late as the reign of Darius (Itti-Nabû-balāṭu in 507 BC) and in AOATS 4, 15, Itti-Nabû-balāṭu and Bēl-kišir are dividing their inheritance. See Paul Koschaker, *Babylonisch-assysisches Bürgschaftrecht* (Leipzig, 1911), pp. 104ff. and 201.

4 See Ungnad, p. 60 and J.N.Strassmaier, "Die Inschriften von Nabuchodonosor, König von Babylon" (=*Babylonische Texte*) (Leipzig, 1890), Heft 5, 107,13.

thereafter he is found heading the operations of the Egibi house and continuing the work of his father, Šulâ (28 July 581).[5] The exact date of his death is, of course, unknown, but it appears that it occurred sometime during the thirteenth year of Nabonidus (543).[6] His son, Itti-Marduk-balāṭu, married Nuptâ, the daughter of the famous Iddina-Marduk of the Nūr-Sin family[7] Over one hundred sixty contract tablets contain mention of him, and in them he is found continuing the banking operations of his father (Nbk 133, 142, 164, 172) and in the purchases of slaves (Nbk. 166, 195, 387, 409), houses or fields (Nbn. 45, 353, 396, 575, etc.) and even as a witness (Nbn 77, 243), or scribe (Nbk. 266, Nbn. 8, etc.).[8] However,as we have already seen,[9] it was during the reigns of Amēl-Marduk and Neriglissar that some of his most important activities occurred, when his time was largely taken up with his duties as Neriglissar's business agent.[10]

Such responsibilities did not prevent him from concluding deals on his own. One such transaction involved the purchase of the slave girl Lītka-idi, and took place during the ninth month of Amēl-Marduk's accession year.[11] While, of course, the sale of the slave is not significant, nevertheless several details deserve comment. It seems that the slave girl was placed at his disposal in the forty-third year of Nebuchadnezzar. In return, he produced twelve shekels of silver, which "guaranteed" the return of the slave. However, in the next year, he bought Litka-idi "for the full

---

5 See Weingort, p. 58 and Ungnad, p. 60. See also *Nbk.* 141-43, 164, 172 and 320.

6 See Kohler and Peiser, *Rechtsleben* 4,, p. 21ff; Weingort, pp. 10-11 and Ungnad, p. 60. The last known text in which he is active is *Nbn.* 680 (purchase of a slave) from his twelfth year. In *Nbn.* 760 (fourteenth year) it appears he has already died. His death probably occurred about the same time as that of his cousin Bēl-aḫḫē-iddina. See Georges Contenau, "Contrats néobabyloniens II Achéménides et Sélucides" in *Textes Cunéiformes, Musée du Louvre 13* (Paris, 1929), no. 120.

7 Although this marriage is referred to in *Nbn.* 755 and *Cyr.* 129, the actual document confirming it still awaits discovery.

8 For further citations, see Weingort, pp. 58-9.

9 See discussion above, Chapter 2.

10 See text 9 ,(BM 30411, 5ff.).

11 See AOATS 4, text 19 (=BM 30254). See also Petschow, *Pfandrecht*, p. 42ff. It is interesting to note that, in the reign of Nabonidus, Nabû-apla-iddina reappears in the contracts selling a slave. See Alfred Moldenke, *Cuneiform Texts in the Metropolitan Museum of Art* (New York, 1893), no. 11/12. See also *Nbn*, 238 and 239 (6th year).

price" (*ana šīmi gamrutu*)[12] of nineteen and one-half shekels of silver. Two other members of the Egibi house, Nabû-zēru-lišir and Balāṭu, served as witnesses to the sale. While Dandamaev has already noted that the price paid for the slave is not that terribly significant, it is nevertheless interesting that prices had more than doubled by the sixth century, B.C., with the average figure being fifty shekels.[13] The reasons for the acceptance of such a small amount in an age in which prices were constantly rising are unknown. However, it appears that extenuating circumstances were involved, given what we know from other sources of Gugua's overall financial condition.[14]

Another "business deal" of Nabû-aḫḫē-iddina involved the lady Inbâ, the daughter of the famous Bēl-ēpuš of the Naggāru family. In Amēl-Marduk's accession year, she borrowed an unknown amount of silver[15] from a certain Bēl-uballiṭ, with the house of a certain Liširu serving as security.[16] However, it seems that she was unable to repay the full amount that she had originally borrowed.[17] Consequently, in the following year she was forced to sell her property (to which Bēl-uballiṭ had a claim) in order to satisfy her obligation. Accordingly, she received three minas, seven shekels of silver and fifteen minas of wool plus a garment

---

12 See Petschow, *Kaufformulare*, p. 45ff. Sometimes the phrase *ana šīmi hariṣ* appears instead (GCCI 2 95). See Mariano San Nicolò, *Babylonische Rechtsurkunden aus dem 6. Jahrhundert vor Christus* (Munchen, 1960), text no. 15.

13 See Dandamaev, *Slavery*, Isaac Mendelsohn, *Slavery in the Ancient Near East* (New York, 1949), p. 114; Bruno Meissner, "Warenpreise in Babylonien" in *Abhandlungen der Preussischen Akademie der Wissenschaften, Jahrgang* 1936, *phil.-hist. Klasse*, p. 34; Waldo H. Dubberstein, "Comparative Prices in Later Babylonia" in *American Journal of Semitic Languages* (1939), vol. 56, p. 34ff. In the reign of Nabonidus the price was fifty shekels. There are instances, however, of higher prices being paid for slaves.

14 See *Nbn.* 65. For a discussion of this text, see Peiser, *Rechtsleben 3, p. 14* and *Knut Tallqvist, Babylonische Schenkungsbriefe* (Helsingfors, 1890), p. 14ff. Here Gugua is found placing one mina of silver "at the disposal of" (*ina pani*) Nabû-aḫḫē-iddina. What the relationship was between these two individuals was is not precisely known.

15 AOATS 4 text 20 (=BM 33909). Due to the text's fragmentary condition, as well as the lack of information in other documents, the exact amount of silver originally borrowed by Inbâ cannot be determined.

16 AOATS 4 20, lines 1-2--- *itti* ^{I}*li-ši-ru ša maš-ka-nu ṣa-ab-tu* "along with Liširu, whose house was held as security." However in BM 31358 and BM 41398, she is mentioned as having sold her property to Nabû-aḫḫē-iddina.

17 See *Ibid.*, text 21, 7 (=BM 31358).

(*lubaru*) and an "additional payment" (*atru*, probably a notarizing fee)[18] What is interesting is that, much like the case involving Nabû-apla-iddina and Neriglissar, Inbâ sold her property to Nabû-aḫḫē-iddina, with the document "being sealed" with the name of Bēl-apla-iddina, another member of the Egibi house.[19] Nabû-aḫḫē-iddina then proceeded to pay the one-third mina four shekels of silver that were still due Bēl-uballiṭ, leaving one mina, thirteen shekels of silver to be paid directly to Inbâ and one mina, ten shekels "charged against" (*ina muḫḫi*) Nabû-aḫḫē-iddina, to be paid at some future date.[20] Thus, once again, a large banking house entered the affairs of a defaulting debtor, purchased property, and satisfied obligations.[21]

During the reign of Neriglissar, Nabû-aḫḫē-iddina appears as a scribe in text 55 (9 Du'uzu, 557), as a banker in text 9 and as the purchaser of slaves and property in texts 23 and 42, respectively. Examples of his varied activities can be seen also in texts 27 (30 Araḫsamnu, 559/8) and in the interesting text 80, where he is found loaning silver, buying a slave girl and acquiring real estate. These documents, together with a few other previously-published tablets, serve to adequately comment on the wide range of activities of not only Nabû-aḫḫē-iddina, but of the Egibi house as well.

Another person whose name constantly appears in the contract tablets of this period is Iddina-[22] Marduk, son of Iqiša of the family of Nūr-Sin. Like Nabû-aḫḫē-iddina and the other members of the Egibi house, Iddina-Marduk was a wealthy banker whose wide range of business activities reached their peak during the reigns of Amēl-Marduk, Neriglissar and Nabonidus. His name appears as early as the eighth year of Nebuchadnezzar (where he is engaged in the purchase of slaves)[23], and he remained the active director of his business operations for almost seventy

---

18 There have been many suggestions as to the meaning of *atru* in these documents. For a summary and discussion of the arguments, see San Nicolò, *Or (N.S.)* 16, p. 286ff.

19 See AOATS 4, p. 38 and text 22,1ff (=BM 41398).

20 This leaves twenty shekels of silver still unaccounted for.

21 Unfortunately, the dates of BM 31358 and BM 41398 are broken off. It is interesting that the same Bēl-apla-iddina is mentioned as having paid out (*ina qati*) the money owed to Inbâ and Bēl-uballiṭ (in BM 41398, lines 33-36) much in the same manner as Nabû-aḫḫē-iddina acted on behalf of Neriglissar.

22 Cf. Ungnad, *AfO* 14, p. 61, Anm. 36 and Mariano San Nicolò and Arthur Ungnad, *Neubabylonische Rechts- und Verwaltungsurkunden, Glossar* (Leipzig, 1937), p. 103.

23 *Nbk.* 67.

years, dying probably towards the end of Cambyses' third year.[24] Through marriage, he was related to both the Egibi and Nabāja families, and his wife, Ina-Esagila-ramat, continues to be mentioned in the documents after her husband's death.[25] His daughter, Nuptâ, married Itti-Marduk-balāṭu, the son of Nabû-aḫḫē-iddina of the Egibi house.[26] In his business dealings, he is frequently found working in partnership with his brothers-in-law Labaši, Bēl-ušallim, and especially Madānu-šuma-iddina. In the contracts from Amēl-Marduk's reign, he is found loaning both commodities (mustard, vats and especially garlic) and silver.[27] In the reign of Neriglissar, he can be found loaning silver and garlic (text 32---2 Kislimu, 558/7) and is again associated with Madānu-šuma-iddina of the Nabaja family in the loaning of dates (text 22---27 Du'uzu, 559/8).[28] Further examples of his activities can be found in text 10 (6 Abu 560 where he loans silver to a member of the Šangû parakki family) and in n. 66 (19 Šabaṭu, 559/8, where he again loans garlic to several individuals).

Two of Iddina-Marduk's business associates appear prominently in the documents from Neriglissar's reign. The first of these, a certain Bēl-ēpuš, son of Rašil of the Nappāḫu family, appears initially in a promissory note for silver as early as the thirty-second year of Nebuchadnezzar.[29] Not surprisingly, the creditor in this instance was Iddina-Marduk himself. His name also appears in a number of documents datable to Amēl-Marduk's first year. In them, he is found loaning silver, sheep or garlic[30] and, in one instance, silver that is said to have been a part of the "business capital" (*ḫarrānu*) of Iddina-Marduk[31]. In the texts from Neriglissar's reign, he appears as a witness to transactions involving Iddina-Marduk (no. 10 and no.43), and as the creditor lending dates (nos. 21 and 22), silver and garlic (no. 35). In two of those instances, the scribes mentioned are both members of the Nūr-Sin family.

---

24 The last certain mention of him is in J.N.Strassmaier, "Die Inschrifted von Cambyses, König von Babylon" in *Babylonische Texte* (Leipzig, Eduard Pfeiffer, 1894), vol. 8, text no. 219.

25 *Camb.* 263 and 279.

26 We have mention of the marriage contract in *Nbn.* 755 and *Cyr.* 130.

27 We know, of course, that it was customary, when silver or commodities were loaned, to demand some sort of security (*maškanu*) that might serve as a guarantee that the loan would be repaid. This security could take the form of houses, fields, gardens, and "all of one's possessions" (*mimma šumšu ša ālu ṣēru mala bašû maškānu*).

28 See *Ner.*12.

29 See *Nbk.*252,4.

30 See BM 30442; BM 33124 and BM 30620 (=AOATS 4, texts 28-30).

31 See *Ibid.*, text 30, 10ff.

Appearing along with Bēl-ēpuš is Madānu-šuma-iddina, son of Zērija, and an important member of the Nabāja house. The earliest known mention of him occurs in a contract datable to the thirty-seventh year of Nebuchadnezzar, where he appears as the scribe.[32] He was Iddina-Marduk's brother-in-law, and would, on occasion, serve as the scribe writing up contracts in which he was involved.[33] In Neriglissar's first year, he is repeatedly mentioned with Bēl-ēpuš in transactions concerning dates (nos. 21 and 22), silver and garlic (no. 35) and is found independently loaning barley (no. 67) and garlic (no. 68). In no. 69, he borrows silver himself. Like Bēl-ēpuš, his resources included the "business capital" of Iddina-Marduk, and witnesses to his transactions could include scribes and other members of the Nūr-Sin house.[34] However, unlike his contemporary and associate (whose name disappears from the documents in Neriglissar's second year)[35], Madānu-šuma-iddina continued to be active in the business of loaning and buying commodities until at least Nabonidus' fourth year.[36]

As an interesting sidelight, one should note the presence of the interesting Nabû-ušallim, son of Pānija, as both witness and "partner" in the documents involving Madānu-šuma-iddina and Bēl-ēpuš. The earliest mention of him occurs in a promissory note datable to Nebuchadnezzar's forty-first year;[37] he, in fact, witnesses a transaction to which Iddina-Marduk is a principal party. Later, in Amēl-Marduk's time, he again witnesses a promissory note for silver[38] loaned by Iddina-Marduk, and even loans barley, sesame oil, and garlic on his own.[39] However, he is most active during the reigns of Neriglissar and Nabonidus. In text no. 8, he borrows silver that is said to come from the "business capital" (*ḫarrānu*) of Iddina-Marduk, and in text 15, the commodities he loans out appear to have come from the same source. In text no 35, he again borrows silver and garlic, this time through Bēl-ēpuš and Madānu-šuma-iddina; he had to return the goods directly to Iddina-Marduk. In nos. 68 and 69, he is found

---

32 See *Nbk.* 326, 11.

33 See *Ibid.*, line 11.

34 This also includes members of the Dabibi family, who witness transactions involving both Iddina-Marduk and Madānu-šuma-iddina. See, for example, text 66, 18 and text 67,14-15.

35 The latest text containing mention of him is text 43, 15.

36 See *Nbn.* 141, 2. Texts published to date indicate that he was quite active in the early years of Nabonidus' reign.

37 See *Nbk.* 384, 9.

38 BM 31103, 13 (=AOATS 4, text 24).

39 See BM 31100 and BM 33124 (=AOATS 4, texts 27 and 29, respectively).

both borrowing and loaning silver or garlic with Madānu-šuma-iddina. Finally, in texts 21 and 22, he appears as a witness (along with other members of the Nūr-Sin house) to transactions involving the loaning of dates by both Madānu-šuma-iddina and Bēl-ēpuš. His activities continued until at least the month of Tašritu of Nabonidus' seventh year;[40] during this time he either borrows commodities himself or witnesses contracts to which members of the Nappāḫu, Nūr-Sin and Nabāja families are a party. What is most intriguing here is that his "family name" is not mentioned anywhere in the documents. While it is certainly likely that he was a member of one of these "banking houses" himself (probably Nūr-Sin, given his repeated association with Iddina-Marduk), one wonders why this information never appears in the contracts.

The Sippar Texts

Of the more than one hundred texts included in this volume, over twenty come from Sippar. While their contents have been known for several years, most are published here in transliteration and translation for the first time. They form a part of the massive Sippar collection of Babylonian tablets presently housed in the British Museum.[41] Unfortunately, most of the documents datable to the reign of Neriglissar are fragmentary, and their contents cannot be adequately or accurately analyzed. In addition, many of the texts described as "complete" or "nearly complete" in the important British Museum Sippar Catalogue are actually in very poor condition. In some cases, they are hardly legible. Nevertheless, the documents photographed and discussed here are among the best preserved of the lot. While they represent a cross-section of categories from promissory notes for silver (nos. 79, 85, 88, 101), garlic (83) or dates (89, 98), to receipts for tithes (*ešrû*, no. 90), provisions (91), hides (94) and barley (104), they are, regrettably, not related directly to one another with regard to subject matter or specific personalities mentioned. While all are identified as "Tablets from Sippar" in the Catalogue, several (including nos. 73-75, 78 and 79) were actually written in Babylon. Of particular interest to me are the persons mentioned both as parties to transactions and as witnesses to them. They mirror the kind of

---

40 See *Nbn.* 261, 3. Like Madānu-šuma-iddina, the bulk of his activities took place in the reigns of Neriglissar and Nabonidus.

41 See Erle V. Leichty and A.K.Grayson, *Catalogue of the Babylonian Tablets in the British Museum, volumes VI-VIII--Tablets from Sippar 1-3* (London the British Museum, 1986-88).

information represented in the documents examined by Evetts and Pinches over a century ago.

We have already noted the presence of prominent families in the texts discussed above. Some of these families, in particular those of the Isinite, Dannēa, Nūr-Sin and Dabibi, turn up in the Sippar material as well. All are important, and all are well-known from the documents written in Babylon.[42] Certainly, the most interesting new text mentioning their activities is no. 87 (record of the sale of a house), since members of three of these families are parties or witnesses to the transaction. In fact, several members of the Isinite house, namely Bălāṭu, Šamaš-udammiq and Arad-Bēl serve as witnesses, as does Nabû-šuma-ukīn of the Dannēa firm, while the scribe Na'id-Marduk of the Iddina-Marduk family is the seller of the property. Also involved are the families Šangû-Sippar and Šangû-Ištar-Bābili, both well known from previously-published contracts.[43] The son of Balāṭu, namely, Nabû-zēru-lišir, also appears prominently in text no. 77, both as the scribe and the party obligated to deliver the barley mentioned in l. 1. In fact, all of the witnesses mentioned in text 77 are members of the same family.

The names of Mukallim, Nūr-Sin and Maštuk occur frequently in the in the Sippar texts as well. In text 101, two members of the Mukallim house are present as witnesses or as the scribe in the transaction. In text 88, Marduk-šuma-ibni of the Nūr-Sin house witnesses a promissory note for silver involving a member of the Šangû-Sippar family. Finally, the interesting text 85 involves two members of the Maštuk family, with one of them, Marduk-bēl-zēri, also serving as scribe. It is indeed unfortunate that more of the texts recorded in the Sippar Catalogue are not in better condition. Since the same families are engaged in business activities in more than one city in northern Babylonia, additional texts could provide us with more information about the extent of those activities.

42 See Knut Tallqvist, *Neubabylonisches Namenbuch* (Helsingfors, 1905) for citations of texts in which these and other prominent "family names" occur.

43 See *Ibid.*, p. 198.

PART TWO
Other Items of Interest

Other sites in Babylonia are also represented in the contracts datable to Neriglissar's reign. These cities include Dilbat[44], Nippur,[45] and Kish[46] as well as Uruk. Without question, some of the most important of these tablets comment on the activities of personnel in the great Eanna sanctuary in Uruk, and we have already had occasion to discuss the implications of the information they contain in the context of Neriglissar's succession to the throne.[47] However, in addition to providing us with specific information as to the nature of duties of important administrative personnel,[48] they also paint an intriguing picture of the involvement of important families in temple affairs. Included among these are Gimil-Nanâ, Bā'iru and, of course, Egibi and Ekur-zākir. One of the most interesting members of the Ekur-zākir house is Nabû-bāni-aḫi, son of Ibnâ. While his occupation and involvement with the hierarchy of Eanna are well-known, several tablets not only elaborate on his activities during the reigns of both Amēl-Marduk and Neriglissar, but also seem to provide us with a few clues as to the nature of the men chosen to occupy the important offices of *qīpu* and *šatammu* of Eanna, as well as the position of *šākin ṭēmi*

---

44 See A.T.Clay, *Babylonian Business Transactions of the First Millennium, B.C. (=Babylonian Records in the Library of J. Pierpont Morgan*, vol I) (New York, 1912), 56. (promissory note for dates-- 29 Ululu, accession year of Neriglissar).

45 See, for example, A.T.Clay, *Legal and Commercial Transactions, dated in the Assyrian, Neo Babylonian and Persian Periods, chiefly from Nippur (=Babylonian Expedition, University of Pennsylvania, vol. 8/1)* (Philadelphia, 1908), no. 36 (promissory note for sesame oil).

46 See Stephen Langdon, *Excavations at Kish*, 3 (Oxford, 1929), W1929, 145 (Nisanu, third year of Neriglissar---testimonial). This text mentions a certain Bēl-kāṣir, the *šākin ṭēmi* of the city of Kish.

47 See above, Chapter 2. It should also be noted that other published contracts (from promissory notes to testimonials) comment on both private and administrative activity in Uruk in the reign of Neriglissar. See, for example, C.E.Keiser, *Letters and Contracts from Erech written in the Neo Babylonian Period (=Babylonian Inscriptions in the collection of J.B.Nies 1)* (New Haven, 1917), no. 123 (promissory note for dates due the treasury of Eanna) and Georges Contenau, *Contrats néo-babyloniens I (de Téglath -phalasar à Nabonide (= Textes cunéiformes, Musée du Louvre 12)* (Paris, 1927, texts 63-69. Text 69, in fact, is a promissory note involving Mušēzib-Marduk, the overseer (*qīpu*) of Eanna and is dated to the tenth of Addaru of Neriglissar's third year. See below for further discussion of his activities.

48 See discussion of the offices of *qīpu* and *šatammu* below and San Nicolò, *Prosopographie*, p. 16ff.

of Uruk. Prior to Neriglissar's accession to the throne, we repeatedly find Nabû-bāni-aḫi in the company of Sin-iddina and a certain Marduk-šuma-iddina[49] son of Nabû-balāssu-iqbi of the Gimil-Nanâ family, who later held the office of *šākin ṭēmi* of Uruk[50]. In this context, we can feel fairly secure in concluding that prominent Uruk families provided both a) the scribes who attended to the daily business of writing up documents and b) the holders of the position of *šākin ṭēmi*, who thus went through an apprenticeship[51] in the temple before assuming their office, probably through royal appointment.[52]

Appearing also with Nabû-bani-ahi is Bānija, son of Tabnēa of the Bā'iru house, whose activities we have already mentioned.[53] He, like Nabû-bāni-aḫi, was a scribe who not only witnessed documents involving the *qīpu* and *šatammu* of Eanna, but also is found associating himself with the temple accountant, Nabû-aḫḫê-bulliṭ and Zērija, who preceeded him as holder of the office of *šatammu*. Banija succeeded to the office of *šatammu* early in Neriglissar's reign and held his office until the accession of Nabonidus. In fact, an important previously-published text, YBC 11526[54], although in fragmentary condition, mentions Zērija as *šatammu* of Eanna in the accession year of Neriglissar and further establishes the fact that he served two terms of office.[55] Also, when taken with another

---

49 Marduk-šuma-iddina appears primarily as a witness in the texts from Nebuchadnezzar's reign. See R.P.Dougherty, *Goucher College Cuneiform Inscriptions I Archives from Erech, time of Nebuchadrezzar and Nabonidus* (New Haven, 1923), 233,14 (26 Du'uzu, 567/6); 261,11 (18 Simanu, 567/6), and 262,9 (568/7).

50 See the relevant discussion in R.H.Sack, "The Scribe Nabû-bāni-aḫi, son of Ibnâ, and the Hierarchy of Eanna as seen in the Erech Contracts" in *Zeitschrift für Assyriologie* 67 (1977), p. 46 and note 9.

For further discussions of these individuals and their offices, see Francis Joannes, *Textes Économiques de la Babylonie Récente (Étude des textes de TEBR-Cahier n. 6)* (Paris, 1982) and, especially, Kümmel, *Familie, Beruf und Amt in spatbabylonischen Uruk* (Berlin, Mann, 1979).

51 Unfortunately, up to this time, it has been difficult to identify with absolute certainty the families to which several holders of the office of *šākin ṭēmi* in the years 602-555 BC belonged. However, it has been known for several years that the Gimil-Nanâ family provided at least two holders of this office, namely, Marduk-šuma-iddina and Šamaš-zēra-iqīša, who held the office during at least the early years of Nebuchadnezzar's reign. See San Nicolò, *Prosopographie*, p. 12.

52 See discussion below concerning probable royal intervention in Eanna.

53 See discussion above, Chapter 2.

54 =ZA 67 (1977), p. 50-1.

55 See *Ibid.*, p. 51-2.

important document dated to the twenty-eighth of Abu, 560/59,[56] where Nabû-bāni-aḫi also appears (this time as a witness) in a text again involving the *šatammu* Zerija, it constitutes the latest mention of Nabû-bāni-aḫi in the Erech contracts. Coincidentally, Sin-iddina, the *qīpu* of Eanna with whom Nabû-bāni-aḫi had been associated for so many years, also disappears[57] at about the same time and is succeeded by Mušēzib-Marduk, who remained as temple overseer during the rest of Neriglissar's reign.[58] Although Zērija subsequently reappears as *šatammu* of Eanna in the reign of Nabonidus,[59] nothing is heard of either Sin-iddina or Nabû-bāni-aḫi again. Perhaps (given Nabû-bāni-aḫi's repeated involvement with Sin-iddina in his official and private affairs) he also was a casualty of what appears to have been a general "housecleaning" done in Eanna shortly after Neriglissar ascended the throne in early 560 BC.[60]

In addition to identifying specific personages, the Uruk contracts datable to Neriglissar's reign give us an indication of a) the specific functions of temple administrators and b) the presence of "royal officials" who would oversee the activities of people in positions of responsibility. They indicate that the *šatammu* (at least in Eanna in Uruk) served as a judicial official, supervised temple estates, had jurisdiction over the *širku*, over the assignment of temple slaves to military service, over the appointment and activities of certain other temple officials, and over the ultimate settling of accounts.[61] Also, while the *qīpu* and *šākin ṭēmi* are frequently found together supervising the delivery of commodities to Uruk or to Eanna specifically, it was the *šatammu* who had ultimate control over the disposition of those goods. The documents from Uruk continue to support the contention that the *šatammu* operated from the temple exclusively, while the *qīpu* was frequently found away from Uruk on official business. Nevertheless, at least one Neriglissar text[62] indicates that

---

56 YBC 3752 (=ZA 66 p.289ff).

57 See *Ibid.*, p.289ff.

58 YBC 4012, 2 (=ZA 66, p. 287). This text, datable to the twenty-second of Ajaru, accession year of Labaši-Marduk, nevertheless refers to the first year of Neriglissar when mentioning what appears to have been the final year of Sin-iddina's term of office.

59 See San Nicolò, *Prosopographie*, p. 16.

60 See discussion above, Chapter 2.

61 In cases involving the *širke* and the settling of accounts, sometimes only the *qīpu* is mentioned. Cf. RA 12 (1915), p. 6ff. and NBC 4897, 45 and AOAT 203, p. 117ff.

62 See V. Scheil, "La libration judiciaire d'un fils donné en gage sous Neriglissor an 558 av. J.-C." in *Revue d'assyriologie et d'archéologie orientale 12* (1915), 1ff.

the overseer, Mušēzib-Marduk, did perform judicial functions on the same level as that of the *šatammu* in Eanna specifically; thus the functions of the two offices could, on occasion, overlap one another.

We have noted above that available evidence seems to justify the contention that the *šatammu*, no less than the *qīpu*, owed his position to royal intervention and that he could be retained or removed in accordance with the king's desires. However, there has long been disagreement as to when this "policy" first went into effect. Years ago, San Nicolò, on limited evidence,[63] concluded that it must have happened either at the end of the Chaldean or the beginning of the Achaemenid period. However, evidence from the reign of Nebuchadnezzar[64] suggests that royal intervention or control of temple affairs was a deliberate policy much earlier than was formerly thought and the relatively small number of Chaldean administrative documents published decades ago distorted our picture of the relations between palace and temple in pre-Achaemenid times.

It would be foolish to suggest that all aspects of Neo Babylonian "economic life" are represented in the texts from Neriglissar's reign. Nevertheless, their contents do allow for several conclusions to be drawn. First, the contracts serve as sufficient commentary not only on normal everyday buying and selling activities, but also on the involvement of the developing banking houses in the affairs of private citizens. They demonstrate that such prominent figures as Nabû-aḫḫē-iddina, Iddina-Marduk and their business associates could take advantage of both the plights of debtor and creditor, while at the same time expanding the material resources at their disposal. Second, we certainly can conclude that the Chaldean economy was not devoid of the "planning element," and that the "administrations," particularly those of the temples, were just as meticulous as in any other period. Finally, as the Uruk contracts clearly show, certain families were also prominent in temple affairs. As we have just seen, men like Nabû-bāni-aḫi, even though not nolding important administrative positions, were nevertheless involved in the affairs of temple officials just as members of the Egibi, Nūr-Sin and Nabāja families were business associates in northern Babylonia. Surely it is clear that these sources from the time of Neriglissar, when treated together, create an intriguing picture of a period about which much still needs to be written.

63 San Nicolò, *Prosopographie*, p. 18ff. and see discussion in *TEBR*, pp. 131-35, 150, 176, 207, 226, etc.

64 See *PTS* 74 where it is now clear that the "office" of *ša rēš šarri bēl piqitti Eanna* was already a fact of life during the reign of Nebuchadnezzar.

Catalogue and Description of Datable Texts

Text Number	Inventory Number	Reign	Year.Month.Day	Description of Contents
1	BM 92791	*Nergel-šarra-uṣur*	Acc. 6. 12	Slave sale
2	BM 30228	" " "	Acc. 6. 16	Slave sale
3	BM 64933	" " "	Acc. 6. 24	Promissory note for dates
4	BM 638.40	" " "	Acc. 6. 24	Promissory note for dates
5	BM 41440	" " "	Acc. 9. 5	Receipt for silver
6	BM 47347	" " "	Acc. 9. 16	Receipt for fodder for oxen
7	BM 31105	" " "	Acc. 10. 23	Slave sale
8	BM 33067	" " "	Acc. 12. 7	Promissory note for silver
9	BM 30411	" " "	Acc. 12. 9	Receipt for silver
10	BM 33910	" " "	Acc.	Promissory note
11	BM 77590	" " "	Acc.	Receipt for grain as food allotment
12	BM 30419	" " "	Acc. 5. 6	Promissory note
13	BM 47517	" " "	1. 1. 1	Record of marriage of Nab-šuma-ukin
14	BM 54178	" " "	1. 1. 25	Promissory note for beer
15	BM 30573	" " "	1. 2. 9	Promissory note for garlic
16	BM 31248	" " "	1. 3. 1	Promissory note for silver
17	BM 54210	" " "	1. 3. 25	Receipt
18	BM 92746	" " "	1. 4. 4	Receipt for barley delivered to Ebabbar

Text Number	Inventory Number	Reign	Year.Month.Day	Description of Contents
19	BM 64730	*Nergel-šarra-uṣur*	1. 4. 8	Receipt for wool and flour
20	BM 31964	" " "	1. 4. 15	Promissory note for silver
21	BM 33562	" " "	1. 4. 17	Promissory note for dates
22	BM 30551	" " "	1. 4. 27	Promissory note for dates
23	BM 30574	" " "	1. 5. 3	Slave sale
24	BM 30252	" " "	1. 5. 15	Record of loan of silver for which house serves as security
25	BM 30525	" " "	1. 6. 6	Dowry document
26	BM 30575	" " "	1. 8. 14	Promissory note for silver
27	BM 31558	" " "	1. 8. 30	Record of loan of silver
28	BM 63834	" " "	1. 9. 16	Record of commodities delivered to Ebabbar
29	BM 63932	" " "	1. 10. 20	Rental agreement
30	BM 30244	" " "	1. 11. 17	Promissory note
31	BM 77303	" " "	1.	Promissory note for dates
32	BM 31308	" " "	2. 1. 10	Promissory note for garlic and silver
33	BM 31143	" " "	2. 2. 23	Promissory note (?)
34	BM 30848	" " "	2. 2. 27	Receipt
35	BM 31084	" " "	2. 3. 25	Promissory note for garlic and silver

Text Number	Inventory Number	Reign	Year.Month.Day	Description of Contents
36	BM 77825	*Nergel-šarra-uṣur*	2. 4. 28	Document concerning loan of silver for which house served as security
37	BM 63933	" " "	2. 5. 11	Receipt
38	BM 31104	" " "	2. 6. 2	Promissory note for silver and garlic
39	BM 30443	" " "	2. 6. 10	Promissory note for silver
40	BM 65260	" " "	2. 7. 3	Receipt for silver
41	BM 63960	" " "	2. 8. 30	Receipt
42	BM 30454	" " "	2. 8. 27	Slave sale
43	BM 30331	" " "	2. 9. 2	Promissory note for silver and barley
44	BM 77304	" " "	2. 9. 7	Promissory note for silver
45	BM 30951	" " "	2. 9. 9	Promissory note
46	BM 72797	" " "	2. 10. 4	Record of payment of dates to Ebabbar
47	BM 38135	" " "	2. 10. 10	Testimonial
48	BM 63830	" " "	2. 10. 19	Receipt
49	BM 75778	" " "	2. 11. 11	Promissory note for gold
50	BM 30526	" " "	2. 11. 19	Promissory note for silver and garlic
51	BM 63931	" " "	2. 12. 22	Record of dates placed at disposal of various individuals
52	BM 31209	" " "	3. 2. 25	Receipt of silver as rent

Text Number	Inventory Number	Reign	Year.Month.Day	Description of Contents
53	BM 63842	*Nergel-šarra-uṣur*	3. 3. 2	Receipt
54	BM 63843	" " "	3. 3. 18	Promissory note for barley and dates
55	BM 31009	" " "	3. 4. 9	Promissory note for hides
56	BM 64956	" " "	3. 4. 25	Receipt for barley
57	BM 63841	" " "	3. 4. 27	Receipt for animals
58	BM 31858	" " "	3. 5. 19	Record of individual placed at disposal of royal official
59	BM 30871	" " "	3. 6. 5	Record of sale of servants
60	BM 31151	" " "	3. 6. 6	Promissory note for silver
61	BM 54259	" " "	3. 6. 13	Receipt of dates
62	BM 54244	" " "	3. 6. 15	Receipt for dates
63	BM 31207	" " "	3. 6. 13	Promissory note for dates
64	BM 64969	" " "	3. 6. 24	Record of linen placed at disposal of individual
65	BM 55712	" " "	3. 8. 12	Receipt
66	BM 30577	" " "	3. 11. 5	Receipt for garlic
67	BM 31044	" " "	3. 12. 12	Receipt for barley
68	BM 41401	" " "	4. 1. 2	Promissory note for garlic
69	BM 30334	" " "	4. 1. 2	Promissory note for silver
70	BM 63831	" " "	... ...	Record of barley delivered to Ebabbar
71	BM 30713	" " "	... ...	Receipt (?) for silver

Text Number	Inventory Number	Reign	Year.Month.Day	Description of Contents
72	BM 64935	*Nergel-šarra-uṣur*	... 12b. ...	Rental agreement
73	BM 54179	" " "	... 9. 14	Sale of property
74	BM 54180	" " "	1. 11. 6	Testimonial
75	BM 75968	" " "	1. ... 28	Loan of silver for which property serves as surety
76	BM 74511	" " "	1. 7. 6	Promissory note (?)
77	BM 74495	" " "	2. 11. 28	Promissory note for barley
78	BM 77626	" " "	Acc. 9. 19	Dowry document
79	BM 77637	" " "	... 5. 21	Promissory note for silver
80	BM 41399	" " "	Acc. 11. 8	Record of real estate sale
81	BM 30215	" " "	1. 11. 18	Slave sale
82	BM 30297	" " "	2. 6. 2	Promissory note
83	BM 30599	" " "	3. 9. 23	Promissory note for garlic
84	BM 74937	" " "	1. 10. 3	Record of non-renewal of litigation concerning property
85	BM 33350	" " "	2. 2. 15	Promissory note for silver
86	BM 32602	" " "	1. 12. 9	Slave sale (?)
87	BM 75509	" " "	2. 5. 20	Sale of a house
88	BM 75757	" " "	Acc. 7. ...	Promissory note for silver
89	BM 33796	" " "	2. 6. ...	Promissory note for dates
90	BM 79569	" " "	... 1. ...	Record of tithe placed at disposal of Marduk

Text Number	Inventory Number	Reign	Year.Month.Day	Description of Contents
91	BM 75489	*Nergel-šarra-uṣur*	Acc. 2. 4	Receipt for provisions
92	BM 74953	" " "	Acc. 5. 24	Receipt
93	BM 75285	" " "	1. 1. ...	Receipt
94	BM 75181	" " "	Acc. 5. 24	Receipt for hides
95	BM 67012	" " "	Acc. 12. 14	Receipt
96	BM 60947	" " "	3. 8. 9	Receipt
97	BM 60231	" " "	Acc. ... 25	Receipt
98	BM 60762	" " "	1. 2. 27	Promissory note for dates
99	BM 75431	" " "	Acc.	Receipt for dates
100	BM 74938	" " "	1. 2. 18	Document concerning silver used for business venture and rental of a house
101	BM 79363	" " "	3. 11. 25	Promissory note for silver
102	BM 74907	" " "	2. 10. 16	Receipt
103	BM 74926	" " "	2. 2. ...	Receipt or accounting of silver
104	BM 75193	" " "	Acc. 6. 2	Receipt for barley brought from the temple of Šamaš

Texts Arranged According to Museum Number

Museum Number	*Catalog Number*
BM 30228	2
30244	30
30252	24
30297	82
30315	81
30331	43
30334	69
30411	9
30419	12
30443	39
30454	42
30525	25
30526	50
30551	22
30573	15
30574	23
30575	26
30577	66
30599	83
30713	71
30848	34
30871	59
30941	67a
30951	45
31009	55
31044	67
31084	35
31104	38
31105	7
31143	33
31151	60
31207	63
31209	52
31248	16
31249	7a
31308	32

	Museum Number	*Catalog Number*
BM	31428	8a
	31558	27
	31858	58
	31964	20
	32602	86
	33167	8
	33350	85
	33562	21
	33796	89
	33910	10
	38135	47
	41399	80
	41400	5
	41401	68
	47347	6
	47517	13
	54178	14
	54179	73
	54180	74
	54210	17
	54244	62
	54259	61
	55712	65
	60231	97
	60762	98
	60947	96
	63830	48
	63831	70
	63834	28
	63840	4
	63841	57
	63842	53
	63843	54
	63931	51
	63932	29
	63933	37
	63960	41
	64730	19
	64933	3

	Museum Number	*Catalog Number*
BM	64931	72
	64956	56
	64969	64
	65260	40
	67012	95
	72797	46
	74495	77
	74511	76
	74907	102
	74926	103
	74937	84
	74938	100
	74953	92
	75181	94
	75193	104
	75285	93
	75431	99
	75489	91
	75509	87
	75757	88
	75778	49
	75968	75
	77303	31
	77304	44
	77590	11
	77626	78
	77637	79
	77825	36
	79363	101
	79569	90
	92746	18
	92791	1

Texts Arranged in Chronological Order

Year	*Month*	*Day*	*Reign*	*Text Number*
Acc	1	26	*Nergal-šarra-uṣur*	97
Acc	2	4	" " "	91
Acc	5	6	" " "	12
Acc	5	24	" " "	92
Acc	5	24	" " "	94
Acc	6	2	" " "	104
Acc	6	12	" " "	1
Acc	6	16	" " "	2
Acc	6	24	" " "	3
Acc	6	24	" " "	4
Acc	7	...	" " "	88
Acc	9	5	" " "	5
Acc	9	16	" " "	6
Acc	9	19	" " "	78
Acc	10	23	" " "	7
Acc	11	8	" " "	80
Acc	12	7	" " "	8
Acc	12	9	" " "	9
Acc	12	14	" " "	95
Acc	...	...	" " "	99
Acc	...	...	" " "	10
Acc	...	...	" " "	11
1	1	1	" " "	13
1	1	25	" " "	14
1	2	9	" " "	15
1	1	...	" " "	93
1	2	18	" " "	100
1	2	27	" " "	98
1	3	1	" " "	16
1	3	25	" " "	17
1	4	4	" " "	18
1	4	8	" " "	19
1	4	15	" " "	20
1	4	17	" " "	21
1	4	27	" " "	22
1	5	3	" " "	23

Year	*Month*	*Day*	*Reign*	*Text Number*
1	5	15	*Nergal-šarra-uṣur*	24
1	6	6	" " "	25
1	7	6	" " "	76
1	8	14	" " "	26
1	8	30	" " "	27
1	9	16	" " "	28
1	10	3	" " "	84
1	10	20	" " "	29
1	1	16	" " "	74
1	11	6	" " "	30
1	1	18	" " "	81
1	12	9	" " "	86
1	...	28	" " "	75
1	...	...	" " "	31
2	1	10	" " "	32
2	2	15	" " "	85
2	2	23	" " "	33
2	2	27	" " "	34
2	2	...	" " "	103
2	3	25	" " "	35
2	4	28	" " "	36
2	4	11	" " "	37
2	5	20	" " "	87
2	6	2	" " "	38
2	6	2	" " "	82
2	6	10	" " "	39
2	6	...	" " "	89
2	7	3	" " "	40
2	8	27	" " "	42
2	8	30	" " "	41
2	9	2	" " "	43
2	9	7	" " "	44
2	9	9	" " "	45
2	10	4	" " "	46
2	10	10	" " "	47
2	10	16	" " "	102
2	10	19	" " "	48
2	11	11	" " "	49
2	11	19	" " "	50

Year	*Month*	*Day*	*Reign*	*Text Number*
2	11	28	*Nergal-šarra-uṣur*	77
2	12	22	" " "	51
3	2	25	" " "	52
3	3	2	" " "	53
3	3	18	" " "	54
3	4	9	" " "	55
3	4	25	" " "	56
3	4	27	" " "	57
3	5	19	" " "	58
3	6	5	" " "	59
3	6	6	" " "	60
3	6	13	" " "	61
3	6	13	" " "	63
3	6	15	" " "	62
3	6	24	" " "	64
3	8	9	" " "	96
3	8	12	" " "	65
3	9	23	" " "	83
3	11	5	" " "	66
3	11	25	" " "	101
3	12	12	" " "	67
4	1	2	" " "	68
4	1	2	" " "	69
...	1	28	" " "	90
...	5	21	" " "	79
...	9	14	" " "	73
...	12	...	" " "	72
...	...	...	" " "	70
...	...	...	" " "	71

Index of Personal Names

Name	*Text*
Abu-ul-idi (wr. **AD-NU-ZU**)	
anc. of Nabû-bēlšunu	74:14
anc. of Bēl-ušallim	74:14
Adad-ēriš (wr.^{d}**IM-KAM**)	
f. of Nabû-zēra-iddina	82:15
Adad-ibni (wr. ^{d}**IŠKUR**-*ib-ni*)	
s. of Zariqu-ibni	2:18
desc. of Šangû-Zariqu	2:18
Adad-šamê (wr. ^{d}**IM**-*šam-me-e*)	
anc. of Arad-Bēl	84:15; 100:16
anc. of Arad-Gula	80:49
anc. of Bēl-aḫḫē-iddina	100:4
anc. of Bēl-ušallim	29:11;84:15;100:2,16
anc. of Marduk-šuma-ibni	100:4
anc. of Nabû-ušabši	29:11;100:2
Adad-šuma-ēriš (wr. ^{d}**IM-MU-KAM**)	
anc. of Marduk-zēri	52:16
anc. of Mušēzib-Bēl	52:16
Adad-šuma-iddina (wr.^{d}**IM-MU-MU**)	
anc. of Nabû-balāssu-iqbi	38:11
anc. of Šūzubu	38:11
Agiri (wr. *a-gi-ri*)	46:8
Aḫa-iddina (wr. **ŠEŠ-MU**)	
ṭupšarru, s. of Ardija	8:13;32:4,13
Aḫa-ittabši (wr. **ŠEŠ**-*i-tab-ši*)	
s. of Nabû-mālik	66:3,13,14;68:9;69:2,83:4

Name	*Text*
Aḫu-bāni (wr.**ŠEŠ**-*ba-ni-i*)	
f. of Rīmūt-bēl-ili	80:45
anc. of Aplâ	42:13
anc. of Bēl-iddina	8:12;33:2;66:16
anc. of Bēlšunu	9:13
anc. of Bēl-uballiṭ	42:13
anc. of Nabû-apla-iddina	79:11
anc. of Nabû-šuma-iddina	79:11
anc. of Nabû-ušallim	8:12;33:2;66:16
anc. of Uššâ	9:13
Aḫu-likin (wr. **ŠES**-*li-kin*$_7$)	
f. of Iddinunu	66:8
Amēl-Marduk (wr.**LÚ-^{d}AMAR.UD**)	
šar Bābili	90:2,6,7,11
Amēlu (wr. **LÚ**-*ú*)	
anc. of Nādin	59:7
anc. of Šulâ	59:7
Apkallu (wr. **NUN.ME**)	
f. of Nabû-ibni	16:10
desc. of Ašlaku	16:10
Aplâ (wr.**A**-*a* or *ap-la-a*)	101:4
f. of Mušēzib-Marduk	25:12
f. of Nabû-nādin-šumi	9:12
f. of Nabû-zēra-ukīn	5:10
f. of Zērūtu	43:21
s. of Bēl-uballiṭ	42:12
s. of Kābtija	58:4,2'
s. of Kudurru	85:13
ṭupšarru, s. of Nabû-šuma-iškun	29:13
desc. of Aḫu-bāni	42:12
desc. of Damiqu	58:4,2'
desc. of Mukallim	43:21
desc. of Nūr-Sin	85:13

Name	*Text*
desc. of Sin-nādin-šumi	9:12
desc. of Šangû-Ninurta	25:12
Appanu (wr. *ap-pa-nu* or *ap-pa-ni*)	18:12;70:6
Arabi (wr. *ar-ra-bi*)	
s. of (name broken)	73:16
Arad-aḫḫēšu (wr.**ÈR-ŠEŠ.MEŠ**-*šú*)	46:6;62:5
Arad-Bēl (wr. **ÈR-**^{d}**EN**)	56:3;75:12
f. of Nabû-aḫḫē-iddina	45:15
f. of Šamaš-aḫa-iddina	17:6
ṭupšarru, s. of Bēl-ušallim	84:14;100:15
s. of Bēl-ušallim	100:6
s. of Kābtija	63:2,7
s. of Nabû-aḫḫē-iddina	87:18
desc. of Adad-šamê	84:14;100:15
desc. of Egibi	45:15
desc. of Isinite	87:18
desc. of Pappāja	63:2,7
Arad-Ea (wr. **ÈR**^{d}**BE**)	
anc. of Ardija	34:10
anc. of Bēl-šarra-uṣur	12:15
anc. of Ea-iddina	58:3
anc. of Labaši	12:15
anc. of Mukīn-zēri	34:10
anc. of Nergal-iddina	58:3
Arad-Gula (wr. **ÈR-**^{d}*gu-la*)	73:6
dajānu, s. of Adad-šamê	80:49,3'
s. of Kiribtu	14:2;73:8
desc. of Dullupu	14:2;73-8
Arad-Marduk (wr. **ÈR-**^{d}**AMAR.UD**)	
anc. of Atkal-ana-Bēl	75:4
anc. of Rīmūt	75:4

Name	*Text*
Ašlaku (wr. **LÚ.TÚG.BABBAR**)	
anc. of Apkallu	16:11
anc. of Nabû-ibni	16:11
Atkal-ana-Bēl (wr. *at-kal-ana-*ᵈ**EN**)	
s. of Rīmūt	75:3
desc. of Arad-Marduk	75:3
Atkal-ana-Marduk (wr. *at-kal-a-na-*ᵈ**AMAR.UD**)	45:4,10
Atkuppu (wr. **LÚ.AD.KID**)	
anc. of Marduk-šākin-šumi	80:47
Babuttu (wr. *ba-bu-ut-tú* or *ba-bu-tu*)	
anc. of Bēl-kāṣir	23:17
anc. of Bēl-rīmanni	23:17;34:14
anc. of Marduk-šuma-ibni	15:5
anc. of Nabû-kišir	15:5
anc. of Šuma-ukīn	34:14
Bā'iru (wr.**LÚ.ŠU.ḪA**)	
anc. of Silim-Bēl	26:10
anc. of Šuma-ukīn	26:10
Bakūa (wr. *ba-ku-ú-a*)	
f.(?) of Bēl...	57:8
qalla of (name broken)	65:6
Balāssu (wr. **TIN**-*su* or *ba-laṭ-su*)	54:7
f. of Etellu	23:8;45:13
f. of Nabû-šumu-lišir	75:17
f. of Nādin	33:3'
f. of Zērija	42:6
desc. of Dannēa	23:8;42:6;45:13
desc. of Rāb-bāni	33:3'
desc. of Šangû Ištar Bābili	75:17

Name	*Text*
Balaṭu (wr. **TIN** or *ba-la-ṭu*)	
f. of Aḫa...	74:11
f. of Labaši	9:2
f. of Nabû-apla-iddina	101:3
f. of Nabû-zēru-lišir	77:5,15
f. of Šamaš-mukīn-apli	84:11
f. of Šamaš-zēra-iqīša	36:25
s. of Bēl-aḫḫē-iddina	74:12
s. of Erība	47:12
s. of Gimillu	32:5
s. of Marduk-erība	14:12
ṭupšarru, s. of Šamaš-iddina	33:4'
s. of Šamaš-uballiṭ	32:9
s. of Zikari	54:15
desc. of Dullupu	74:12
desc. of Isinite	54:15;77:5,15
desc. of Nabunnāja	74:11
desc. of Nabû-ušēzib	84:11
desc. of Nappāḫu	14:12
desc. of Šanašišu	9:2
desc. of Šigūa	36:25
Baltumu' (wr. *bal-tú-mu-'*)	
f. of Šalammanu	82:12
Bānija (wr. *ba-ni-ia* or *ba-ni-ía*)	44:5
f. of Marduk-iqīšanni	2:15;86:11
s. of Marduk...	27:7
s. of Rīmūt	34:10
s. of Šulâ	24:19
desc. of Epeš-ili	34:10
desc. of Illat-na'id	2:15;86:11
desc. of Marduk...	27:7
desc. of Si'atum	24:19
Bānitum-guzzu (wr. **DÙ**-*tum-gu-uz-zu*)	59:4
Bānitum-umma (wr. **DÙ**--*tum-um-ma*)	
w.(?) of Nabû-edu-uṣur	2:4

Name	*Text*
Banunu (wr. *ba-nu-nu*)	
s. of Ṣillâ	42:11;55:14;58:3';81:10
desc. of Rāb bāni	42:11;55:14;58:3';81:10
Bariqi (wr. *ba-ri-qi*)	
f. of Nabû-zēra-iddina	66:6
Basija (wr. *ba-si-ía*)	
anc. of Itti-Bēl-lumur	85:16
anc. of Nergal-uballiṭ	85:16
Ba'ti-ili (wr. *ba-'-ti*-**DINGIR.MEŠ**)	28:36
Bazitum (wr. *ba-zi-tum*)	
m. of Nādin	36:8
Bazuzu (wr. *ba-zu-zu*)	
qalla	23:2,7
Bēl-aḫa-ušabši (wr. **dEN-ŠEŠ-GÁL**-*ši*)	
f. of Bēl-zēra-ibni	16:8
f. of Lūṣu-ana-nūri	31:10
desc. of Bēl-ēṭir	16:8
desc. of Kassidakku	31:10
Bēl-aḫḫē-bulliṭ (wr. **dEN-ŠEŠ.MEŠ-TIN**-*iṭ*)	102:12
Bēl-aḫḫē-erība (wr. **dEN-PAP.ME-SU**)	
f. of Ea-šuma-iddina	14:18
Bēl-aḫḫē-iddina (wr. **dEN-ŠEŠ.MEŠ-MU**)	
f. of Ardija	71:13
f. of Balāṭu	74:12
f. of Bēlšunu	7:18
f. of Marduk-šuma-ibni	100:3
f. of Mušēzib	43:18
f. of Šamaš-zēra-ibni	100:6
f. of Zērūtu	22:11

Name	*Text*
	43:15
desc. of Mušēzib	47:12
desc. of Nappāḫu	10:10;21:2;22:4;35:3; 43:15
Bēl-erība (wr. ^{d}**EN-SU**)	
f. of Bēl-iddina	35:15
s. of (name broken)	63:11
desc. of Dabibi	35:15
desc. of (name broken)	63:11
Bēl-ēriš (wr. ^{d}**EN-APIN**-*eš*)	
f. of Kalbâ	39:15
Bēl-ēṭir (wr. ^{d}**EN-SUR** or ^{d}**EN**-*e-ṭè-ru*)	
f. of Bēl-aḫḫē-iqīša	39:17
f. of Zērūtu	38:3,4
s. of Ina-tēšî-ēṭir	83:9
s. of Nergal-aba-uṣur	82:13
desc. of Damqa	83:9
desc. of Suḫāja	38:3,4
anc. of Bēl-aḫa-ušabši	16:9
anc. of Bēl-zēra-ibni	16:9
anc. of Iddinunu	80:6
anc. of Kalbâ	80:8
anc. of Marduk-ēṭir	60:22
anc. of Marduk-zēra-uṣur	80:6
anc. of Nādin-aḫi	72:2
anc. of Nergal-uballiṭ	60:22
anc. of Rīmūt	78:17
anc. of Saggilu	72:2
anc. of Tabnēa	78:17
anc. of Zakir	80:8
Bēl-ibni (wr. ^{d}**EN-DÙ**)	
s. of Nādin	22:5
Bēl-iddina (wr. ^{d}**EN-MU**)	37:3
f. of Marduk-šarrāni	36:23

Name	*Text*
ṭupšarru, s. of Bēl-erība	35:15
ṭupšarru,s. of Bēl-upaḫḫir	66:18;67:14
s. of Bēl-ušallim	2:17
s. of Nabû-aḫḫē-bulliṭ	26:4
s. of Nabû-ušallim	8:11;33:1';66:15
s. of Nabû...	98:5
s. of Nergal-ušēzib	84:3,5
ṭupšarru, s. of (name broken)	71:15
desc. of Aḫu-bāni	8:11;33:1';66:15
desc. of Dabibi	35:15;66:18;67:14
desc. of Eṭēru	36:23
desc. of Šangû-zariqu	2:17
Bēlilitum (wr. *be-li-li-tum*)	
d. of Bēl-ušēzib	23:1;42:4
m. of Zērija	42:4
desc. of šanašišu	23:1
Bēl-iqīša (wr. ᵈ**EN-BA**-*ša*)	
f. of Nādin	36:5,17
s. of Nabû-ušallim	36:1
ṭupšarru, s. of Nergal-ušallim	86:13
desc. of Mudammiq-Adad	36:1
desc. of Sin-karābi-išemme	86:13
Bēlit (wr. *be-lit*)	
d. of Marduk-bēl-zēri	85:10
Bēlit-iqbi (wr. ᵈ**GAŠAN**-*iq-bi*)	54:6
Bēl-iti (wr. ᵈ**EN-UŠ.SA.DU**)	
f. of Bunene-ibni	47:14
Bēl-kāṣir (wr.ᵈ**EN**-*ka-ṣir* or **KÁD**)	
f. of Iqīša	10:3;43:3;71:4
f. of (name broken)	63:13
s. of Bēl-rīmanni	23:16
desc. of Babutti	23:16
desc. of Šangû parakki	10:4;43:3;71:4

Name	*Text*
desc. of (name broken)	63:13
Bēl-mukīn-apli (wr. ^{d}**EN-DU-DUMU.UŠ**)	
s. of Rašil	26:2
desc. of Nappāḫu	26:2
Bēl-mukīn-zēri (wr. ^{d}**EN-DU-NUMUN**)	
s. of Nabû-mukīn-apli	21:4
desc. of Arad-Nergal	21:4
Bēl-nādin-apli (wr. ^{d}**EN**-*na-din*-**A**)	
f. of (name broken)	30:6
ṭupšarru, s. of Kalbâ	101:13
s. of Nabû-ušabši(!)	59:17
s. of (name broken)	79:7
desc. of Egibi	59:17
desc. of Mukallim	101:13
desc. of Rē'û sīsi	79:7
Bēl-rīmanni (wr.^{d}**EN**-*ri-man-ni*)	
f. of Bēl-kāṣir	23:16
f. of Šuma-ukīn	34:13
s. of Nabû-ēṭir-napšāti	42:13
desc. of Arad-Nergal	42:13
desc. of Babutti	23:16;34:13
Bēl-šāpik-zēri (wr. ^{d}**EN-DUB.NUMUN**)	
s. of Gimillu	12:10
Bēl-šarra-uṣur (wr. ^{d}**EN-LUGAL-ŠEŠ**)	
f. of Labaši	12:14
desc. of Arad-Ea	12:14
Bēl-šulum-šukun (wr. ^{d}**EN**-*šu-lum-šu-kun*)	28:1
Bēl-šuma-iškun (wr. ^{d}**EN-MU-GAR**-*un*)	24:15,16
s. of Marduk-nādin-šumi	24:2
s. of (name broken)	74:2
desc. of Sippê	24:2

Name	*Text*
desc. of (name broken)	74:2
Bēlšunu (wr. ^{d}**EN**-*šú-nu*)	
s. of Bēl-aḫḫē-iddina	7:18
s. of Nabû-zēra-ušabši	7:19;55:15;60:18;86:12
s. of Uššâ	9:12
desc. of Aḫu-bāni	9:12
desc. of Isinite	7:19;55:15;60:18;86:12
desc. of Sin-imitti	7:18
Bēl-šūzibanni (wr. ^{d}**EN**-*šu-zib-an-ni*)	
s. of Šuma-ukin	26:12
Bel-uballiṭ (wr. ^{d}**EN-TIN**-*iṭ*)	18:18;70:15
f. of Aplâ	42:12
f. of Nabû-mukīn-zēri	24:22
f. of (name broken)	77:12
s. of Bēl-zēra-ibni	38:8
s. of Nabû-gamil	81:1,9
desc. of Aḫu bāni	42:12
desc. of Dannēa	25:7
desc. of Egibi	81:1,9
desc. of Isinite	77:12
desc. of Naš paṭri	38:8
Bēl-udammiq (wr. ^{d}**EN-SIG$_5$**-*iq*)	
s. of Šamaš-apla-iddina	66:8
Bēl-upaḫḫir (wr. ^{d}**EN-NIGIN**-*ir*)	
f. of Bēl-iddina	66:19;67:15
desc. of Dabibi	66:19;67:15
Bēl-ušallim (wr. ^{d}**EN-GI** or *ú-šal-lim*)	52:5,10
f. of Arad-Bēl	84:14;100:6,15
f. of Bēl-iddina	2:17
f. of Nabû-bēlšunu	74:14
f. of Nabû...	36:19
f. of Sikkuti	29:4
f. of Silim-Bēl	100:7

Name	*Text*
s. of Nabû-ušabši	29:10
desc. of Abu-ul-idi	74:14
desc. of Adad-šamê	84:14;100:2,7
desc. of Suḫāja	36:19
desc. of Šangû-zariqu	2:17
Bēl-ušēzib (wr. ^{d}**EN**-*ú-še-zib*)	
f. of Bēlilitum	23:1;42:5
desc. of Šanašišu	23:1
Bēl-zēra-ibni (wr. ^{d}**EN-NUMUN-DÙ**)	
f. of Bēl-uballiṭ	38:9
s. of Bēl-aḫa-ušabši	16:7
desc. of Bēl-ēṭir	16:7
desc. of Naš paṭri	38:9
Bēl-zēra-ušabši (wr. ^{d}**EN-NUMUN-TIL**)	18:20
Bēl-zēru (wr. ^{d}**EN-NUMUN**)	5:4
Bēl-zēru-lišir (wr. ^{d}**EN-NUMUN-SI.SÁ**)	
f. of Ea-zēra-ibni	60:3
desc. of Egibi	60:3
Biriqu (wr. *bi-ri-qu-ʾ*)	
f. of Ḫumḫumia-aḫa-iddina	88:4
Bulluṭu (wr. *bul-lu-ṭu*)	
f. of Šamaš-udammiq	87:20
f. of Šullumu	52:13
desc. of Isinite	87:20
desc. of Nūr Sin	52:13
Bulṭâ (wr. *bul-ṭa-a*)	
f. of Nabû-mīti-bulliṭ	15:14
s. of Nabû-zēra-ušabši	54:10
desc. of Dannēa	54:10
Bunene-ibni (wr. ^{d}*bu-ne-ne*-**DÙ**)	

Name	*Text*
s. of Bēl-iti	47:13
s. of Nabû-udammiq	10:12
desc. of Sisû	10:12
Bunene-šarra-uṣur (wr. ^{d}*bu-ne-ne-* **LUGAL-ŠEŠ**)	96:10
Burašu (wr. *bu-ra-šú*)	
w. of Ili-qanûa	82:4
Busasa (wr. *bu-sa-sa*)	
d. of Ḫundari	76:1
Dabibi (wr. *da-bi-bi*)	
anc. of Bēl-erība	35:16
anc. of Bēl-iddina	35:16;66:19;67:15
anc. of Bēl-upaḫḫir	66:19;67:15
anc. of Ea-iddina	79:3
anc. of Nabû-nāṣir	98:9
anc. of Nabû-zēra-ušabši	98:9
anc. of ... Marduk(?)	79:3
Dajān-Marduk (wr. **DI.KU$_5$-^{d}AMAR.UD**)	
f. of Esagila-šuma-ibni	83:14
f. of Labaši	36:22
desc. of Mušēzib	83:14
desc. of (name broken)	36:22
Damiqu (wr. *da-mi-qu*)	
anc. of Aplâ	58:5
anc. of Kābtija	58:5
Damqa (wr. *dam-qa*)	
anc. of Bēl-ēṭir	83:10
anc. of Ina-tēš-ēṭir	83:10
Damqu (wr. *dam-qu*)	
anc. of Mušēzib-Bēl	31:13
anc. of Šamaš-ēriš	31:13

Name	*Text*
anc. of Ardija	1:2,4,10,13
anc. of Gimillu	1:2,4,10,13
Ea-iddina (wr. ^{d}**BE-MU**)	
f. of Nabû-šuma-ukīn	14:7
f. of ...Marduk	79:2
s. of Nergal-iddina	58:2
desc. of Arad-Ea	58:2
desc. of Dabibi(?)	79:2
desc. of Mukallim	14:7
Ea-ilūtu-ibni (wr. ^{d}**BE-DINGIR**-*ti*-**DÙ**)	
anc. of Nabû-ēṭir	89:15
anc. of Nabû-šumu-lišir	89:15
anc. of Nergal-uballiṭ	86:4
anc. of (name broken)	86:4
Ea-pattanu (wr. ^{d}**BE**-*pat-ta-nu*)	
anc. of Nabû...	1:25
anc. of Rīmūt	1:25
Ea-qalu-išemme (wr.^{d}**BE**-*qa-lu-i-šem-me)*	
anc. of Mušēzib-Marduk	81:13
anc. of Nūrea	81:13
Ea-šuma-iddina (wr. ^{d}**BE-MU-MU**)	
s. of Bēl-aḫḫē-erība	14:17
Ea-zēra-ibni (wr. ^{d}**BE-NUMUN-DÙ**)	
f. of Šulâ	20:2'
s. of Bēl-zēru-lišir	60:3,5,11,16
s. of Marduk	30:2
desc. of Egibi	60:3,5,11,16
desc. of (name broken)	30:2
Ebabbar-šadunu (wr. **É.BABBAR.RA**-*šá-du-nu*)	
f. of Nabû-nāṣir	49:10
desc. of Šangû Sippar	49:10

Name	*Text*
Egibi (wr. *e-gi-bi* or *e-gì-bi*)	
Anc. of Arad-Bēl	45:15
anc. of Bēl-aḫḫē-iddina	58:6'
anc. of Bēl-nādin-apli	59:18
anc. of Bēl-uballiṭ	81:2
anc. of Bēl-zēru-lišir	60:4(?)
anc. of Ea-zēra-ibni	60:4(?)
anc. of Ina-tēšî-ēṭir	60:21
anc. of Itti-Šamaš-balāṭu	34:12
anc. of Libluṭ	16"12
anc. of Liširu	59:28
anc. of Marduk-zēra-ibni	58:6'
anc. of Nabû-aḫḫē-bulliṭ	60:25
anc. of Nabû-aḫḫē-iddina	2:8;7:15;9:6;23:5;27:3,9; 34:2;39:13;42:3;45:3;55: 17;58:7';59:17;60:13;80: 23,27;86:2
anc. of Nabû-apla-iddina	45:15
anc. of Nabû-ēṭir	16:12;59:28
anc. of Nabû-gamil	81:2
anc. of Nabû-šuma-uṣur	85:15
anc. of Nabû-ušabši	59:18
anc. of Nabû-zēru-lišir	34:12;60:21,25
anc. of Rīmūt-Bēl	59:20
anc. of Šamaš-inammir	59:20
anc. of (name broken)	85:15
Ekurrata (wr. *e-kur-ra-ta*)	
f. of Nabu-nāṣir	88:2
desc. of Šangû Sippar	88:2
Eli-ilāni-rābi-Marduk (wr. *e-li-* **DINGIR.MEŠ**-*ra-bi-*^{d}**AMAR.UD**)	
f. of Mušēzib-Bēl	80:44
Epeš-ili (wr. **DÙ**-*eš*-**DINGIR**)	
anc. of Ardija	44:4
anc. of Bānija	34:11

Name	*Text*
anc. of Gimillu	30:4;44:4;78:3
anc. of Marduk	27:2
anc. of Marduk-zēra-ibni	24:24;30:9
anc. of Nabû-bēlšunu	63:4
anc. of Nabû-mušētiq-uddê	24:24
anc. of Nabû-šuma-uṣur	27:2
anc. of Nādin-apli	63:4
anc. of Rīmūt	34:11
anc. of Šamaš-iddina	30:19
anc. of Šulâ	30:4;44:4;78:3
Erība (wr. *eri$_4$-ba*)	46:15(?)
f. of Balāṭu	47:13
Eribšu (wr. *e-rib-šú*)	
s. of Nabû-mālik	68:11
Erišu (wr. *e-ri-šú*)	
s. of Nabû-mālik	69:11
Esagila (wr. **É.SAG.ÍL**-*a-a*)	
anc. of Labaši	79:4
anc. of (name broken)	79:4
Esagila-šuma-ibni (wr. **É.SAG.ÍL-MU-DÙ**)	
f. of Bēl-aḫḫē-iddina	2:1,10
f. of Nabû-aḫḫē-bulliṭ	2:1
ṭupšarru,s. of Dajān-Marduk	83:13
desc. of Mušēzib	83:13
desc. of Sin-damāqu	2:1
Etilpi (wr. *e-til-pi*)	
f. of Nabû-zēra-ušabši	24:14
s. of Nabû-kāṣir	24:4
s. of Šulâ	7:2,9,13
desc. of Gallābu	24:4
desc. of Nūbu	7:2,9,13
anc. of Rašil	36:3
anc. of Zēr-Bābili	36:3

Name	*Text*
Etillu (wr. *e-til-lu*)	23:8
s. of Balāssu	23:7;45:13
desc. of Dannēa	23:7;45:13
Eṭēru (wr. *e-ṭi-ru*)	36:13(?)
anc. of Bēl-apla-iddina	36:21
anc. of Bēl-iddina	36:23
anc. of Iqīša-Marduk	80:22,29,41
anc. of Kinâ	36:20
anc. of Marduk-ēṭir	80:22,29,41
anc. of Marduk-šākin-šumi	80:22,29,41
anc. of Marduk-šāpik-zēri	36:7,18
anc. of Marduk-šarrāni	36:23
anc. of Nabû-bāni-aḫi	80:22,29,41
anc. of Nabû-ēṭir-napšāti	80:22,29,41
anc. of Na'id-Marduk	36:21
anc. of Nergal-ēṭir	36:7,18
anc. of anc. of Zakir	36:20
Etillitum (wr. *e-til-li-tum*)	96:4
Gabbija (wr. *gab-bi-ia*)	
f. of Kalbâ	55:5
Gaḫul (wr. *ga-ḫul*)	
anc. of Nabû-šuma-iškun	2:19;7:17
anc. of Rīmūt	2:19;7:17
Gaḫul-Marduk (wr. *ga-ḫul*-^{d}TU.TU)	
f. of Nabû-muṭir-gamil	80:52
Gallābu (wr. **LÚ.ŠU.I**)	
anc. of Etilpi	24:5
anc. of Iqīša	7:21
anc. of Nabû-kāṣir	24:5
anc. of Nabû-nādin-aḫi	7:21
Gigitum (wr. *gi-gi-i-tum*)	

Name	*Text*
w. of Silim-Bēl	7:3,10,14
Ḫašdâ (wr. *ḫaš-da-a*)	
s. of (name broken)	12:13
Ḫiptâ (wr. *ḫi-ip-ta-a*)	7:5,6,13
w. of Nergal-uballiṭ	86:5(?)
Ḫumḫumia-aḫa-iddina (wr. ᵈ*ḫum-ḫum-ia-* **ŠEŠ-MU**)	
s. of Biriqu	88:4
Ḫundari (wr. (*ḫu-un-da-ri*)	
f. of Busasa	76:2
Ibni-ili (wr. *ib-ni-***DINGIR**)	
anc. of Arad-Nergal	80:5
anc. of Silim-Bēl	80:5
Iddin (wr. *i-di-in*)	
f. of Kābtija	66:5
Iddina-Bēl (wr. **MU-ᵈEN**)	12:5(?)
s. of Marduk-šarrāni	75:16
desc. of Šangû-parrakki	75:16
Iddina-Marduk (wr. **MU-ᵈAMAR.UD**)	15:3;21:10;26:8;35:5,7
f. of (name broken)	20:3
s. of Iqīša	8:1,4;10:2;12:1,6;22:8;24: 13;30:4,7,8,11;32:2;43: 2,11;66:1;67:9;71:2,7,9; 83:2
s. of Nergal-ušēzib	30:16
desc. of Illat-na'id	30:16
desc. of Nūr Sin	8:1,4;10:2;12:1,6;22:8; 30:4,7,8,11;32:2,43:2,11; 66:1;71:2,7,9; 83:2
anc. of Na'id-Marduk	54:21

Name	*Text*
anc. of Marduk-iqīšanni	2:15;86:12
anc. of Marduk-zēra-ibni	44:13
anc. of Mukīn-zēri	54:18
anc. of Nabû-nipšari	54:18
anc. of Nergal-ušēzib	30:17
Immadubu (wr. *im-ma-du-bu*)	
f. of Kidinni	20:3'
Ina-Esagila (wr. *ina*-**É.SAG.ÍL**)	11:4
Ina-ṣillâ (wr. *ina*-**GIŠ.GE**$_6$-*a-a*)	51:2
Ina-tēšî-ēṭir (wr. *ina*-**SÙḪ-SUR**)	
f. of Bēl-ēṭir	83:9
f. of Ṣillâ	52:14
s.. of Nabû-zēru-lišir	60:20
desc. of Damqa	83:9
desc. of Egibi	60:20
desc. of Šigûa	52:14
Iqīša (wr. **BA**-*šá* or **BA**-*šá-a*)	70:19
f. of Gula-balāssu-iqbi	45:12
f. of Iddina-Marduk	8:2;10:2;12;22:9;24:13;30:5;32:3;42:2;66:2;67:10;72:2;83:3
f. of Kāṣir	69:10
f. of Nabû-balāssu-iqbi	9:15
f. of Nabû-nādin-aḫi	7:20
f. of Nabû-qa...	63:10
f. of Šamaš-uballiṭ	39:15
s. of Bēl-kāṣir	10:3;43:3;71:4,5,7,10
s. of Gilûa	9:1
s. of Kudurru	24:21
s. of Ša-Nabû-šū	92:2
desc. of Gallābu	7:20
desc. of Nūr-Sin	8:2;10:2;12:2;22:9;24:21;30:5;32:3;66:2;69:10:71:2;83:3

Name	*Text*
desc. of Rāb-bāni	45:12
desc. of Sin-šadûnu	9:1,15
desc. of Šangû parakki	10:3;43:3
desc. of (name broken)	63:10
Iqīša-Marduk (wr. **BA**-*ša*-'[d]**AMAR.UD**)	
f. of Mušallim-Marduk	42:16
s. of Marduk-ēṭir	80:20,28,58
desc. of Eṭēru	80:20,28,58
desc. of Sin-nāṣir	42:16
Irani-Marduk (wr. *ir-an-ni*-[d]**AMAR.UD**)	
anc. of Gimil-Gula	80:50
Isinite (wr. **LÚ.PA.ŠE.KI**)	
anc. of Arad-Bēl	87:18
anc. of Balāṭu	54:16;77:5,15;87:15
anc. of Bēlšunu	7:19;55:16;60:19;86:13
anc. of Bēl-uballiṭ	77:12
anc. of Bulluṭu	87:20
anc. of Gugûa	60:2
anc. of Marduk-erība	77:14
anc. of Nabû-aḫḫē-iddina	87:18
anc. of Nabû-zēra-ušabši	7:19;55:16;60:19;86:13
anc. of Nabû-zēru-lišir	77:5,15
anc. of Nabû...	77:14
anc. of Šamaš-udammiq	87:20
anc. of Zakir	60:2
anc. of Zikari	54:16;87:15
anc. of (name broken)	77:12
Itinnu (wr. **LÚ.DÍM**)	
anc. of Marduk-šarrāni	80:7
anc. of Nabû-apla-iddina	80:7
anc. of Nabû-nāṣir	30:15
anc. of Šulâ	
Itti-Bēl-kinu (wr. **KI**-[d]**EN**-*ki-nu*)	50:2

Name	*Text*
Itti-Bel-lummir (wr. **KI-^{d}EN**-l*um-mir*)	
f. of Nergal-uballiṭ	85:16
desc. of Basija	85:16
Itti-Marduk-balāṭu (wr. **KI-^{d}AMAR.UD-TIN**)	
f. of Širiktum	25:14
s. of Šuma-iddina	85:1,4
desc. of Maštuk	85:1,4
desc. of Sin-udammiq	25:14
Itti-Šamaš-balāṭu (wr. **KI-^{d}UTU-TIN**)	
f. of Liširu	49:5
s. of Nabû-zēru-lišir	34:11
desc. of Egibi	34:11
Kābtija (wr.**BE**-*ia*)	
f. of Aplâ	58:5,2'
f. of Arad-Bēl	63:2
s. of Iddin	66:5
desc. of Damiqu	58:5,2'
desc. of Pappāja	63:2
Kābti-ilāni-Marduk (wr. *kab-ti-* **DINGIR.MEŠ-^{d}AMAR.UD**)	
ṭupšarru, desc. of Suḫāja	80:54
Kalbâ (wr. *kal-ba-a*)	
f. of Bēl-nādin-apli	101:14
s. of Bēl-ēriš	39:15
s. of Gabbija	55:4
s. of Gimillu	32:11
s. of Marduk-nāṣir	12:3,7
s. of Marduk-zēra-ibni	34:3
s. of Nabû-tukte-erība	55:3
s. of Zakir	80:8
desc. of Bēl-eṭir	80:8
desc. of Mukallim	32:11;101:14
*Kalbija (*wr. *kal-bi-ia)*	

Name	*Text*
s. of Šamaš-iddina	98:2
Kanak-bābi (wr. *ka-nak*-**KÁ**)	
anc. of Nabû-kišir	1:23
anc. of Šamaš-šuma-ibni	1:23
Kassidakku (wr. *kas-si-dak-ku*)	
anc. of Bēl-aḫa-ušabši	31:11
anc. of Lūṣu-ana-nūri	31:11
Kāṣir (wr. *ka-ṣir*)	
s. of Iqīša	69:9
desc. of Nūr-Sin	69:9
Kidin (wr. *ki-din*)	
f. of Sin-apla-iddina	49:14
Kidin-Marduk (wr. *ki-din*-^{d}**AMAR.UD**)	
s. of Marduk-zēra-ibni	44:12
desc. of Illat-na'id	44:12
Kidinnu (wr. *ki-di-ni*)	
s. of Immadubu	20:3'
Kinâ (wr. *ki-na-a*)	18:18;46:12
f. of Zakir	36:20
desc. of Eṭēru	36:20
ša rēš šarri	55:7,12
zaqippanu	61:5'
Kinenunâ (wr. *ki-ne-nu-na-a-a*)	
f. of Nabû-dīni-ēpuš	67:12
Kiribtu (wr. *ki-rib-tu*)	
f. of Arad-Gula	14:3;73:8
f. of Tabnēa	87:13,19;88:9
desc. of Arad-Nergal	87:19;88:9
desc. of Dullupu	14:3;73:8
Kisrinni (wr. *ki-is-ri-in-ni*)	2:5

Name	*Text*
Kudurru (wr. **NÍG.DU**)	
f. of Aplâ	85:13
f. of Iqīša	24:21
f. of Mušēzib-Marduk	27:8
f. of Nergal-uballiṭ	7:4
s. of (name broken)	25:10
desc. of Dikî	25:10
desc. of Nūr-Sin	24:21;85:13
desc. of (name broken)	27:8
Labaši (wr. *la-a-ba-ši*)	28:34;95:2
f. of Ṣillâ	74:9
s. of Balāṭu	101:3
ṭupsšarru,s. of Bēl-šarra-uṣur	12:14
s. of Dajān-Marduk	36:22
s. of Marduk-zēra-ibni	34:2
s. of Nabû-mušētiq-uddê	16:3
s. of Šuma-ukīn	5:10
desc. of Arad-Ea	12:14
desc. of Esagila	79:3
desc. of Šamaš-dari	74:9
desc. of (name broken)	36:22
Liblut (wr. *lib-luṭ*)	96:9
f. of Šamaš-udammiq	76:2'
s. of Nabû-ēṭir	16:11
desc. of Egibi	16:11
desc. of Rē'û sīsi	76:2'
Li'ea (wr. **Á.GAL**-*e-a*)	
anc. of Mušibši	84:10
anc. of Nabû-mukku-ēlip	84:10
Liširu (wr. *li-ši-ru*)	18:8;70:8
s. of Itti-Šamaš-balāṭu	49:4
s. of Nabû-ēṭir	59:26
šatammu of ᵈ*NIN.GAL*	49:4
desc. of Egibi	59:26

Name	*Text*
Lūṣu-ana-nūri (wr. *lu-ú-ṣu-ana-***ZALÁG**)	
s. of Bēl-aḫa-ušabši	31:9
desc. of Kassidakku	31:9
Luttû (wr. *lu-ut-tu-*ú)	
f. of Gimillu	67:4
Madānu-šuma-iddina (wr. ^{d}**DI.KU$_5$-MU-MU**)	
s. of Zēr-Bābili	9:10
ṭupšarru,s. of Zērija	21:3;22:2;24:1,7,8,11; 26:13;33:5;35:5;35:2; 67:1; 68:2;69:3
desc. of Nabāja	21:3;22:2;24:1,7,8,11; 26:13;33:5;35:5;35:2; 67:1;68:2;69:3
desc. of Naš-paṭri	9:10
Marduk (wr. *mar-duk*)	90:3,12
f. of Ea-zēra-ibni	30:2
f. of Nabû-šuma-uṣur	27:2
desc. of Epeš-ili	27:2
desc. of (name broken)	30:2
anc. of Bēl-aḫḫē-iddina	44:11
anc. of Marduk-šuma-ibni	44:11
Marduk-bēlšunu (wr. ^{d}**AMAR.UD-EN-***šú-nu*)	
s. of *Nabû-ēṭir*	78:12
desc. of Sin-šadûnu	78:12
Marduk-bēl-zēri (wr. ^{d}**AMAR.UD-EN-NUMUN**)	
f. of Bēlit	85:10
s. of Munnabiti	85:11
ṭupšarru,s. of Mušēzib-Marduk	85:2,8,10,12,18
desc. of Maštuk	85:2,8,10,12,18

Name	*Text*
Marduk-erība (wr. ^{d}**AMAR.UD-SU**)	
f. of Balāṭu	14:13
f. of Rīmūt	8:11,14;43:17
f. of Uballissu-Gula	8:14
s. of Nabû...	77:13
s. of Nādin	22:12;43:4
s. of (name broken)	71:3,5,6,10
desc. of Isinite	77:13
desc. of Nappāḫu	14:13
desc. of Sin-ili	8:11,14;43:17
Marduk-ēṭir (wr. ^{d}**AMAR.UD-SUR** or *e-ṭi-ir*)	
f. of Iqīša-Marduk	80:21,29,41
f. of Marduk-šākin-šumi	80:21,29,41
f. of Marduk-šarrāni	85:17
f. of Nabû-bāni-aḫi	80:21;29,41
f. of Nabû-etir-napšati	80:21;29,41
s. of Marduk-šuma-ibni	1:20
ṭupšarru,s. of Nergal-uballiṭ	60:21
nappāḫu,	102:4
desc. of Asû	85:17
desc. of Bēl-ēṭir	60:21
desc. of Eṭēru	80:21,29,41
desc.of Šigûa	1:20
Marduk-iddina (wr. ^{d}**ŠÚ-MU**)	51:6
Marduk-iqīšanni (wr. ^{d}**AMAR.UD-BA**-*šá an-ni*)	
s. of Bānija	2:15;86:11
desc. of Illat-na'id	2:15;86:11
Marduk-nādin-šumi (wr. ^{d}**AMAR.UD**-*na-din*-**MU**)	
f. of Bēl-šuma-iškun	24:3
desc. of Sippê	24:3
Marduk-nāṣir (wr. ^{d}**AMAR.UD**-*na-ṣir*)	

Name	*Text*
f. of Nabû-šuma-ukīn	87:17
f. of Nuptâ	59:3
s. of Bēl-aḫḫē-iddina	100:3,10
s. of Nabû-kišir	15:4,6,8,11,24
s. of Nergal-uballiṭ	88:7
s. of Šākin-šumi	1:6,9,11,17
desc. of Adad-šamê	100:3,10
desc. of Babuttu	15:4,6,8,11,24
desc. of Dannēa	87:17
desc. of Marduk	44:11
desc. of Nūr-Sin	88:7
desc. of Paḫāru	59:3
desc. of Šigūa	1:6,9,20,22
Marduk-šuma-iddina (wr. ^{d}AMAR.UD-MU-MU)	
f. of Mušallim-Marduk	89:13
s. of Marduk-šarrāni	55:1,10(?)
desc. of Šigūa	89:13
Marduk-šuma-uṣur (wr. ^{d}AMAR.UD-MU-ŠEŠ)	41:7
s. of Marduk-zēra-ibni	101:1,8
desc. of Mukallim	101:1,8
Marduk-zēra-ibni (wr. ^{d}AMAR.UD-NUMUN-DÙ)	
f. of Bēl-aḫḫē-iddina	36:24;58:5'
f. of Kalbâ	34:3
f. of Kidin-Marduk	44:12
f. of Labaši	34:3
f. of Marduk-šuma-uṣur	101:2
f. of Nabû-zēra-ukīn	19:9
ṭupšarru,son of Nabû-mušētiq-uddê	24:23
ṭupšarru,s. of Šamaš-iddina	30:18
s. of ...-ušallim	75:13
desc. of Egibi	58:5'
desc. of Epeš-ili	24:23;30:18
desc. of Illat-na'id	44:12

Name	Text
desc. of Mukallim	101:2
desc. of Uṣur-amat-Ea	36:24
Marduk-zēra-uṣur (wr. ^{d}AMAR.UD-NUMUN-*ú-ṣur*)	
s. of Iddinunu	80:5
desc. of Bēl-ēṭir	80:5
Marduk-zēri (wr. ^{d}AMAR.UD-NUMUN)	
f. of Mušēzib-Bēl	52:16
desc. of Adad-šuma-ēriš	52:16
Maṣṣar-bābi (wr. **LÚ.EN.NUN.KÁ.GAL**)	
anc. of Nabû-šuma-ibni	35:14
anc. of Rīmūt-Bēl	35:14
Maštuk (wr. *maš-tuk*)	
anc. of Itti-Nabû-balāṭu	85:2
anc. of Marduk-bēl-zēri	85:3,19
anc. of Mušēzib-Marduk	85:3,19
anc. of Šuma-iddina	85:2
Miṣirāja (wr. *mi-ṣir-a-a*)	
anc. of Zērūtu	88:12
anc. of ...-ušallim	88:12
Mudammiq-Adad (wr. *mu-dam-mi-iq-*^{d}IM)	
anc. of Bēl-iqīša	36:2
anc. of Nabû-iddina	80:51
anc. of Nabû-ušallim	36:2
Mukallim (wr. *mu-kal-lim*)	
anc. of Aplâ	43:21
anc. of Bēl-nādin-apli	101:14
anc. of Ea-iddina	14:7
anc. of Gimillu	32:12
anc. of Kalbâ	32:12;101:14
anc. of Marduk-šuma-uṣur	101:2
anc. of Marduk-zēra-ibni	101:2

Name	*Text*
anc. of Nabû-šuma-ukīn	**14:7**
anc. of Nadnâ	**101:10**
anc. of Pir'	**101:10**
anc. of Zērūtu	**43:21**
Mukīn-zēri (wr. **DU-NUMUN**)	
f. of Ardija	**34:9**
f. of Nabû-nipšari	**54:17**
desc. of Arad-Ea	**34:9**
desc. of Illat-na'id	**54:17**
Mukkēa (wr. *muk-ki-e-a*)	
s. of Šamaš-riṣūa	**72:2**
Munnabitti (wr. *mun-na-bit-ti*)	
m. of Marduk-bēl-zēri	**85:11**
Muranu (wr. *mu-ra-nu*)	
s. of Mukallim(?)	**73:15**
s. of Ninurta-aḫa-iddina	**30:3,6,11,12**
desc. of Paḫāru	**30:3,6,11,12**
Mušallim (wr. *mu-šal-lim*)	
f. of Šuma-iddina(?)	**6:3**
Mušallim-ili (wr. *mu-šal-lim*-**DINGIR**)	
f. of Šuma-ukīn	**39:4**
Mušallim-Marduk (wr. *mu-šal-lim*-[d]**AMAR.UD**)	
ṭupšarru, s. of Iqīša-Marduk	**42:15**
s. of Marduk-šuma-iddina	**89:12**
s. of Šamaš-šuma-ukīn	**49:2;75:1,9;87:6,13,14**
desc. of Sin-nāṣir	**42:15**
desc. of Šangû-Sippar	**49:2;75:1,9;87:6,13,14**
desc. of Šigūa	**89:12**
Mušēzib (wr. *mu-še-zib*)	
s. of Bēl-aḫḫē-iddina	**43:18**

Name	*Text*
desc. of Qaqqadinu	43:18
anc. of Bēl-ēpuš	47:12
anc. of Dajān-Marduk	83:14
anc. of Esagila-šuma-ibni	83:14
anc. of Nabû-na'id	47:12
Mušēzib-Bēl (wr. *mu-še-zib-*^{d}EN)	
šākin ṭēmi Bābili,s. of Eli-ilāni-rābi-Marduk	80:44,8'
ṭupšarru,s. of Marduk-zēri (KAR-^{d}EN)	52:15
ṭupšarru,s. of Šamaš-ēriš	31:12
desc. of Adad-šuma-ēriš	52:15
desc. of Damqu	31:12
Mušēzib-Marduk (wr. *mu-še-zib-*^{d}AMAR.UD or ^{d}ŠÚ)	
f. of Marduk-bēl-zēri	85:3,19
f. of Šāpik-zēri	81:11
s. of Aplâ	25:12
s. of Kudurru	27:8
s. of Marduk-šuma-ibni	1:21
s. of Nabû-nipšari	40:5
s. of Nūrea	81.12
s. of Šamaš-zēra-ibni	87:16
desc. of Ea-qalu-išemme	81:12
desc. of Maštuk	85:3,19
desc. of Suḫāja	81:11
desc. of Šangû Ištar Bābili	87:16
desc. of Šangû Ninurta	25:12
desc. of Šigûa	1:21
desc. of (name broken)	27:8
Mušibši (wr. *mu-šib-ši*)	
f. of Nabû-mukku-ēlip	84:10
desc. of Li'ea	84:10
Nabāja (wr. *na-ba-a-a*)	
anc. of Madānu-šuma-iddina	21:4;22:3;24:2;26:14;33:6; 35:3;67:2;68:3;69:4

Name	*Text*
anc. of Zērija	21:4;22:3;24:2;26:14;33:6; 35:3;67:2;68:3;69:4; 99:7
Nabû-aḫa-iddina (wr. ^{d}**AG-ŠEŠ-MU**)	
f. of Ili-adinu	66:6
Nabû-aḫḫē-bulliṭ (wr. ^{d}**AG-ŠEŠ.MEŠ-TIN**-*iṭ* or *bul-liṭ*)	
f. of Bēl-aḫḫē-iddina	100:14
f. of Bēl-iddina	26:5
f. of Nabû-ēṭir-napšāti	15:15
s. of Esagila-šuma-ibni	2:1,10
s. of Nabû-zēru-lišir	60:24
desc. of Egibi	60:24
desc. of Nabû-nāṣir	15:15
desc. of Sin-damāqu	2:2,10
Nabû-aḫḫē-iddina (wr. ^{d}**AG-ŠEŠ.MEŠ-MU**)	
f. of Arad-Bēl	87:18
ṭupšarru, s. of Šulâ	2:7;7:15;9:5,9:23:4;27:2,9; 34:1,8;39:12;42;2,9; 45:2,7;55:16;58:6';59:16; 12,14;80:22,27;86:1,8
desc. of Egibi	2:7;7:15;9:5,9:23:4;27:2,9; 34:1,8;39:12;42;2,9; 45:2,7;55:16;58:6';59:16; 12,14;80:22,27;86:1,8
desc. of Isinite	87:18
Nabû-aḫḫē-šullim (wr. ^{d}**AG-ŠEŠ.MEŠ-GI**)	28:3
f. of Bēl-aḫḫē-iddina	100:13
desc. of Šangû Šamaš	100:13
Nabû-ajalu (wr. ^{d}**AG**-*a-a-lu*)	
s. of Sin-ēṭir	16:1
Nabû-ālik-pāni (wr. ^{d}**AG-DU-IGI**)	
s. of Ili-iddina	84:1,6

Name	*Text*
Nabû-dīni-ēpuš (wr. ^{d}**AG**-*di-i-ni*-**DÙ**-*uš*)	1:3,16
s. of Kinenunâ	67:11
Nabû-edu-uṣur (wr. ^{d}**AG**-*e-du*-**ŠEŠ**)	2:4
Nabû-ēriš (wr. ^{d}**AG**-*e-ri-iš*)	
s. of Šulâ	80:9
s. of (name broken)	87:3
desc. of Sin-imitti	87:3
desc. of Sin-nādin-šumi	80:9
Nabû-ēṭir (wr. ^{d}**AG-SUR**)	
f. of Iddina-Nabû	31:5
f. of Ilat	34:6
f. of Libluṭ	16:12
f. of Liširu	59:27
f. of Marduk-bēlšunu	78:13
f. of Marduk-šarra-uṣur	24:1
f. of Nabû-šumu-lišir	89:14
s. of Šulâ	14:4
desc. of Ea-ilūtu-ibni	89:14
desc. of Egibi	16:12;59:27
desc. of Sin-imitti	14:4
desc. of Sin-šadûnu	78:13
Nabû-ēṭir-napšāti (wr. ^{d}**AG-KAR-ZI.MEŠ**)	
f. of Bēl-rīmanni	42:14
s. of Marduk-ēṭir	80:21;28,59
s. of Nabû-aḫḫē-bulliṭ	15:14
desc. of Arad-Nergal	42:14
desc. of Eṭēru	80:21,28,59
desc. of Nabû-nāṣir	15:14
Nabû-gamil (wr. ^{d}**AG**-*ga-mil*)	
f. of Bēl-uballiṭ	81:1
desc. of Egibi	81:1
Nabû-ibni (wr. ^{d}**AG-DÙ**)	

Name	*Text*
s. of Apkallu	16:10
desc. of Ašlaku	16:10
Nabû-iddina (wr. ^{d}**AG-SUM.NA**)	
dajānu,s. of Mudammiq-Adad	80:51,5'
Nabû-kāṣir (wr. ^{d}**AG-KÁD**)	
f. of Etilpi	24:5
desc. of Gallābu	24:5
Nabû-kî-ilāni (wr. ^{d}**AG**-*ki-i*-**DINGIR.MEŠ**)	
f. of Nabû-zēra-iddina	66:4
Nabû-kišir (wr. ^{d}**AG**-*ki-šir*)	
f. of Marduk-šuma-ibni	15:4
f. of Šamaš-šuma-ibni	1:23
desc. of Babuttu	15:4
desc. of Kanak-bābi	1:23
Nabû-kudurri-uṣur (wr. ^{d}**AG.NÍG.DU-ŠEŠ**)	
šar Bābili	36:3
Nabû-le'i (wr. ^{d}**AG-DA**)	
ṭupšarru,s. of Ardija	38:12
desc. of Šigûa	38:12
Nabû-mālik (wr. ^{d}**AG**-*ma-lik*)	
f. of Aḫa-ittabši	66:3;68:10;69;2;83:4
f. of Eribšu	68:11
f. of Erišu	69:11
f. of Nabû-bāni-aḫi	68:5
f. of Rīmūt	69:13
Nabû-mīti-bulliṭ (wr. ^{d}**AG-UŠ**-*bul-liṭ*)	
s. of Bultâ	15:13
Nabû-mukīn-apli (wr. ^{d}**AG-DU-DUMU.UŠ**)	

Name	*Text*
f. Bēl-mukīn-zēri	21:5
f. of Nabû-bāni-aḫi	20:5'
desc. of Arad-Nergal	21:5
Nabû-mukīn-zēri (wr. ^{d}**AG-DU-NUMUN**)	
s. of Bēl-uballiṭ	24:22
s. of Nabû-zēra-iddina	15:16
desc. of Dannēa	25:6,8
desc. of Nappāḫu	15:16
Nabû-mukku-ēlip (wr. ^{d}**AG-MUG**-*e-lip*)	
s. of Mušibši	84:9
desc. of Li'ea	84:9
Nabû-mušallim (wr. ^{d}**AG**-*mu-šal-lim*)	
s. of Nabû-mušētiq-uddê	21:11
desc. of Nūr-Sin	21:11
Nabû-mušētiq-uddê (wr. ^{d}**AG**-*mu-še-tíq*-**UD.DA** or *mu-še-ti-iq*)	
f. of Iddina-Nabû	66:17;83:11
f. of Labaši	16:3,6
f. of Marduk-zēra-ibni	24:24
f. of Nabû-mušallim	21:12
f. of Nergal-nāṣir	21:16
f. of Šamaš-udammiq	22:15
desc. of Epeš-ili	24:24
desc. of Nuḫašu	66:17;83:11
desc. of Nūr-Sin	21:12,16;22:15
Nabû-muṭir-gamil (wr ^{d}**AG**-*mu-ṭir-ga-mil*)	
ṭupšarru,s. of Gaḫul-Marduk	80:52,6'
Nabû-nādin-aḫi (wr. ^{d}**AG**-*na-din*-**ŠEŠ**)	74:5
ṭupšarru, s. of Iqīša	7:20
desc. of Gallābu	7:20
Nabû-nādin-šumi (wr. ^{d}**AG**-*na-din*-**MU**)	
s. of Aplâ	9:11

Name	*Text*
desc. of Sin-nādin-šumi	9:11
Nabû-na'id (wr. ^{d}**AG-I**)	61:2'(?)
s. of Bēl-ēpuš	47:11
desc. of Mušēzib	47:11
Nabunnāja (wr. ^{d}*na-bu-un-na-a-a*)	
anc. of Aḫa...	74:11
anc. of Balāṭu	74:11
anc. of Nabû-šuma-uṣur	49:12
anc. of Nabû-zēru-lišir	80:55
anc. of Nergal-iddina	49:12
Nabû-nāṣir (wr. ^{d}**AG**-*na-ṣir* or **PAP**)	46:7
f. of Nabû-zēra-ušabši	25:16;98:8
s. of Ebabbar-šadûnu	49:9
s. of Ekurrata	88:2
s. of Šulâ	30:14
desc. of Bēl-apla-uṣur	25:16
desc. of Dabibi	98:9
desc. of Itinnu	30:14
desc. of Šangû-Sippar	49:9;88:2
anc. of Nabû-aḫḫē-bulliṭ	15:16
anc. of Nabû-ēṭir-napšāti	15:16
Nabû-nipšari (wr. ^{d}**AG**-*ni-ip-ša-ri*)	
f. of Mušēzib-Marduk	40:6
s. of Mukīn-zēri	54:17
desc. of Illat-na'id	54:17
Nabû-rīmu-šukun (wr. ^{d}**AG-AMA**-*šu-kun*)	59:5
Nabû-ṣabit-qatê (wr. ^{d}**AG**-*ṣa-bit*-**ŠU**^{II})	
rāb bīti	38:2,10
ša rēš šarri	7:8;58:6
Nabû-šarra-uṣur (wr. ^{d}**AG-LUGAL-ŠEŠ**)	
dajānu, s. of (name broken)	13:2'

Name	*Text*
Nabû-šeme (wr. ^{d}**AG**-*še-me*)	
anc. of Na'id-Bēl	23:12
anc. of Šamaš-aḫa-iddina	23:12
Nabû-šuma-ibni (wr. ^{d}**AG-MU-DÙ**)	
s. of Rīmūt-Bēl	35:13
desc. of Maṣṣar-bābi	35:13
Nabû-šuma-iddina (wr. ^{d}**AG-MU-MU**)	
f. of Nabû-apla-iddina	79:11
desc. of Aḫu-bāni	79:11
kabšarru(?)	70:32
Nabû-šuma-iškun (wr. ^{d}**AG-MU-GAR**-*un*)	
f. of Aplâ	29:13
f. of Rīmūt	2:19;7:17
s. of Nabû-zēra-ibni	50:6
desc. of Gaḫul	2:19;7:17
desc. of Nūr-Sin	50:6
Nabû-šuma-ukīn (wr. ^{d}**AG-MU-DU**)	
s. of Ea-iddina	14:6
s. of Marduk-šuma-ibni	87:17
s. of Šamaš-šākin-šumi	29:1
s. of Širikti-Marduk	13:1,7
desc. of Arkat-ilāni-damqa	13:1,7
desc. of Dannēa	87:17
desc. of Mukallim	14:6
ērib bīti Nabû	13:1,7
šatammu Ezida	13:1,7
Nabû-šuma-uṣur (wr. ^{d}**AG-MU-ŠEŠ** or *ú-ṣur*)	
s. of Marduk	27:1
s. of Nabû-ušallim	73:3,6,7,10
s. of Nergal-iddina	49:11
s. of (name broken)	85:14
desc. of Dullupu	73:3,6,7,10
desc. of Egibi	85:14

Name	*Text*
desc. *of Epeš-ili*	27:1
desc. *of Nabunnāja*	49:11
ṭupšarru,desc. *of Ina...*	13:3'
Nabû-šumu-lišir (wr. dAG-MU-SI.SÁ)	28:28;53:2
ṭupšarru,s. *of Balāssu*	75:17
s. *of Nabû-ēṭir*	89:14
s. *of (name broken)*	13:1'
desc. *of Ea-ilūtu-ibni*	89:14
desc. *of Šangû-Ištar-Bābili*	75:17
Nabû-tukte-erība (wr. d*AG-tuk-te-eri*$_4$*-ba*)	
f. of Kalbâ	55:4
f. of Nabû-zēra-iddina	55:3
Nabû-uballiṭ (wr. dAG-TIN-*iṭ*)	
s. *of Na'id-Marduk*	12:11
desc. *of Ur-Nannar*	12:11
Nabû-udammiq (wr. dAG-SIG$_5$-*iq*)	
f. of Bunene-ibni	10:13
desc. *of Sisû*	10:13
Nabû-ušabši (wr. dAG-GÁL-*ši*)	
f. of Bēl-nādin-apli	59:18
f. of Bēl-ušallim	29:10;100:2
desc. *of Adad-šamê*	29:10;100:2
desc. *of Egibi*	59:18
Nabû-ušallim (wr. dAG-GI or *ú-šal-lim*)	
f. of Bēl-iddina	8:12;33:2';66:16
f. of Bēl-iqīša	36:1
f. of Nabû-šuma-uṣur	73.3,7
f. of Tabnēa	60:7,19
s. *of Pānija*	8:3;15:2,8,11,23;21:13;22-13;36:6;38:4;50:3;68:3;69:5;71:14
desc. *of Aḫu-bāni*	8:12;33:2';66:16
desc. *of Dullupu*	73:3,7

Name	*Text*
desc. of Mudammiq-Adad	36:1
desc. of Sin-šadûnu	60:7,19
Nabû-ušēzib (wr. ^{d}AG-*ú-še-zib*)	61:4
anc. of Balāṭu	84:12
anc. of Šamaš-mukīn-apli	84:12
Nabû-zēra-ibni (wr. ^{d}AG-NUMUN-DÙ)	
f. of Nabû-šuma-iškun	50:6
f. of Nādin	58:4
desc. of Nūr-Sin	50:6
Nabû-zēra-iddina (wr. ^{d}AG-NUMUN-MU)	
f. of Gimil-Šamaš	68:122;69:12
f. of Nabû-mukīn-zēri	15:17
ṭupšarru,s. of Adad-ēriš	82:15
s. of Bariqi	66:5
s. of Nabû-kī-ilāni	66:4
s. of Nabû-tukte-erība	55:2,11
s. of Šamaš-erība	49:13
desc. of Nappāḫu	15:17
Nabû-zēra-ukīn (wr. ^{d}AG-NUMUN-DU)	99:4
s. of Aplâ	5:9
s. of Marduk-zēra-ibni	19:8
s. of Šamaš-šuma-ibni	54:18
desc. of Dannēa	54:18
Nabû-zēra-ušabši (wr. ^{d}AG-NUMUN-GÁL-*ši*)	
f. of Bēlšunu	7:19;55:15;60:18;86:12
f. of Bulṭâ	54:10
f. of Nergal-aḫa-iddina	15:18
f. of Šamaš-aḫḫē-iddina	16:14
f. of Šamaš-šumu-lišir	89:2
s. of Etilpi	24:14
ṭupšarru,s. of Nabû-nāṣir	25:15
desc. of Bēl-apla-uṣur	25:15
desc. of Dannēa	54:10

Name	Text
desc. of Isinite	7:19;55:15;60:18;86:12
desc. of Nappāḫu	15:18
desc. of Paḫāru	16:14
Nabû-zēru-lišir (wr. ^{d}AG-NUMUN-SI.SÁ)	
f. of Ina-tēšî-ēṭir	60:20
f. of Itti-Šamaš-balāṭu	34:12
f. of Nabû-aḫḫē-bulliṭ	60:25
ṭupšarru,s. of Balāṭu(?)	77:4,14(?)
desc. of Egibi	34:12;60:20,25
desc. of Isinite	77:14,14
ṭupsarru,desc. of Nabunnāja	80:55
Nadnâ (wr. *na-da-a*)	
w. of Ea-zēra-ibni	30:3,10
Nādin (wr. *na-din*)	
f. of Bēl-ibni	22:5
f. of Marduk-erība	22:12;43:5
s. of Balāssu	33:3'
s. of Bēl-iqīša	36:5,8,9,17,19(?)
s. of Dannāja(?)	75:15
s. of Nabû-zēra-ibni	58:4,11'(na-di-nu)
ṭupšarru, s. of Rīmūt	44:14
s. of Šulâ	59:7,9,10,13,15,25
s. of Šuma-ukīn	50:7
desc. of Amēlu	59:7,9,10,13,15,25
desc. of Naggāru	50:7'
desc. of Paḫāru	44:14
desc. of Rāb-bāni	33:3'
Nādin-aḫi (wr. SUM-ŠEŠ)	
f. of Saggilu	72:1
desc. of Bēl-ēṭir	72:1
Nādin-apli (wr. MU-A)	52:5,11
s. of Nabû-bēlšunu	63:3(na-din-A)
desc. of Epeš-ili	63:3

Name	*Text*
Nadnâ (wr. *nad-na-a*)	
f. of Zērija	35:12
s. of Pir'	101:9
desc. of Mukallim	101:9
desc. of Rāb-bāni	35:12
Naggāru (wr. **LÚ.NAGAR**)	
anc. of Nādin	50:8
anc. of Šuma-ukīn	50:8
Na'id-Bēl (wr. *na-'-id*[d]**EN**)	
s. of Šamaš-aḫa-iddina	23:11
desc. of Nabû-šemê	23:11
Na'id-Marduk (wr. *na-'-id*-[d]**AMAR.UD** or **I**)	
f. of Bēl-apla-iddina	36:21
f. of Nabû-uballiṭ	12:12
ṭupšarru,s. of Šulâ	54:20;87:2,11,21
desc. of Eṭēru	36:21
desc. of Iddina-Marduk	54:20;87::2,11,21
desc. of Ur-Nannar	12:12
Nanâ-riṣuni (wr. [d]*na-na-a-ri-ṣu-ni*)	
w. of Nūr-Bēl-lumur	42:1
Nappāḫu (wr. **LÚ.SIMUG**)	
anc. of Balāṭu	14:14
anc. of Bēl-ēpuš	10:11;21:2;22:4;43:16
anc. of Bēl-mukīn-apli	26:3;35:4
anc. of Marduk-ēṭir	14:14
anc. of Nabû-mukīn-zēri	15:17
anc. of Nabû-zēra-iddina	15:17
anc. of Nabû-zēra-ušabši	15:19
anc. of Nergal-aḫa-iddina	15:19
anc. of Rašil	10:11;21:2;22:4;26:3; 35:4;43:16
Naš-Paṭri (wr. **LÚ.GÍR.LÁ**)	
anc. of Bēl-aḫḫē-iddina	22:11

Name	*Text*
anc. of Bēl-uballiṭ	38:9
anc. of Bēl-zēra-ibni	38:9
anc. of Madānu-šuma-iddina	9:11
anc. of Zēr-Bābili	9:11
anc. of Zērūtu	22:11
Nergal-aba-uṣur (wr. ᵈ**IGI.DU-AD-ŠEŠ**)	
f. of Bēl-ēṭir	82:13
Nergal-aḫa-iddina (wr. ᵈ**U+GUR-ŠEŠ-MU**)	
ṭupšarru,s. of Nabû-zēra-ušabši	15:18
desc. of Nappāḫu	15:18
Nergal-bāni-aḫi (wr. ᵈ**U+GUR-DÙ-ŠEŠ**)	
f. of Rīmūt	20:4
Nergal-ēṭir (wr. ᵈ**U+GUR-SUR**)	
f. of Marduk-šāpik-zēri	36:6,18
desc. of Eṭēru	36:6,18
Nergal-iddina (wr. ᵈ**U+GUR-MU**)	
f. of Ea-iddina	58:3
f. of Nabû-šuma-uṣur	49:12
desc. of Arad-Ea	58:3
desc. of Nabāja	49:12
Nergal-ina-tēšî-ēṭir (wr. ᵈ**U+GUR**-*ina*-**SÙḪ-KAR**-*ir*)	
dajānu, desc. of Rāb-bāni	80:46,10'
Nergal-nāṣir (wr. ᵈ**U+GUR**-*na-ṣir*)	
ṭupšarru, s. of Nabû-mušētiq-uddê	21:15
desc. of Nūr-Sin	21:15
Nergal-šarra-uṣur (wr. ᵈ**U+GUR-LUGAL-ŠEŠ** or **IGI.DU**)	
s. of Šalammanu	82:14

Name	*Text*
šar Bābili	1:26;2:21;3:5;4:4;5:7;6:7; 7:22;8:17;9:17;10:18; 11:15;12:17;13:3,6,5'; 14:20;15:21;16:17;17:8; 18:3,19:11;20:7'21:18; 22:18;23:18;24:26;25:18; 26:16;27:11;28:6;28:15; 30:20;31:15;32:15;33:7'; 34:15;35:18;36:26;37:7; 38:15;39:18;40:8;41:10; 42:18;43:7;44:16;45:17; 46:4;47:3;48:9;49:16; 50:12;51:14;52:2;4,9,18; 53:6;54:22;55:19;56:5; 57:14;58:9';59:1,22;60:23; 61:3;62:4;63:15;64:5; 65:16;66:21;67:18;68:16; 69:17;70:2;71:18;72:14; 73:19;74:16;75:20;76:7'; 77:17;78:19;79:13;80:57 (usur);81:17;82:17;83:16; 84:17;85:21;86:16;87:23; 88:15;89:18;90:14;91:10; 92:6;93:9;94:9;95:6;96:7; 97:9;98:11;99:11;100:17; 101:16;102:9;103:2;104:15
Nergal-uballiṭ (wr. ^{d}**U+GUR-TIN**-*iṭ*)	
f. of Marduk-ēṭir	60:22
f. of Marduk-šuma-ibni	88:7
f. of Rīmūt	29:12
s. of Itti-Bēl-lummur	85:15
s. of Kudurru	7:4,6,12
s. of (name broken)	86:3
desc. of Basija	85:15
desc. of Bēl-ēṭir	60:22
desc. of Ea-ilūtu-ibni	86:3
desc. of Nūr-Sin	88:7
desc. of Paḫāru	29:12

Name	*Text*
s. of Šulâ	14:14
desc. of Sin-imitti	14:14
ameluttum of Nabû-aḫḫē-iddina	42:1
Nūrea (wr. **ZALÁG**-*e-a*)	89:4
f. of Mušēzib-Marduk	81:13
desc. of Ea-qalu-išemme	81:13
Nūr-Sin (wr. **ZALÁG-ᵈ30**)	
s. of Tabnēa	30:15
desc. of Nūr-Sin	30:15
anc. of Aplâ	85:14
anc. of Bulluṭu	51:13
anc. of Iddina-Marduk	8:2;10:3;12:2;22:9;30:5; 32:3;43:2;66:2;71:2;83:3
anc. of Iqīša	8:2;10:3;12:2;22:9;24:21; 30:5;32:3;43:2;66:2;69:10; 71:2;83:3
anc. of Kāṣir	69:10
anc. of Kudurru	24:21;85:14
anc. of Marduk-šuma-ibni	88:8
anc. of Nabû-mušallim	21:13
anc. of Nabû-mušētiq-uddê	21:17;22:16
anc. of Nabû-šuma-iškun	50:7
anc. of Nabû-zēra-ibni	50:7
anc. of Nergal-nāṣir	21:17
anc. of Nergal-uballiṭ	88:8
anc. of Nūr-Sin	30:16
anc. of Šamaš-udammiq	22:16
anc. of Šullumu	51:13
anc. of Tabnēa	30:16
Nūr-Šamaš (wr. **ZALÁG-ᵈUTU**)	65:11
Nusku-iddina (wr. **ᵈŠEŠ.DU-MA.AN.SUM**)	
anc. of Marduk-šākin-šumi	80:48
Paḫāru (wr. **LÚ.DUG.QA.BUR**)	

Name	*Text*
anc. of Marduk-šuma-ibni	59:3
anc. of Nabû-zēra-ušabši	16:14
anc. of Nergal-uballiṭ	29:12
anc. of Nuptâ	59:3
anc. of Rīmūt	29:12
anc. of Šamaš-aḫḫē-iddina	16:14
Pānija (wr. **IGI**-*ni-ia*)	
f. of Nabû-ušallim	8:3;15:2;21:14;22:13;35:6;38:5;50:3;68:4;69:5;71:14
Pāni-Nabû (wr. *pa-ni*[d]**AG**)	
šabû	64:3
Pāni-Nabû-ṭēmu (wr. *pa-ni-*[d]**AG**-*tè-e-mu*)	
b. of Ili-qanūa	82:1,6,7,9
Pappāja (wr. *pap-pa-a-a*)	
anc. of Arad-Bel	63:3
anc. of Kābtija	63:3
Pir' (wr. **NUNUZ**-')	
f. of Nadnâ	101:10
desc. of Mukallim	101:10
Qaqqadinu (wr. *qaq-qa-di-nu*)	
anc. of Bēl-aḫḫē-iddina	43:19
anc. of Mušēzib	43:19
Qarbēa (wr. *qar-bi-e-a*)	
f. of Nabû-balāssu-iqbi	24:6
Rāb-bāni (wr. **LÚ.GAL.DÙ**)	
anc. of Balāssu	33:4'
anc. of Banunu	42:12;55:15;58:4';81:11
anc. of Gula-balāssu-iqbi	45:12
anc. of Iqīša	45:12
anc. of Nādin	33:4'
anc. of Nadnâ	35:12
anc. of Nergal-ina-tēšî-ēṭir	80:46

Name	*Text*
anc. of Ṣillâ	42:12;55:15;58:4';81:11
anc. of Zērija	35:12
Rašil (wr. *ra-šil*)	
f. of Bēl-ēpuš	10:11;21:2;22:4;43:16
f. of Bēl-mukīn-apli	26:3;35:4
f. of Šamaš-aḫa-iddina	68:14;69:15
f. of Zēr-Bābili	36:3
desc. of Etilpi	36:3
desc. of Nappāḫu	10:11;21:2;22:4;26:3;35:4; 43:16
Rē'û(?) (wr. **LÚ.SIPA**-*i*)	66:23
anc. of Ardija	71:13
anc. of Bēl-aḫḫē-iddina	71:13
Rē'û-sīsi (wr. **LÚ.SIPA.ANŠE.KUR.RA**)	
anc. of Bēl-nādin-apli	79:8
anc. of Libluṭ	76:3'
anc. of Šamaš-udammiq	76:3'
anc. of (name broken)	79:8
Rikis-kalāmu-Bēl (wr. *ri-kis-ka-la-mu-*^{d}**EN**)	11:6,8
Rīmat (wr. *ri-mat*)	
m. of Bēl-aḫḫē-iddina	2:2,11
m. of Nabû-aḫḫē-bulliṭ	2:2,11
Rīmūt (wr. *ri-mut* or *ri-mu-tu*)	104:10
f. of Atkal-ana-Bēl	75:3
f. of Bānija	34:11
f. of Nabû...	1:24
f. of Nādin	44:14
f. of Šamaš-uballiṭ	19:6
f. of Tabnēa	78:17
s. of Marduk-erība	8:10;43:16
s. of Nabû-mālik	69:13
ṭupšarru,s. of Nabû-šuma-iškun	2:19;7:17

Name	*Text*
s. of Nergal-bāni-aḫi	20:4
s. of Nergal-uballiṭ	29:11
s. of (name broken)	75:14;78:4
des. of Arad-Marduk	75:3
desc. of Bēl-eṭir	78:17
desc. of Ea-pattanu	1:24
desc. of Epeš-ili	34:11
desc. of Gaḫul	2:19;7:17
desc. of Paḫāru	29:11;44:14
desc. of Sin-ili	8:10
Rīmūt-Bēl (wr. *ri-mut-*[d]EN or *ri-mu-ú-tu*)	73:4
f. of Nabû-šuma-ibni	35:13
f. of Šamaš-inammir	59:20
ṭupsarru,s. of šarru...	72:10
desc. of Egibi	59:20
desc. of Maṣṣar-bābi	35:13
desc. of Uballissu-Gula(?)	72:10
Rīmūt-Bēl-ili (wr. *ri-mut-*[d]EN-DINGIR.MEŠ)	
dajānu,s. of Aḫu-bāni	80:45:9'
Rīmūt-Gula (wr. *ri-mut-*[d]*gu-la*)	
f. of Niqudu	58:2
Saggilu (wr. *sag-gil-lu*)	
s. of Nādin-aḫi	72:1,5
desc. of Bēl-ēṭir	72:1,5
Si'atum (wr. *si-'-a-tum*)	
anc. of Bānija	24:20
anc. of Šulâ	24:20
Sikkuti (wr. *sik-ku-ti*)	
d. of Bēl-ušallim	29:4
Silim-Bēl (wr.*si-lim-*[d]EN)	
s. of Arad-Nergal	80:4

Name	*Text*
s. of Šuma-ukīn	26:9
desc. of Bā'iru	26:9
desc. of Ibni-ili	80:4
qalla of Etilpi	7:1
Sin-apla-iddina (wr. ᵈ**30-A-MU**)	
ṭupšarru, s. of Kidin	49:14
Sin-damāqu (wr. ᵈ**30**-*da-ma-qu*)	
anc. of Bēl-aḫḫē-iddina	2:2,11
anc. of Esagila-šuma-ibni	2:2
anc. of Nabû-aḫḫē-bulliṭ	2:2
Sin-ēṭir (wr. ᵈ**30-SUR**)	
f. of Nabû-ajalu	16:2
Sin-ili (wr. ᵈ**30-DINGIR**)	
anc. of Marduk-erība	8:11,14;43:17
anc. of Rīmūt	8:11
anc. of Uballissu-Gula	8:14
Sin-imitti (wr. ᵈ**30-ZAG.LU**)	
anc. of Bēl-aḫḫē-iddina	7:18
anc. of Bēlšunu	7:18
anc. of Nabû-ēriš	87:3
anc. of Nabû-ēṭir	14:5
anc. of Nūr-Bēl-lummur	14:15
anc. of Šulâ	14:5,15
anc.of (name broken)	87:3
Sin-karābi-išemme (wr. ᵈ**30**-*ka-ra-bi-iš-me*)	
anc. of Bēl-iqīša	86:14
anc. of Nergal-ušallim	2:16;86:14
anc. of Šāpik-zēri	2:16
Sin-kidiri (wr. ᵈ**30**-*ki-di-ri*)	
ša rēš šarri	101:11
Sin-nādin-šumi (wr. ᵈ**30**-*na-din*-**MU** or *šu-mi*)	

Name	*Text*
anc. of Aplâ	9:12
anc. of Nabû-ēriš	80:10
anc. of Nabû-nādin-šumi	9:12
anc. of Šulâ	80:10
Sin-nāṣir (wr. ^{d}**30-PAP**)	
anc. of Iqīša-Marduk	42:16
anc. of Mušallim-Marduk	42:16
Sin-šadûnu (wr. ^{d}**30**-*šá-du-nu*)	
anc. of Gilūa	9:2
anc. of Iqīša	9:2,15
anc. of Marduk-bēlšunu	78:13
anc. of Nabû-balāssu-iqbi	9:15
anc. of Nabû-ēṭir	78:13
anc. of Nabû-ušallim	60:7,20
anc. of Nergal-ušallim	78:15
anc. of Tabnēa	60:7,20
anc. of (name broken)	78:15
Sin-udammiq (wr. ^{d}**30-SIG**$_5$-*iq*)	
anc. of Itti-Marduk-balāṭu	25:14
anc. of Širiktum	25:14
Sippê (wr. *sip-pi-e*)	
anc. of Bēl-šuma-iškun	24:3
anc. of Marduk-nādin-šumi	24:3
Sisû (wr. **ANSE.KUR.RA**)	
anc. of Bunene-ibni	10:13
anc. of Nabû-udammiq	10:13
Suḫāja (wr. *su-ḫa-a-a*)	
anc. of Bēl-ēṭir	38:3
anc. of Bēl-ušallim	36:19
anc. of Kābti-ilāni-Marduk	80:54
anc. of Mušēzib-Marduk	81:12
anc. of Nabû...	36:19
anc. of Šāpik-zēri	981:12

Name	*Text*
desc. of Nabû-ušēzib	84:11
Šamaš-nāṣir (wr. [d]UTU-PAP or *na-ṣir*)	
f. of Šamaš-šumu-lišir	76:4
ṭupšarru,s. of Širiktum	47:14
desc. of Paḫāru	47:14
desc. of Šangû-Sippar	76:4
Šamaš-rīmi-šukun (wr. [d]UTU-AMA-*šu-kun*)	51:4
Šamaš-riṣūa(?) (wr. [d]UTU-*ru-ṣu-ú-a*)	
f. of Mukkēa	72:3
Šamaš-šākin-šumi (wr. [d]UTU-GAR-MU)	
f. of Nabû-šuma-ukīn	29:1
Šamaš-šuma-ibni (wr. [d]UTU-MU-DÙ)	
f. of Nabû-zēra-ukīn	54:19
s. of Nabû-kišir	1:23
desc. of Dannēa	54:19
desc. of Kanak-bābi	1:23
Šamaš-šuma-ukin (wr. [d]UTU-MU-*ú-kin*)	
f. of Mušallim-Marduk	49:3;75:2
f. of Nidintum-Bēlit	89:3,5
desc. of Šangû-Sippar	49:3;75:2;87:6
Šamaš-šumu-lišir (wr. [d]UTU-MU-GIŠ)	
s. of Nabû-zēra-ušabši	89:1
s. of Šamaš-nāṣir	76:3
desc. of Šangû-Sippar	76:3
Šamaš-uballiṭ (wr. [d]UTU-TIN-*iṭ*)	3:8;41:3;65:14;70:10,31;93:7
f. of Balāṭu	32:10
nukaribbu,s. of Ardija	3:9;57:11,15
s. of Iqīša	39:14
s. of Rīmūt	19:5

Name	*Text*
Šamaš-udammiq (^{d}**UTU-SIG**$_5$-*iq*)	
s. of Bulluṭu	87:20
s. of Libluṭ	76:2'
ṭupšarru,s. of Nabû-mušētiq-uddê	22:14
desc. of Isinite	87:20
desc. of Nūr-Sin	22:14
desc. of Rē'û-sīsi	76:2'
Šamaš-ušallim (wr. ^{d}**UTU-GI**)	18:16
Šamaš-zēra-ibni (wr. ^{d}**UTU-NUMUN-DÙ**)	
f. of Mušēzib-Marduk	87"16
s. of Bēl-aḫḫē-iddina	100:5
desc. of Šangû-Ištar-Bābili	87:16
Šamaš-zēra-iqīša (wr. ^{d}**UTU-NUMUN-BA**-*šá*)	
f. of Iddina-Nabû	81:14
ṭupšarru,s. of Balāṭu	36:25
desc. of Dannu-Adad	81:14
desc. of Šigûa	36:25
Ša Nabû šū (wr. *šá*-^{d}**AG**-*šu-ú*)	
f. of Iqīša	92:2
f. of Šuma-ukīn	43:20
Šanašišu (wr. *šá-na-ši-šú*)	
anc. of Balāṭu	9:3
anc. of Bēlilitum	23:2
anc. of Bēl-ušēzib	23:2
anc. of Nabû-apla-iddina	9:3
Šangû-Gula (wr. **LÚ.É.MAŠ**-^{d}*gu-la*)	
anc. of Šušranni-Marduk	80:53
Šangû-ili (wr. **LÚ.ŠID.DINGIR**)	
anc. of Ašarid	2:14

Name	*Text*
anc. of Ašarid	2:14
anc. of Marduk-nāṣir	2:14;23:15
anc. of Šāpik	23:15
Šangû-Ištar-Bābili (wr. **LÚ.ŠID ^{d}INNIN TIN.TIR.KI**)	
anc. of Balāssu	75:18
anc. of Gimil-Marduk	76:5'
anc. of Mušēzib-Marduk	87:16
anc. of Nabû-šumu-lišir	75:18
anc. of Šamaš-bani-aḫi	76:5'
anc. of Šamaš-zēra-ibni	87:16
Šangû-Ninurta (wr. **LÚ.ŠID-^{d}MAŠ**)	
anc. of Aplâ	25:13
anc. of Mušēzib-Marduk	25:13
Šangû-parakki (wr. **LÚ.ŠID.BÁR**)	
anc. of Bēl-kāṣir	10:5;43:4
anc. of Iddina-Bēl	75:16
anc. of Iqīša	10:5;43:4
anc. of Marduk-šarrāni	75:16
anc. of Nabû-bāni-aḫi	2:13
anc. of Rīmat	2:3
anc. of Šūzubu	2:3,13
Šangû-Sippar (wr. **LÚ.ŠID.UD.KIB.NUN.KI** or *sip-par* **KI**)	
anc. of Ebabbar-šadûnu	49:11
anc. of Ekurrata	88:3
anc. of Mušallim-Marduk	49:3;75:2;87:7
anc. of Nabû-nāṣir	49:11;88:3
anc. of Šamaš-nāṣir	76:4
anc. of Šamaš-šuma-ukīn	49:3;75:2
anc. of Šamaš-šumu-lišir	76:4
Šangû-Šamaš (wr. **LÚ.ŠID-^{d}UTU**)	
anc. of Bēl-aḫḫē-iddina	100:13
anc. of Nabû-aḫḫē-šullim	100:13

Name	*Text*
ᵈ**AMAR.UD**)	
f. of Nabu-šuma-ukīn	13:2
desc. of Arkat-ilāni-damqa	13:2
Širiktum (wr. *ši-rik-tum*)	
f. of Šamaš-nāṣir	47:15
s. of Itti-Marduk-balāṭu	25:13
desc. of Paḫāru	47:15
desc. of Sin-udammiq	25:13
Šulâ (wr. *šu-la-a*)	18:14;28:31;70:12
f. of Bānija	24:20
f. of Etilpi	7:2
f. of Nabû-aḫḫē-iddina	2:7;7:15;9:6;23:5;27:3,9; 34:1;39:13;42:3;45:3; 55:17;58:7';59:16;60:12; 80:22,27;86:2(!)
f. of Nabû-ēriš	80:10
f. of Nabû-ēṭir	14:5
f. of Nabû-nāṣir	30:14
f. of Nādin	59:7
f. of Na'id-Marduk	54:20;87:2,12,21
f. of Nūr-Bēl-lummur	14:15
s. of Ea-zēra-ibni	20:2'
s. of Gimillu	31:3;44:3;78:2
desc. of Amēlu	59:7
desc. of Egibi	2:7;7:15;9:6;23:5;27:3,9; 34:1;39:13;42:3;45:3; 55:17;58:7';59:16;60:12; 80:22,27;86:2(!)
desc. of Epeš-ili	31:3;44:3;78:2
desc. of Iddina-Marduk	54:20;87:2,12,21
desc. of Itinnu	30:14
desc. of Nūbu	7:2
desc. of Si'atum	24:20
desc. of Sin-imitti	14:5,15
desc. of Sin-nādin-šumi	80:10

Name	*Text*
Šullumu (wr. *šul-lu-mu*)	
s. of Bulluṭu	52:12
desc. of Nūr-Sin	52:12
Šuma-iddina (wr. **MU-MU**)	17:4
f. of Itti-Nabû-balāṭu	85:2
s. of Mušallim(?)	6:2
desc. of Maštuk	85:2
Šuma-ukīn (wr. **MU-DU** or **MU-GI.NA**)	
f. of Labaši	5:11
f. of Nādin	50:8
f. of Nergal-ušallim	81:6
f. of Silim-Bēl	26:10
f. of (name broken)	79:9
ṭupšarru,s. of Bēl-rīmanni	34:13
s. of Mušallim-ili	39:3
s. of Ša-Nabû-šū	43:19
s. of Zērija	67:13
s. of (name broken)	70:21
desc. of Babuttu	34:13
desc. of Bā'iru	26:10
desc. of Ili-Marduk	81:6
desc. of Naggāru	50:8
desc. of ...-Ea	79:9
Šušranni-Marduk (wr. *šu-uš-ra-an-ni-*ᵈ**AMAR.UD**)	
ṭupšarru,desc. of Šangû-Gula	80:53,7'
Šūzubu (wr. *šu-zu-bu*)	
f. of Nabû-balāssu-iqbi	38:10
f. of Nabû-bāni-aḫi	2:13
f. of Rīmūt	2:3
desc. of Adad-šuma-iddina	38:10
desc. of Šangû-parakki	2:3,13
Tabnēa (wr. *tab-ni-e-a*)	
f. of Nūr-Sin	30:15

Name	*Text*
f. of (name broken)	79:6
s. of Kiribti	87:12,19;88:8
s. of Nabû-ušallim	60:7,19
ṭupšarru,s. of Rīmūt	78:16
desc. of Arad-Nergal	87:12,19;88:8
desc. of Bēl-ēṭir	78:16
desc. of Nūr-Sin	30:15
desc. of Sin-šadûnu	60:7,19
Taplušu (wr. *ta-ap-lu-šú*)	
lamutanu	85:3
Taqiš (wr. *ta-qiš*)	93:3
Taqiš-Gula (wr. *ta-qiš-*^{d}*gu-la*)	
f. of Bēl-aḫḫē-iddina	23:3
desc. of Šigūa	23:13
Tašlimu (wr. *taš-li-mu*)	
lamutanu	81:3,8
Ṭābatum (wr. **DÙG**-*ba-tum*)	16:5
Uballissu-Gula (wr. **TIN**-*su-*^{d}*gu-la*)	72:12(?)
ṭupšarru,s. of Marduk-erība	8:14
desc. of Sin-ili	8:14
Ur-Nannar (wr. **UR-**^{d}**ŠEŠ.KI**)	
anc. of Nabû-uballiṭ	12:12
anc. of Na'id-Marduk	12:12
Uṣur-amat-Ea (wr. *ú-ṣur-a-mat-*^{d}**BE**)	
anc. of Bēl-aḫḫē-iddina	36:24
anc. of Marduk-zēra-ibni	36:24
Uššâ (wr. *uš-šá-a-a*)	
f. of Bēlšunu	9:13
desc. of Aḫu-bāni	9:13
Zakir (wr. *za-ki-ru* or *za-kir*)	

Name	*Text*
f. of Guguā	60:12
f. of Kalbâ	80:8
s. of Kinâ	36:20
desc. of Bēl-ēṭir	80:8
desc. of Eṭēru	36:20
desc. of Isinite	60:2
Zariqu-zēra-ibni (wr. ^{d}*za-ri-qu*-NUMUN-DÙ)	
f. of Adad-ibni	2:18
desc. of Šangû-zariqu	2:18
Zēr-Bābili (wr. NUMUN-TIN.TIR.KI)	97:5
f. of Madānu-šuma-iddina	9:11
s. of Rašil	36:2
desc. of Etilpi	36:2
desc. of Naš-paṭri	9:11
Zērija (wr. NUMUN-*ia*)	
f. of Gimil-Gula	34:5
f. of Madānu-šuma-iddina	21:3;22:3;24:2;26:14;33:6; 35:2;67:2;68:2;69:4
f. of Marduk-šuma-...	10:15
f. of Šuma-ukīn	67:13
s. of Balāssu	42:5,10
s. of Nadnâ	35:11
s. of (name broken)	99:6
desc. of Dannēa	42:5,10
desc. of Nabāja	21:3;22:3;24:2;26:14;33:6; 35:2;67:2;68:2;69:4;99:7
desc. of Rāb-bāni	35:11
Zērūtu (wr. NUMUN-*ú-tu* or NUMUN-*tú*)	
f. of ...-ušallim	88:11
ṭupšarru,s. of Aplâ	43:20
s. of Bēl-aḫḫē-iddina	22:10
s. of Bēl-ēṭir	38:2
desc. of Miṣirāja	88:11
desc. of Mukallim	43:20
desc. of Naš-paṭri	22:10

Name	*Text*
PARTIALLY BROKEN NAMES	
Ana...	74:10
s. of Balāṭu	74:10
desc. of Nabunnāja	
Bēl...	
s. of Bakūa	57:7
E...	
s. of Šamaš-iddina	98:2
Ina...	
f. of Nabû-šuma-uṣur	13:3'
Marduk...	
s. of Bānija	27:6
desc. of Marduk	27:6,9
anc. of Bānija	27:7
anc. of Marduk	27:7
Marduk-aḫḫē...	
f. of (name broken)	77:2
desc. of Šigūa	77:2
Marduk-šuma...	51:9
s. of Zērija	10:14
Nabû...	94:6
f. of Bēl-iddina	98:6
f. of Marduk-erība	77:13
s. of Bēl-ušallim	36:19
ṭupšarru, s. of Rīmūt	1:24
desc. of Ea-pattanu	1:24
desc. of Isinite	77:13
desc. of Suḫāja	36:19
Nabû-qa...	

Name	*Text*
s. of Iqīša	63:10
desc. of (name broken)	63:10
Nabû-ša...	12:8
Šamaš...	18:21;70:17
Šamaš-...-uṣur	46:14
Šarru...	
f. of Rīmūt-Bēl	72:11
desc. of Uballissu-Gula(?)	7
	2:11
...-aḫḫē-iddina	46:16
...-Ea	
anc. of Šuma-ukīn	79:10
anc. of (name broken)	79:10
...-erība	74:6
...kallim	
f. of Muranu	73:15
...Marduk	
s. of Ea-iddina	79:2
desc. of Dabibi(?)	79:2
...-na-a-a	
f. of Arabi	73:16
...-nādin-apli(?)	
f. of Rīmūt(?)	75:15
...-nāṣir	62:6
...qar	
f. of Nergal-ušallim	78:14
desc. of Sin-šadûnu	78:14

Name	*Text*
...-šumišu	65:7
...-ukīn	
f. of Nergal-uballiṭ	86:3
desc. of Ea-ilūtu-ibni	86:3
...-ušallim	
s. of Marduk-zēra-ibni	75:13
ṭupšarru, s. of Zērūtu	88:11
desc. of Miṣirāja	88:11

Name	*Text*

PROFESSIONS AND FUNCTIONARIES

Ameluttum (wr. *a-me-lut-tum*)	1:12;2:5,9;42:2;59:11,12; 85:5
Bappiru (wr. **LÚ.BAPPIR.MEŠ**)	70:25,34
Dajānu (wr. **LÚ.DI.KU**$_5$)	13:2';80:45,46,47,48,49, 50,51,1',2',3',4',5',9',10'
Erib-bīti-Nabû (wr. **LÚ.TU.É-**^{d}**AG**)	13:1,7
Errešu (wr. **LÚ** *ir-ri-še-e*)	18:24
Ḫarranāja (wr. **LÚ** *ḫar-ra-na-a-a*)	1:2,5,8,18
Ikkāru (wr. **LÚ.APIN.MEŠ**)	18:1,4;70:4
Kabšarru (wr. **LÚ.KAB.SAR**)	70:32
Lamutani (wr. *la-mu-ta-ni*)	1:3;81:3,8;85:3
Maluḫḫutu (wr. **LÚ.MA.LAḪ**$_4$*-ú-tu*)	51:6
Mār-šarri (wr. **LÚ.DUMU.LUGAL**)	39:1,3,7
Mušakil-iṣṣuri (wr. **LÚ** *mu-šá-kil-iṣ-ṣur*)	48:6
Naggāru (wr. **LÚ.NAGAR**)	96:12
Nappāḫu (wr. **LÚ.SIMUG**)	102:4
Nuḫatimmutu (wr. **LÚ.MU**-*ú-tu*)	96:3,99:3(?)
Nukaribbu (wr. **LÚ.NU.GIŠ.SAR**)	3:10;61:2;62:2
Qalla (wr. **LÚ** *qal-la*)	20:2;23:3;65:7;86:1,10(?)

Name	*Text*
WATERCOURSES	
Nār Borsippa (wr. *bar-sip* **KI**)	22:6;66:10;67:15;83:6
Nār Bīt-ṭābi-Bēl (wr. **É.DU$_{10}$.GA-^{d}EN**)	21:7
Nār Eššu (wr. *eš-šú*)	63:14;80:2
Nār Gubbu (wr. *gub-bu*)	62:2
Nār Madanu (wr. ^{d}**DI.KU$_{5}$**)	31:2,14
Nār Palkatkatum (wr. *pal-kat-ka-tum*)	3:3;4:2;70:10
Nār Sumanbandu (wr. *su-man-ban-dù*)	70:14
DEITIES	
Aja (wr. ^{d}**A**-*a*)	65:34
Bēl (wr. ^{d}**EN**)	47:2
Bēlit (wr. ^{d}**GAŠAN.AN.NA**)	19:3
Bunene (wr. ^{d}*bu-ne-ne*)	65:3
Gula (wr. ^{d}*gu-la*)	40:2
Marduk (wr. ^{d}**AMAR.UD**)	80:39
Nabû (wr. ^{d}**AG**)	47:2
Nergal (wr. ^{d}**U+GUR** or **IGI.DU** or **GIR$_{4}$KÙ**)	47:2
Šamaš (wr. ^{d}**UTU**)	3:3;4:2;18:1;46:2;47:2; 54:3;65:3

Name	*Text*
TEMPLES	
Bīt-Gula (wr. **É-**^{d}*gu-la*)	104:13
Ebabbar (wr. **É-BABBAR.RA**)	18:2;28:4;37:4;40:3;46:2; 47:5;65:12;70:3;92:3; 95:3';102:5
Esagila (wr. **É.SAG.ÍL**)	80:42
Ezida (wr. **É.ZI.DA**)	13:2,7,5'
GATES	
Abul Enlil (wr. **KÁ.GAL**^{d}**EN.LIL**)	80:3
Bāb bīt mār šarri (wr. **KÁ.É.DUMU.LUGAL**)	55:5

Texts in Transliteration and Translations

1

BM 92791 (Collated)
Published as Evetts, *Ner.* 1. Published in translation by Peiser, KB 4, 202ff and *Rechtsleben* 2 48ff.

1) ⸢*x*⸣ MA.NA 5 GÍN KÙ.BABBAR *šá* ^{I} ÈR-*ia* A-*šú šá* ^{I} *gi-mil-lu*[...]
2) A ^{Id}BE-DÙ-*eš*-DINGIR *ina* ŠU^{II} LÚ *ḫar-ra-na-a-a iš-šu* [...]
3) *u* ^{Id}AG-*di-i-nu*-DÙ-*uš* DAM-*šú u* DUMU.SAL-*šú* LÚ *la-mu-[ta-ni]*
4) ⸢*šá*⸣ ^{I}ÈR-*ia* A-*šú šá* ^{I}*gi-mil-lu* A ^{Id}BE-DÙ-eš-DINGIR
5) *a-na* ŠÁM *ḫa-ri-iṣ a-na* LÚ *ḫar-ra-na-a-a*
6) *id-di-nu u* ^{Id}AMAR.UD-MU-DÙ A-*šú šá* ^{I}GAR-MU A ^{I}*ši-gu-ú-a*
7) *pu-ut a-ba-ku šá* ^{Id}AG-*di-i-ni*-DÙ-*uš* DAM-*šú u* DUMU.SAL-*šú*
8) *ina* ŠU^{II} LÚ *ḫar-ra-na-a-a na-šu-ú ul* GUR-*ma*
9) ^{Id}AMAR.UD-MU-DÙ A-*šú šá* ^{I}GAR-MU A ^{I}*ši-gu-ú-a*
10) *it-ti* ^{I}ÈR-*ia* A-*šú šá* ^{I}*gi-mil-lu* A ^{I}<^{d}BE>-DÙ-eš-DINGIR
11) *ul i-dab-bu-ub* ^{Id}AMAR.UD-MU-DÙ 1/3 MA.NA [5 GÍN KÙ.BABBAR]
12) ŠÁM *a-me-lut-tum ina* ŠU^{II} ^{I}ÈR-*ia u* [...]
13) DUMU.MEŠ *šá* ^{I}*gi-mil-lu* A ^{I}<^{d}BE>-DÙ-eš-[DINGIR] [...]
14) *ma-ḫir*
15) *ina* UD-*mu ú-ìl-tim lu-ú* GABA.RI *ú-ìl-[tim]* [...]
16) *šá* ^{Id}AG-*di-i-nu*-DÙ-*uš* DAM-*šú u* DUMU.SAL-*šú* [...]
17) *ina* È ^{Id}AMAR.UD-MU-DÙ A-*šú šá* ^{I}GAR-MU [A ^{I}*ši-gu-ú-a*]
18) *u* LÚ *ḫar-ra-na-a-a* ⸢*x*⸣ *tan-ma-ru šá* ^{I}ÈR-[*ia*]
19) *u* ^{I}[...] *a* DUMU.MEŠ *šá* ^{I}*gi-mil-lu ši-[i]*
20) LÚ *mu-kin-nu* ^{Id}AMAR.UD-SUR A-*šú šá* ^{Id}AMAR.UD-MU-DÙ
21) A ^{I}*ši-gu-ú-a* ^{I}*mu-še-zib*-^{d}AMAR.UD A-*šú*
22) *šá* ^{Id}AMAR.UD-MU-DÙ A ^{I}*ši-gu-ú-a*
23) ^{Id}UTU-MU-DÙ A-*šú šá* ^{Id}AG-*ki-šir* A ^{I}*ka-nak*-KÁ
24) LÚ.ŠID ^{Id}AG-[...] A-*šú šá* ^{I}*ri-mu-tu*

25) A ^{Id}BE-*pat-ta-nu* TIN.TIR.KI ITU.KIN UD.12.KAM
26) MU.SAG.NAM.LUGAL.LA ^{Id}U+GUR-LUGAL-ŠEŠ
27) LUGAL TIN.TIR.KI

Translation

(Document concerning) two-thirds(?) mina, five shekels of silver, which Ardija, son of Gimillu, descendant of Ea-epeš-ili received (lit., has) from the man from Ḫarran, ⌜and⌝ for which Ardija, son of Gimillu, descendant of Ea-epeš-ili sold (lit., gave) Nabû-dīni-ēpuš, his wife and his daughter, (his) slaves, for the full price to the man from Ḫarran. Marduk-šuma-ibni, son of Šākin-šumi, descendant of Šigūa, bears the responsibility of delivering Nabû-dīni-ēpuš, his wife and his daughter to the man from Ḫarran. Marduk-šuma-ibni, son of Šākin-šumi, descendant of Šigūa, will not make a claim against Ardija, son of Gimillu, descendant of Ea(!)-epeš-ili and there will be no litigation. Marduk-šuma-ibni has received two-thirds mina, [five shekels of silver], the full price of the slaves, from Ardija and [...] sons of Gimillu, descendants of Ea(!)-epeš-ili. Whenever a contract or a copy [of a contract] concerning Nabû-dīni-ēpuš, his wife and his daughter [turns up(?)] in the house of Marduk-šuma-ibni, son of Šākin-šumi, [descendant of Šigūa] and the man from Ḫarran sees it, it is the property of Ard[ija] and [...], sons of Gimillu. Witnesses (are) Marduk-ēṭir, son of Marduk-šuma-ibni, descendant of Šigūa, Mušēzib-Marduk, son of Marduk-šuma-ibni, descendant of Šigūa, Šamaš-šuma-ibni, son of Nabû-kišir, descendant of Kanak-bābi, (and) the scribe, Nabû-[...] son of Rīmūt, descendant of Ea-pattanu. Babylon, month of Ululu, twelfth day, accession year of Nergal-šarra-uṣur, king of Babylon.

Commentary

1) Although the tablet is now broken off here, restoration is based on the contents of l. 11.

10, 13) Readings of the personal name based on l.2 (correctly copied by Evetts).

2

BM 30228 (Collated)
Published as Evetts, *Ner.* 2 and Dandamaev, *Slavery*, p. 188 ff.

1) ^{Id}EN-ŠEŠ.MEŠ-MU *u* ^{Id}AG-ŠEŠ.MEŠ-*bul-liṭ* DUMU.MEŠ [*šá* ^{I}É.SAG.ÍL-MU-DÙ]

2) A ^{Id}30-*da-ma-qu u* SAL *ri-mat* AMA[-*šú*]-*nu* [DUMU.SAL-*su*]
3) *šá* ^{I}*šu-zu-bu* A LÚ.ŠID.BAR *ina ḫu-ud lìb-bi-*[*šú-nu*]
4) ^{Id}AG-*e-du*-ŠEŠ SAL ^{d}DÙ-*tum-um-ma* DAM-[*su*]
5) SAL *ki-iṣ-ri-in-ni u* SAL *gi-mil-in-ni* DAM
6) PAP 4 *a-me-lut-tum a-na* 2 MA.NA KÙ.BABBAR *a-na* ŠÀM
7) *gam-ru-tu a-na* ^{Id}AG-ŠEŠ.MEŠ-MU A-šú šá ^{I}*šu-la-a*
8) A ^{m}*e-gi-bi id-di-nu pu-ut si-ḫi-i pa-qír-ra-nu*
9) *u* DUMU.DÙ-*ú-tu ša a-me-lut-tum* ^{Id}EN-ŠEŠ.MEŠ-MU
10) *u* ^{Id}AG-ŠEŠ.MES-*bul-liṭ* DUMU.MEŠ *šá* ^{I}É.SAG.ÍL.MU-DÙ
11) A ^{Id}30-SIG$_5$ *u* SAL *ri-mat* AMA-*šü-nu na-šu-ú*
12) [*1-e*]*n pu-ut 2-u na-šu-ú*
13) LÚ *mu-kin-nu* ^{Id}AG-DÙ-ŠEŠ A-*šú šá* ^{I}*šu-zu-bu* A LÚ.ŠID.BAR
14) [^{I}*a-šá*]-*ri-du* A-*šú šá* ^{Id}AMAR.UD-*na-ṣir* A LÚ.ŠID.DINGIR
15) ^{Id}AMAR.UD-BA-*šá-an-ni* A-*šú šá* ^{I}*ba-ni-ia* A ^{Id}ILLAT-I
16) ^{I}DUB-NUMUN A-*šú šá* ^{Id}U+GUR-GI A ^{Id}30-*ka-ra-bi-iš-me*
17) ^{Id}EN-MU A-*šú šá* ^{Id}EN-*ú-šal*(!)(*text:me*)-*lim* A LÚ.ŠID ^{d}*za-ri-qu*
18) ^{Id}IŠKUR-*ib-ni A-šú šá* ^{Id}*za-ri-qu*-NUMUN-DÙ A LÚ.SID ^{d}*za-ri-qu*
19) *u* LÚ.ŠID ^{I}*ri-mut* A-*šú šá* ^{Id}AG-MU-GAR-*un* A ^{I}*ga-ḫul*
20) TIN.TIR.KI ITU.KIN UD.16.KAM MU.SAG.NAM.LUGAL.[LA]
21) ^{Id}U+GUR-LUGAL-ŠEŠ LUGAL TIN.TIR.KI

Translation

Bēl-aḫḫē-iddina and Nabû-aḫḫē-bulliṭ, sons of [Esagila-šuma-ibni], descendant of Sin-damāqu and the lady Rīmat, [their] mother, [daughter of] Šūzubu, descendant of Šangû-parakki have, of [their] own free will, sold (lit., given) Nabû-edu-uṣur, the lady Bānitum-umma, his (?) wife, the lady Kiṣrinni and the lady Gimillinni, total of four slaves, to Nabû-aḫḫē-iddina, son of Šulâ, descendant of Egibi for the full price of two minas of silver. Nabû-aḫḫē-bulliṭ and Bēl-aḫḫē-iddina, sons of Esagila-šuma-ibni, descendant of Sin-damāqu and their mother, the lady Rīmat, bear responsibility for claims against the legality of the sale, claimant and personal freedom that (might arise against) the slaves, (and) [one] shall bear the responsibility for the other. Witneses are Nabû-bāni-aḫi, son of Šūzubu, descendant of Šangû-parakki, [Aša]ridu, son of Marduk-nāṣir, descendant of Šangû-ili, Marduk-iqīšanni, son of Bānija, descendant of

Illat-na'id, Šāpik-zēri, son of Nergal-ušallim, descendant of Sin-karābi-išemme, Bēl-iddina, son of Bēl-ušallim, descendant of Šangû-Zariqu, Adad-ibni, son of Zariqu-zēra-ibni, descendant of Šangû-Zariqu and the scribe, Rīmūt, son of Nabû-šuma-iškun, descendant of Gaḫul. Babylon, month of Ululu, sixteenth day, accession year of Nergal-šarra-uṣur, king of Babylon.

Commentary

1) Restoration is based on the contents of l. 10.
2) Restoration is based on contents of l. 11.
8) For a commentary on *siḫu* see AOATS 4, text No. 19.

3

BM 64933 (Collated)
Published as Evetts, *Ner.* 3

1) 47 GUR ZÚ.LUM.MA
2) ZAG.LU *la gam-mar-ru-tú*
3) *šá* ^{d}UTU *šá ina* ÍD *pal-kat-ka-tum*
4) ITU.KIN UD.24.KAM MU.SAG.NAM.LUGAL.LA
5) ^{d}U+GUR-LUGAL-ŠEŠ LUGAL TIN.TIR.KI
6) *ki-i pi 6 ma-ši-ḫi*
7) *šá* ZAG.LU ⸢*a-na* 1⸣ [GUR *mi-šil*]
8) *ša* ŠE.NUMUN-*šú* DÙ -[*uš*]
9) ^{Id}UTU-TIN-*iṭ* A ^{I}ÈR-*ia*
10) LÚ.NU.GIŠ.SAR

Translation

(Document concerning) forty-seven *kurru* of dates, the incomlete estimated yield of (a field) of Šamaš situated on the Palkatkatum canal (for) the month of Ululu, twenty-fourth day, accession year of Nergal-šarra-uṣur, king of Babylon. Šamaš-uballiṭ, son of Ardija, the gardener, ⸢will produce⸣ an additional six measures of the estimated yield for every [*kurru* in half] of his field.

Commentary

7) the restorations here are based on the contents of lines 8-9 of Evetts, *Ner.* 4.

4

BM 63840 (Collated)
Published as Evetts, *Ner.* 4.

1) ZÚ.LUM.MA ZAG.LU
2) *šá* ^{d}UTU *šá* ÍD *pal-kat-ka-tum*
3) ITU.KIN UD.24.KAM MU.⌜SAG.⌝NAM.LUGAL.LA
4) ^{d}U+GUR-LUGAL-ŠEŠ LUGAL TIN.[TIR.]KI
5) 47 GUR ZÚ.LUM.MA
6) *la gam-mar-ru ki-i pi*
7) ⌜*6*⌝ *ma-ši-ḫi šá* ZÍZ ZAG.LU
8) ⌜*a*⌝*-na* 1 GUR ^{Id}UTU-TIN.*iṭ*
9) ⌜*mi*⌝*-šil* ŠE.NUMUN-*šú* DÙ-*uš*

Translation

(Document concerning) dates, estimated yield of (a field of) Šamaš (located) on the Palkatkutum canal, month of Ululu, twenty-fourth day, accession year of Nergal-šarra-uṣur, king of Babylon. (With regard to) the forty-seven *kurru* of dates, the incomplete (estimated yield), Šamaš-uballiṭ will produce an additional ⌜six⌝ measures of the estimated yield ⌜for⌝ each *kurru* in half of his field.

5

BM 41440 (Collated)
Published as Evetts, *Ner.* 5

1) 8 GÍN 4-*ut bit-qa* KÙ.BABBAR
2) ^{Id}AG-ŠEŠ.MEŠ-MU
3) *ina i-di* É-*šú ina* ŠU^{II}
4) ^{Id}EN-NUMUN *ma-ḫi-ir*
5) ITU.GAN UD.5.KAM
6. MU.SAG.NAM.LUGAL.LA
7) ^{Id}U+GUR-LUGAL-ŠEŠ
8) LUGAL TIN.TIR[.KI]
9) *šá* ^{Id}AG-NUMUN-DU ⌜A-⌝*šú šá*
10) ^{I}A-*a* ^{I}*la-a-ba-ši*
11) A-*šú šá* ^{I}MU-GI.NA

Translation

(Document concerning) eight and three-eighths shekels of silver, belonging to Nabû-zēra-ukīn, ⸢son⸣ of Aplâ (and) Labaši, son of Šuma-ukīn (which) Nabû-aḫḫē-iddina received from Bēl-zēru (as a portion of) the rent of his house. Month of Kislimu, fifth day, accession year of Nergal-šarra-uṣur, king of Babylon.

Commentary

lines 9-11) these lines, although inadvertently put at the end of the text by the scribe, appear to properly belong after line 1.

6

BM 47347 (Collated)
Published as Evetts, *Ner. 6*

1) ⸢2⸣(PI) 4(BÁN) ŠE.BAR *ki-is-sat*
2) *šá* GUD.[MEŠ] *ina* IGI ^{I}⸢MU-MU⸣
3) A ^{I}*mu-šal-lim* [...]
4) ITU.GAN *ta* [...]
5) [UD.16.] KAM
6) MU.SAG.NAM.LUGAL.LA
7) ^{Id}U+GUR-LUGAL-ŠEŠ
8) LUGAL TIN.TIR.KI

Translation

(Document concerning) ⸢two⸣ *pi*, twenty-four *qa* of barley, fodder for the oxen, placed at the disposal of ⸢Šuma-iddina⸣, son of Mušallim. Month of Kislimu, [...] ⸢sixteenth⸣ [day,] accession year of Nergal-šarra-uṣur, king of Babylon.

Commentary

5) Only the last five verticals are left on the tablet. It is possible the date was the sixteenth day.

7

BM 31105 (Collated)

Published as Evetts, *Ner.* 7; published with translation or commentary by Peiser, *Rechtsleben* 3, 2 and Marx, *BA* 4, 15ff as well as Dandamaev, *Slavery*, p. 201 and 210.

1) ^{I}⌜*si-*⌝*lim-*^{d}EN LÚ *qal-la šá*
2) ^{I}⌜e-⌝*tel-pi* A-*šú šá* ^{I}*šu-la-a* A ^{I}*nu-ú-bu*
3) *u* SAL *ḫa-*[*na-šu*] DAM-*šú šá a-na nu-dun-ni-e*
4) *a na* [^{Id}U+GUR-TIN-]*iṭ* A-*šú šá* ^{I}NÍG.DU *it-ti*
5) [SAL *ḫi-ip-ta*]*-a* DUMU-SAL-*an-ni-šú-nu id-di-nu*
6) *u* ^{Id}U+GUR-TIN-*it u* SAL *ḫi-i-p-ta-a*
7) DAM-*šú a-na* 1/3 *ma.na* 5 GÍN KÙ.BABBAR *a-na*
8) [SAM] *gam-ru-tú a*⌜*-na*⌝ ^{Id}AG-*ṣa-bit*-ŠU^{II}
9) [LÚ.SAG] ⌜LUGAL⌝ *id-di-*[*nu*]-⌜*ma*⌝ ^{I}*e-tel-pi*
10) [*u* SAL *ḫa*]*-na-šu* DAM-*šú ina lìb-bi a-na*
11) [*si-bu-tu*] ⌜*áš*⌝*-bu* KÙ.BABBAR-'
12) [1/3 MA.NA 5 GÍN] ^{Id}U+GUR-TIN-*iṭ ù*
13) SAL *ḫi-ip-ta-a* DAM-*šú* ^{I}*e-tel-pi*
14) ⌜*ù*⌝ SAL *ḫa-na-šu* DAM-*šú ina* ŠU^{II}
15) ^{Id}AG-ŠEŠ.MEŠ-MU A-*šú šá* ^{I}*šu-la-a* A ^{I}*e-gi-bi*
16) *e-ṭi-ir-'* LÚ *mu-kin-nu*
17) ^{I}*ri-mut* A-*šú šá* ^{Id}AG-MU-GAR-*un* A ^{I}*ga-ḫal*
18) ^{I}EN-*šú-nu* A-*šú šá* ^{Id}EN-ŠEŠ.MEŠ-MU A ^{Id}30-ZAG.LU
19) ^{I}EN-*šú-nu* A-*šú šá* ^{Id}AG-NUMUN-GÁL-*ši* A LÚ.PA.ŠE.KI
20) [*u*] LÚ.ŠID ^{Id}AG-*na-din*-ŠEŠ A-*šú šá* ^{I}BA-*šá-a*
21) [A LÚ.]ŠU.ḪA TIN.TIR.KI ITU.AB.E UD.23.KAM
22) [MU.]SAG.NAM.LUGAL.E ^{Id}U+GUR-LUGAL-ŠEŠ
23) LUGAL TIN.TIR.KI

Translation

(Document concerning) ⌜Silim-⌝Bēl, slave of Etilpi, son of Šulâ, descendant of Nūbu and the lady Ḫa[našu,] his wife, who were presented to [Nergal-ubal]liṭ, son of Kudurru, along with their daughter, the [Lady Ḫiptâ,] as a wedding present, and who Nergal-uballiṭ and the lady Ḫiptâ, his wife, (subsequently) sold (lit., gave) to Nabû-ṣabit-qāte, the ⌜royal official-⌝, ⌜for⌝ the full [price] of one-third mina, five shekels of silver. Etilpi and the [lady Ḫa]našu, his wife; ⌜were present⌝ as [witnes]ses (to the above-mentioned sale.) [The one-third mina, five shekels] of silver was paid to Nabû-aḫḫē-iddina, son of Šulâ, descendant of Egibi (to) Nergal-uballiṭ and the lady Ḫiptâ, his wife, (as well as) Etilpi ⌈and⌉ the lady Ḫanašu, his wife. Witnesses (are) Rīmūt, son of Sin-imitti, Bēlšunu, son of Nabû-zēra-ušabši, descendant of the Isinite, [and] the scribe, Nabû-nādin-aḫi, son of Iqīša, [descendant] of Bā'iru. Babylon, month of Ṭebetu, twenty-third day, [accession year] of Nergal-sarra-uṣur, king of Babylon.

8

BM 33067 (Collated)
Published as Evetts, *Ner. 8*

1) 2 5/6 MA.NA KÙ.BABBAR *šá ina* 1 GÍN *bit-qa šá* ^{I}MU-^{d}[AMAR.UD]
2) A-*šú šá* ^{I}BA-*šá-a* DUMU ^{I}ZÁLAG-^{d}30
3) *ina* UGU ^{Id}AG-GI A-*šú šá* ^{I}IGI-*ni-ia*
4) *ù* KASKAL^{II} *šá* ^{I}MU-^{d}AMAR.UD
5) *ina* ITU.BÁR *ina* GIS.MÁ-*šú*
6) *ḫa-ru-up-tum i-nam-din e-lat* 5 5/6 MA.NA 2 GÍN KÙ.BABBAR
7) *ša muḫ-ḫi* KASKAL^{II} *u e-lat* 3 1/2 MA.NA KÙ.BABBAR
8) *šá* KASKAL^{II} 1 LIM *gid-lu šá* SUM.SAR *nu-up-tum*
9) *ina muḫ-ḫi i-nam-din*
10) LÚ *mu-kin-nu* ^{I}*ri-mut* A-*šú šá*
11) ^{Id}AMAR.UD-SU A ^{Id}30-DINGIR ^{Id}EN-MU
12) A-*šú šá* ^{Id}⌈AG-⌉GI A ^{I}SES-*ba-ni-*⌈'⌉
13) ^{I}⌈ŠEŠ-MU⌉ A-*šú šá* ^{I}ÈR-*ia u* LÚ.ŠID
14) ^{I}TIN-*su-*^{d}*gu-la* A-*šú šá* ^{Id}AMAR.UD-SU
15) A ^{Id}30-DINGIR TIN.TIR.KI ITU.ŠE
16) UD.7.KAM MU.SAG.NAM.LUGAL.LA
17) ^{Id}U+GUR-LUGAL-ŠEŠ LUGAL TIN.TIR.KI

Translation

(Document concerning) two and five-sixths minas of silver which have one-eighth alloy (per shekel), property of Iddina-[Marduk], son of Iqīša, descendant of Nūr-Sin, charged against Nabû-ušallim, son of Pānija and (which) is (a portion of) the business capital of Iddina-Marduk. He will repay (the silver) at an early sailing of his boat in the month of Nisanu. (This is) apart from the five and five-sixths minas, two shekels of silver, charged against the business capital. He will (also) deliver an additional payment charged against (him) of one thousand strings of garlic. Witnesses are Rīmūt, son of Marduk-erība, descendant of Sin-ili, Bēl-iddina, son of ⌜Nabû⌝-ušallim, descendant of Aḫu-bāni, ⌜Aḫa-iddina,⌝ son of Ardija and the scribe, Uballissu-Gula, son of Marduk-erība, descendant of Sin-ili. Babylon, month of Addaru, seventh day, accession year of Nergal-šarra-uṣur, king of Babylon.

Commentary

12) Collation shows ^{Id}AG-GI, as in Ev M 20, 12-13.

9

BM 30411

Published as Evetts, *Ner.* 9, and Strassmaier, Liverpool, n. 110; Translation and Commentary by Peiser, *Rechtsleben* 3, p. 26

1) 52 1/2 GÍN KÙ.BABBAR *šá* ^{I}BA-*šá-a* A-*šú šá* ^{I}*gi-lu-*⌜*u-*⌝*a*
2) A ^{Id}30-*šá-du-nu šá ina* UGU ^{Id}AG-A-MU A-*šú šá* ^{I}TIN
3) A LÚ-*šá*-KAŠ-*na-ši-šu ina* ŠÁM É ^{Id}AG-A-MU *šá a-na*
4) É.GAL *a-na* KÙ.BABBAR *in-na-ad-nu a-ki-' ra-šu-ta-nu*
5) 1/3 6 GÍN 4-*ut* KÙ.BABBAR *ina* ŠU^{II} ^{Id}AG-ŠEŠ.MEŠ-MU A-*šú šá*
6) ^{I}*šu-la-a* A ^{I}*e-gi-bi* ^{I}BA-*šá-a* A-*šú šá* ^{I}*gi-lu-ú-a*
7) A ^{Id}30-KUR-*nu ma-ḫir u* ⌜*ú*⌝*-ìl-tim*
8) *ša* 52 1/2 GÍN KÙ.BABBAR *šá* ^{Id}AG-A-MU
9) *a-na* ^{Id}AG-ŠEŠ.MEŠ-MU *id-din*
10) LÚ *mu-kin-nu* ^{Id}DI..KU_5-MU.MU A-*šú šá*
11) ^{I}NUMUN-TIN.TIR.KI A LÚ.GÍR.LÁ ^{Id}AG-*na-din*-MU
12) A-*šú šá* ^{I}A-*a* A ^{Id}30-*na-din*-MU ^{I}EN-*šú-nu* A-*šú*
13) *šá* ^{I}*uš-šá-a-a* A ^{I}ŠEŠ-*ba-ni-i*
14) LÚ.ŠID ^{Id}AG-TIN-*su-iq-bi* A-*šú šá*
15) ^{I}BA-*ša-a* A ^{Id}30-*šá-du-nu* TIN.TIR.KI
16) ITU.ŠE.GUR_{10}.KUD UD.9.KAM MU.SAG.NAM.LUGAL.LA
17) ^{Id}U+GUR-LUGAL-ŠEŠ LUGAL TIN.TIR.KI

Translation

(Document concerning) fifty-two and one-half shekels of silver, belonging to Iqīša, son of Gilūa, descendant of Sin-šadûnu, which was charged against Nabû-apla-iddina, son of Balāṭu, descendant of Šanašišu, a portion of the price of the house of Nabû-apla-iddina which was given to the palace for silver. According to the rate set by the creditor, twenty-six and one-fourth shekels of silver were received (by) Iqīša, son of Gilūa, descendant of Sin-šadûnu from Nabû-aḫḫē-iddina, son of Šulâ, descendant of Egibi and he gave (i.e., Iqiša) the contract for fifty-two and one-half shekels of silver concerning Nabû-aplâ-iddina to Nabû-aḫḫē-iddina. Witnesses are Madānu-šuma-iddina, son of Zēr-Bābili, descendant of Naš-paṭri, Nabû-nādin-šumi, son of Aplâ, descendant of Sin-nādin-šumi, Bēlšunu, son of Uššâ, descendant of Aḫu-bāni, and the scribe, Nabû-balāssu-iqbi, son of Iqīša, descendant of Sin-šadûnu. Babylon, month of Addaru, ninth day, accession year of Nergal-šarra-uṣur, king of Babylon.

10

BM 33910 (Collated)
Published as Evetts. *Ner. 10*

1) 2 GÍN KÙ.BABBAR *šá ina* 1 [GÍN *bit-qa*]
2) *ša* ^{I}MU-^{d}AMAR.UD A-*šú šá* ^{I}[BA-*šá-a*]
3) A ^{I}ZALÁG-^{d}30 *ina* UGU ^{I}BA-*šá-a*
4) A-*šú šá* ^{Id}EN-*ka-ṣir*
5) A LÚ.ŠID.BÁR *ina* ITU.BÁR
6) *a-ki-i e-te-ti-iq*
7) *pi-i-tum šá* SUM.SAR
8) *i-nam-din e-lat*
9) *ú-ìl-tim maḫ-ri-i-tum*
10) LÚ *mu-kin-nu* ^{Id}EN-DÙ-*uš*
11) A-*šú šá* ^{I}[*ra-šil* A] LÚ.SIMUG
12) ^{Id}*bu-ne-ne*-DÙ A-*šú-šá*
13) ^{Id}AG-SIG$_5$-*iq* A ^{I}ANŠE.[KUR.RA]
14) *u* LÚ.ŠID ^{Id}AMAR.UD-MU [...]
15) A-*šú šá* ^{I}NUMUN-*ia* [...]
16) TIN.TIR.KI ITU.[...] [UD] [...] [KAM]
17) MU.SAG.NAM.LUGAL.LA
18) ^{d}U+GUR-LUGAL-ŠEŠ LUGAL TIN.TUR.KI

Translation

(Document concerning) two shekels of silver, which has [one-eighth alloy (per shekel)] property of Iddina-Marduk, son of [Iqīša], descendant of Nūr-Sin, charged against Iqīša, son of Bēl-kāṣir, descendant of Šangû-parakki. When he crosses in the month of Nisanu, he will deliver the strings of garlic. (This is) apart from the former contract. Witnesses are Bēl-ēpuš, son of [Rašil, descendant of] Nappāḫu, Bunene-ibni, son of Nabû-udammiq, descendant of [Sisû] and the scribe, Marduk-šuma- [...] son of Zērija [...]. Babylon, month of [...] [day] accession year of Nergal-šarra-uṣur, king of Babylon.

Commentary

2) Restoration of [BA-*šá-a*] is based on Nbk.67,6; 258,3; 265,2, etc. See Tallqvist, NBN 71b.

11) Although the text is no longer preserved at this point, if it originally read ^{Id}DI.KU$_5$-MU, as Evett's copy shows, it most certainly was a scribal error for ^{I}[ra-šil] as correctly interpreted by Tallqvist, NBN 36a. The name occurs in *Nbk.* 252-4; *EvM* 12,3; 20, 5; *Ner.* 21, 2; 22, 4; 26, 2, etc. where he is associated in business dealings with Madānu-šuma-iddina of the Nabāja family. For a further discussion and interpretation of the writings of this name, see AOATS 4, p. 74 (Note to text 30).

11

BM 77590 (Collated)
Published as Evetts, *Ner. 11*

1) [...] *ma-áš-šar-tum šá* ITU.⌜KIN⌝ [...]
2) [...] *i-bu-ú-a ša* ^{d}GAŠAN *ak* ⌜*ka*⌝ [...]
3) [UD].21.KAM *im-du-du ina* lìb-[*bi*] [...]
4) [...] ⌜GUR⌝ ŠE.BAR ^{I}*ina* É.SAG.ÍL *pu*⌜*x*⌝ [...]
5) [...] *i-bu-ú-a ma-ḫir* [...]
6) [...] ^{I}*ri-kis-ka-la-mu-*^{d}⌜EN⌝ [...]
7) [...] *ši li-'-*[...]
8) [^{I}*ri*]-⌜*kis*⌝*-ka-la-mu-*[^{d}EN] [...]
9) [...] *li e* ⌜x⌝ [...]
10) [...] ITU.⌜APIN⌝ [...]
11) [...] *ma is* [...]
12) [...] ŠE.BAR [...]
13) [...] *i-bu-ú-a* [...]
14) [...] *mu ma-ḫir* [...]
15) [MU.SAG.]NAM.LUGAL.LA ^{Id}U+GUR-LUGAL-ŠEŠ
16) LUGAL TIN.TIR.KI

Translation

(Document concerning) the food allotment for the month of ⌜Ululu⌝ [...] ... measured of the lady, ... [...] twenty-first [day.] From the ⌜amount⌝ [...] ⌜*kurru*⌝ of barley Esagila [...] ... received [...] Rikis-kalāmu-[Bēl] [...] Rikis-kalāmu-[Bēl] [...] month of ⌜Araḫsamnu⌝ [...] barley [...] ... [...] received [...] accession [year] of Nergal-šarra-uṣur, king of Babylon.

12

BM 30419 (Collated)
Published as Evetts, *Ner.* 12

1) 1/2 MA.NA ⌜6⌝ GÍN KÙ.BABBAR *šá* [^{I}MU-^{d}AMAR(!).UD(!) (*text:* MU)]
2) *A-šú šá* ^{I}BA-*šá-a* A ^{I}ZALÁG-^{d}30
3) [*ina*] ⌜*muḫ*⌝*-ḫi* ^{I}*kal-ba-a A-šú šá* ^{Id}[AMAR.UD-*na-ṣir*]
4) *a-ki-i qí-it šá* ITU.DU$_6$ ⌜*x x*⌝
5) 5 ⌜GÍN⌝ KÙ.BABBAR ⌜*x*⌝ ^{I}MU-^{d}EN
6) *ma-la [i]-*⌜*ru*⌝*-bu* ^{I}MU-^{d}AMAR.UD
7) *ina* ŠU^{II} ^{I}*kal-ba-a i-na* ⌜*x x*⌝
8) [...] *šá* ^{Id}AG ⌜*ša*⌝ [...]
9) [...] ^{Id}EN-*bul-*[*liṭ*] [...]
10) [...] ^{Id}EN-⌜DUB-NUMUN⌝
11) *A-šú šá* ^{I}*gi-mil-lu* ^{Id}AG-⌜TIN-*iṭ*⌝
12) *A-šú šá* ^{I}*na-'-id-*^{d}AMAR.UD A ^{I}⌜UR⌝-^{d}ŠEŠ.KI
13) ^{I}*ḫaš-da-a A-šú šá* [...] ⌜*su ru x*⌝
14) ^{I}*la-a-ba-ši* [LÚ.ŠID] *A-šú šá* ^{Id}EN-LUGAL-ŠEŠ
15) A ^{I}ÈR-^{d}BE TIN.TIR.KI ITU.NE
16) UD.6.KAM MU.SAG.NAM.LUGAL.LA
17) ^{d}U+GUR-LUGAL-ŠEŠ LUGAL TIN.[TIR.KI]

Translation

(Document concerning) one-half mina, six shekels of silver, property of [Iddina-Marduk,] (!) son of Iqīša, descendant of Nūr-Sin, ⌜charged against⌝ Kalbâ, son of [Marduk-nāṣir.] At the end of the month of Tašritu, five ⌜shekels⌝ of silver [...] silver [...] Iddina-Bēl (?), as much as it has ⌜increased⌝ (against him) [...] Iddina-Marduk from Kalbâ [...] Nabû [...] (Witnesses are) Bēl-bul[liṭ] [...] Bēl-[šāpik-zēri] son of Gimillu, Nabû-⌜uballiṭ,⌝ son of Na'id-Marduk, descendant of ⌜Ur⌝-

Nannar, Ḫašdija, son of [...] (and) [the scribe], Labaši, son of Bēl-šarra-uṣur, descendant of Arad-Ea. Babylon, month of Abu, sixth day, accession year of Nergal-šarra-uṣur, king of Baby[lon.]

13

BM 47517 (Collated)
Published as Evetts, *Ner.* 13
Translated in Kohler and Peiser, *Rechtsleben* III, p. 10 and T.G. Pinches, "Babylonian Contracts and Tablets with Historical References" in *Records of the Past New Series* 4 (1890), p. 101

1) ⌈^{Id}AG⌉-MU-DU LÚ.TU.É ^{d}AG LÚ.ŠÀ.TAM
2) É.ZI.DA A-*šú šá* ^{I}*ši-rik-tum*-^{d}AMAR.UD A ^{I}EGIR.MEŠ-DINGIR.MEŠ-SIG$_5$
3) *a-na* ^{Id}U+GUR-LUGAL-ŠEŠ LUGAL TIN.TIR.KI *iq-bi*
4) SAL *gi-gi-i-tum* DUMU.SAL-*ka ba-tul-tum*
5) *a-na áš-šu-tu bi-nam-ma lu-ú* DAM *ši-i*
6) ^{Id}U+GUR-LUGAL-ŠEŠ LUGAL TIN.TIR.KI *a-na*
7) [^{Id}AG-MU-DU] LÚ.TU.É ^{d}AG LÚ.ŠÀ.TAM É.ZI.[DA]

-- rest of observe broken --

1') [...] ⌈x⌉ DUMU ^{Id}AG-MU-SI.[SÁ] [...]
2') [...] *ri* DUMU *šá* ^{Id}AG-LUGAL.ŠEŠ LÚ.DI.[KU$_5$] [...]
3') ^{Id}AG-[MU]-*ú-ṣur* LÚ.DUB.SAR A ^{I}*ina*-⌈*x*⌉ [...]
4') ⌈KÁ.DINGIR.RA⌉.KI ITU.BÁR UD.1.KAM MU.I.KAM
5') [^{Id}U+GUR-LUGAL]-ŠEŠ LUGAL TIN.⌈TIR⌉.KI GABA.RI É.ZI.DA

Translation

⌈Nabû⌉-šuma-ukīn, the priest of Nabû, the administrator of Ezida, son of Širikti-Marduk, descendant of Arkat-ilāni-damqa spoke (as follows) to Nergal-šarra-uṣur, king of Babylon: "please give me (the hand of) your nubile daughter Gigitum, in marriage; let her be (my) wife." Nergal-šarra-uṣur, king of Babylon, to [Nabû-šuma-ukīn], the priest of Nabû, the administrator of ⌈Ezida⌉; [...] son of Nabû-šumu-lišir [...] son of Nabû-šarra-uṣur, the ⌈judge⌉ [...] Nabû[-šuma]-uṣur, the scribe, son of Ina [...]. ⌈Babylon⌉, month of Nisanu, first day, first year of [Nergal-šarra]-uṣur, king of Babylon. Copy (of the contract is for) the Ezida.

14

BM 54178 (Collated)
Published as Evetts, *Ner. 14*

1) 10 *dan-nu-tu šá ši-ka-ri*
2) *šá* 1 GUR.A *šá-bat šá* ^{I}ÈR-^{d}[*gu-la*]
3) A-*šú šá* ^{I}*ki-rib-tu* A ^{I}*dul-lu-pu*
4) *ina muḫ-ḫi* ^{Id}AG-SUR A-*šú šá*
5) ^{I}*šu-la-a* A ^{Id}30-ZAG.LU
6) *u* ^{Id}AG-MU-DU A-*šú šá*
7) ^{Id}BE-MU A ^{I}*mu-kal-lim*
8) *ina qí-it šá* ITU.ŠU
9) *i-nam-din pu-ut*
10) *šá ab-bi u*
11) *mar* (!) (text: *ḫar*)-*su na-šu-ú*
12) LÚ *mu-kin* ^{I}*ba-la-ṭu*
13) A-*šú šá* ^{Id}AMAR.UD-SU
14) A LÚ.SIMUG $^{I(!)}$(text: LÚ) ZÁLAG.^{d}EN-[*lu-mur*]
15) A-*šú šá* ^{I}*šu-la-a* A ^{Id}30-[ZAG-LU]
16) 1-*en pu-ut* 2-*ú na-šu-ú*
17) *u* LÚ.ŠID ^{Id}BE-MU-[MU A-*šú šá*]
18) ^{Id}EN-PAP.ME-SU TIN.[TIR.KI]
19) ITU.BÁR UD.25.KAM
20) MU.1.KAM ^{d}U+GUR-LUGAL-PAP
21) LUGAL E.KI

Translation

(Document concerning) ten vats of beer, each holding one *kurru*, belonging to Arad[Gula], son of Kiribtu, descendant of Dullupu, charged against Nabû-ēṭir, son of Šulâ, descendant of Sin-imitti and Nabû-šuma-ukīn, son of Ea-iddina, descendant of Mukallim. They (!) will deliver (the beer) at the end of the month of Du'uzu (and) they warrant that they (the vats) are leaky and broken. One shall bear the responsibility for the other. Witnesses are Balāṭu, son of Marduk-erība, descendant of Nappāḫu, Nūr-Bel-[lummur], son of Šulâ, descendant of Sin-[imitti,] and the scribe, Ea-šuma- ⌜iddina⌝, [son of] Bēl-aḫḫē-erība. Bab[ylon,] month of Nisanu, twenty-fifth day, first year of Nergal-šarra-uṣur, king of Babylon.

Commentary

2) For the restoration ^{d}[*gu-la*], see Tallquist, NBN 13b and cf. *Nbn* 6: 4 and Peiser, *Verträge*, text no. 9: 14 where the same person and family name occur.

9) The verb *nadānu* should here be plural to agree with the subject in lines 4-7 and with l. 11.

9-11) For parallel uses of this phrase, see *Dar.* 543:9, *Nbn* 600: 6-8 and *Nbn* 334 and cf. AJSL 43, p. 215.

16) This line property belongs after l. 11.

15

BM 30573 (Collated)
Published as Evetts, *Ner. 15* and as Strassmaier, *Liverpool*, no. 111

1) 20 LIM I LIM 2 ME *gid-dil šá* SUM.SAR
2) ZAG *šá* ^{Id}AG-GI A-*šú šá* ^{I}IGI-*ni-ia*
3) *šá* KASAL^{II} *šá* ^{I}MU-^{d}AMAR.UD *ina* IGI
4) ^{Id}AMAR.UD-MU-DÙ A-šú *šá* ^{Id}AG-*ki-šìr*
5) ^{I}*ba-bu-ut-tú* UD.15.KAM *šá* ITU.GUD
6) *gíd-dil šá* SUM.SAR ^{Id}AMAR.UD-MU-DÙ
7) *i-man-ni- -ma a-na*
8) ^{Id}AG-GI *ina* ⌜SAG.DU⌝ ^{Id}AMAR.UD-MU-DÙ
9) *i-nam-din pu-ut nu-uḫ-ḫi-tum*
10) ⌜*ši-*⌝*bir-tum šá ina* 1 GÍN *bit-qa*
11) *šá ina* IGI ^{Id}ŠÚ-MU-DÙ ^{Id}AG-GI
12) *na-ši*
13) LÚ *mu-kin-ni* ^{Id}AG-ÚŠ(!) (text: DU)-*bul-liṭ*
14) A-*šú šá* ^{I}*bul-ṭa-a* ^{Id}AG-KAR-ZI.MEŠ
15) A-*šú šá* ^{Id}AG-ŠEŠ.MEŠ-*bul-liṭ*
16) A ^{Id}AG(!) (text: DA)-*na-ṣir* ^{Id}AG-DU-NUMUN
17) A-*šú šá* ^{Id}AG-NUMUN-MU A LÚ.SIMUG
18) *u* LÚ.ŠID ^{Id}U+GUR-ŠEŠ-MU A-*šú šá* ^{Id}AG-NUMUN.TIL
19) A LÚ.SIMUG URU *šaḫ-ri-ni* ITU.GUD
20) UD.9.KAM MU.1.KAM
21) ^{d}U+GUR-LUGAL-ŠEŠ LUGAL E.KI
22) ⌜*pu*⌝*-ut e-ṭè-ru ša* 1/2 MA.NA 1 GÍN KÙ.BABBAR
23) *šá ina* 1 GÍN *bit-qa* ^{Id}AG-GI
24) *ina* ŠU^{II} ^{I}[^{d}AMAR.UD-MU-DÙ] [...]
25) *nu-uḫ-ḫi-tum šá ši-[bir-tum na-ši]*

Translation

(Document concerning) twenty-one thousand, two hundred strings of garlic, estimated yield of Nabû-ušallim, son of Pānija, from the business capital of Iddina-Marduk, and placed at the disposal of Marduk-šuma-ibni, son of Nabû-kišir, descendant of Babuttu. Marduk-šuma-ibni will total up the strings of garlic (on) the fifteenth day of the month of Ajaru and Marduk šuma-ibni will deliver (them) to Nabû-ušallim from (his) ⌈capital⌉. Nabû-ušallim guarantees that the block (of silver) which has one-eighth alloy in every shekel (and which was) placed at the disposal of Marduk-šuma-ibni is not of poor quality. Witnesses are Nabû-mīti (!)-bulliṭ, son of Bulṭâ, Nabû-ēṭir-napšāti, son of Nabû-aḫḫē-bulliṭ, descendant of Nabû(!)-nāṣir, Nabû-mukīn-zēri, son of Nabû-zēra-iddina, descendant of Nappāḫu, and the scribe, Nergal-aḫa-iddina, son of Nabû-zēra-ušabši, descendant of Nappāḫu. City of Saḫrinu, month of Ajaru, ninth day, first year of Nergal-šarra-usur, king of Babylon. Nabû-ušallim [bears] the ⌈responsibility⌉ for the payment of one-half mina, one shekel of silver which has one-eighth alloy (per skekel), which is a [block of good quality and which he received(?)] from [Marduk-šuma-ibni].

Commentary

9,10) For *nuḫḫutu*, meaning "of poor quality" see von Soden, AHw 801a("minderwertig"). On occasion, the negative *la* is omitted from the phrase. See Ungnad, NRV *Glossar* p.p. 79 and 114. Cf also BE 8/I 138::12 VAS 5 118: 5,9. For further discussion of these words, see MSL I, p. 138, *Landsberger*, ZA 39 (1930) p.285 and Ungnad, NRV *Glossar* p.p. 107 and 125.

24) The restoration of [^{d}AMAR.UD-MU-DÙ] is based on the information contained in lines 9-12.

16

BM 31248 (Collated)

Published as Evetts, *Ner*. 16 and Strassmaier, *Liverpool*, p. 112.

1) 5 GÍN KÙ.BABBAR ^{Id}AG-*a-a-lu*
2) *A-šú šá* ^{Id}*30-SUR* *ina* UGU
3) ^{I}*la-ba-ši A-šú šá* ^{Id}AG-*mu-še-ti-iq*-UD.DA
4) *ina* ITU.DU$_6$ *i-nam-din*
5) SAL DÙG-*ba-tum pu-ut* ANŠE

6) *šá ^{I}la-a-ba-ši na-šá-a-ta*
7) LÚ *mu-kin-nu* ^{Id}EN-NUMUN-DÙ
8) *A-šú šá* ^{Id}EN-ŠEŠ-GÁL-ši
9) A ^{Id}EN-[*e-ṭè*]*--ru*
10) ^{Id}AG-DÙ [*A-šú šá*] ^{I}NUN.ME
11) A LÚ.TUG.BABBAR ^{I}⸢*lib*⸣-[*luṭ*]
12) *A-šú šá* ^{Id}AG-SUR ⸢A^{I}*e-gì*⸣*-bi*
13) *u* LÚ.ŠID ⸢^{Id}⸣UTU-ŠEŠ.MEŠ-MU
14) *A-šú šá* ^{Id}⸢AG-NUMUN⸣-GÁL-*ši* A LU.DUG.QA.BUR
15) TIN.TIR.KI ITU.SIG$_4$
16) UD.I.KAM MU.I.KAM
17) ^{Id}U+GUR-LUGAL-ŠEŠ LUGAL E.KI

Translation

(Document concerning) five shekels of silver, belonging to Nabû-ajalu, son of Sin-ēṭir, charged against Labaši, son of Nabû-mušētiq-uddê. He will deliver (the silver) in the month of Tašritu (and) the lady Tabatum bears the responsibility for the donkey of Labaši. Witnesses are Bēl-zēra-ibni, son of Bēl-aḫa-ušabši, descendant of Bēl-[ēṭir], Nabû-ibni, [son of] Apkallu, descendant of Ašlaku, ⸢Liblut⸣, son of Nabû-ēṭir, ⸢descendant of⸣ Egibi and the scribe, Šamaš-aḫḫē-iddina, son of ⸢Nabû-zēra⸣-ušabši, descendant of Paḫāru. Babylon, month of Simanu, first day, year of Nergal-šarra-uṣur, king of Babylon.

17

BM 54210 (Collated)
Published as Evetts, *Ner.* 17

1) 9 GUR 1(PI)5(BÁN) ŠE.BAR
2) *na-áš-par-*⸢*tum*⸣ [*ša* ...] ^{d}⸢xx⸣
3) ^{I}*ni-qu-du ina* ŠU^{II}
4) ^{I}MU-MU *ma-ḫir*
5) *ina* GUB-*su šá* ^{Id}UTU-PAP-MU A
6) ^{I}ÈR-^{d}EN
7) ITU.SIG$_4$ UD.25.KAM
8) MU.1.KAM ^{d}U+GUR-LUGAL-ŠEŠ
9) LUGAL TIN.TIR.KI
10) *taḫ-sis-si*
11) ⸢*la*⸣ [*ma*]*-še-e*

Translation

(Document concerning) nine *kurru*, one *pi*, thirty *qa* of barley (which) Niqudu received from Šuma-iddina (by) order of [...] ... in the presence of Šamaš-aḫa-iddina, son of Arad-Bēl. Month of Simanu, twenty-fifth day, first year of Nergal-šarra-uṣur, king of Babylon. The entry (in the ledger) is not to be ⌈forgotten].

Commentary

5-6) See parallel in *Dar*. 53, 16 and see Tallqvist, NBN, 188a.

18

BM 92746 (Collated)
Published as Evetts, *Ner*. 18

1) ŠE.BAR *šá* LÚ.APIN.MEŠ *šá* ^{d}UTU ⌈*a-na*⌉
2) É.BABBAR.RA *id-di-nu* ITU.ŠU
3) UD.4.KAM MU.1.KAM ^{Id}U+GUR-LUGAL-ŠEŠ LUGAL ⌈TIN.TIR.KI⌉
4) 7ME 80 GIŠ.BAR *šá* LÚ.APIN.MEŠ
5) ^{Id}UTU-MU
6) 1ME 68 GUR ^{Id}UTU-MU
7) 32 GUR ŠE.BAR ⌈*ri*⌉-*ḫi*
8) 1ME 50 GUR ^{I}*li-ši-ru*
9) 50 GUR *ri-ḫi*
10) 1ME 76 ⌈GUR⌉ ^{Id}UTU-ZALÁG-*ir*
11) ⌈24⌉ GUR *ri-ḫi*
12) 1ME 23 GUR ^{I}*ap-pa-nu*
13) 27 GUR *ri-ḫi*
14) 4 ME 48 GUR ^{I}*šu-la-a*
15) KAR
16) ⌈x⌉.ME ⌈x⌉ GUR [^{Id}UTU-GI]
17) KAR
18) ⌈20⌉GUR ^{Id}EN-TIN-*iṭ šá bil-tum ša* ^{I}*ki-na-a*
19) ^{Id}UTU-ZALÁG-*ir šá ha-sa-pi-e*
20) ^{Id}UTU-MU *šá* ^{d}EN-⌈NUMUN⌉- TIL
21) 55GUR 3(PI) 2(BÁN) ^{Id}UTU[...]
22) *šá bal-lu-ka-tum* 62 GUR ⌈*ri-ḫi*⌉
23) 2ME 50 ŠE.BAR *šá eš-ru-ú*

24) 3ME 80 ŠE.BAR *šá* LÚ ⸢*ir-ri-še*⸣*-e*

25) PAP 3 LIM 1 ME ŠE.BAR MU.1.[KAM]

Translation

(Document concerning) barley which the farmers of (the field of) Šamaš delivered (i.e., gave) ⸢to⸣ the Ebabbara, month of Du'uzu, fourth day, first year of Nergal-šarra-uṣur, king of ⸢Babylon⸣. Seven hundred eighty (*kurru*) are the rent of the farmers (under the supervision of) Šamaš-iddina; one hundred sixty eight *kurru* (are from) Šamaš-iddina, (with) thirty-two *kurru* ⸢remaining⸣ (to be paid); one hundred fifty *kurru* (are from) Liširu, (with) fifty *kurru* (remaining to be paid), one hundred seventy-six ⸢*kurru*⸣ (are from) Šamaš-unammir, (with) ⸢twenty-four⸣ *kurru* remaining (to be paid), one hundred twenty-three *kurru* (are from) Appanu, (with twenty-seven *kurru* remaining (to be paid), four hundred forty-eight *kurru* Šulâ paid, [...] hundred [...] *kurru* Šamaš-ušallim paid, ⸢twenty⸣ *kurru* (are from) Bēl-uballiṭ from the outlying district of Kinâ, Šamaš-unammir, the official (?), Šamaš-iddina, (and) Bēl-⸢zēra⸣-ušabši (?), fifty-five *kurru*, three *pi*, twelve *qa* (are from) Šamaš [...] sixty-two *kurru* ⸢remain⸣ (to be delivered). Two hundred fifty (*kurru*) of barley constitute the tithe, three hundred eighty (*kurru*) of barley are from the ⸢farmers⸣-- total of three thousand, one-hundred (*kurru*) of barley (for) the first year.

19

BM 64730 (Collated)
Published as Evetts, *Ner.* 19

1) [...][MA].NA SÍG.ḪI.A *a-na*

2) [TÚG] *ú-za-ri šá mu-ḫu-ú*

3) *šá an-dul-lum šá* ^{d}GAŠAN.AN.NA

4) *šá* ITU.ŠU *a-na*

5) ^{Id}UTU-TIN-*it* A-*šú šá*

6) ^{I}*ri-mut* SUM-[*na*]

7) 1 *ma-ši-ḫi* ZÍZ.ÀM

8) *a-na* ^{Id}AG-NUMUN-DU

9) A-*šú šá* ^{Id}AMAR.UD-NUMUN-DÙ

10) SUM-*in* ITU.ŠU UD.8.KAM

11) MU.1.KAM ^{d}U+GUR-LUGAL-ŠEŠ

12) LUGAL TIN.TIR.KI

Translation

(Document concerning) [...] minas of wool for the cover over the canopy of the goddess which was delivered to Šamaš-uballiṭ, son of Rīmūt (in) the month of Du'uzu.One measure of flour was delivered to Nabû-zēra-ukīn, son of Marduk-zēra-ibni. Month of Du'uzu, eigth day, first year of Nergal-šarra-uṣur, king of Babylon.

20

BM 31964 (Collated)

Published as Evetts, *Ner.* 20 and as Strassmaier, *Liverpool*, no. 116

1) 2 GÍN *gi-ru-ú* KÙ.BABBAR *šá*
2) [...] ^{Id}AG-DU-ŠEŠ LÚ *qal-la*
3) [...] A-*šú šá* ^{I}MU-^{d}AMAR.UD *ina muḫ-ḫi*
4) ^{I}*ri-mut* A-*šú šá* ^{Id}U+GUR-DÙ-ŠEŠ
5) [...] LÚ *mu* ⌜*x*⌝ KÙ.BABBAR *ina* SAG.DU

(remainder broken away)

1') [...] *u* LÚ *mu-kin-nu* [...]
2') ^{I}*šu-la-a* A-*šú šá* ^{Id}BE-NUMUN-DÙ
3') ^{I}*ki-di-ni* A ^{I}*im-ma-du-bu*
4') LÚ.ŠID ^{Id}AG-DÙ-ŠEŠ A-*šú šá*
5') ^{Id}AG-DU-DUMU.UŠ TIN.TIR.KI
6') ITU.ŠU UD.15.KAM MU.1.KAM
7') ^{d}U+GUR-LUGAL-ŠEŠ LUGAL TIN.TIR.KI

Translation

(Document concerning) two and one twenty-fourth shekels of silver, which [...] Nabû-mukīn-aḫi, slave of [...] son of Iddina-Marduk, charged against Rīmūt, son of Nergal-bāni-aḫi.[...] the silver from the capital [...] Witnesses [...] Šulâ, son of Ea-zēra-ibni, Kidinni, son of Immadubu, (and) the scribe, Nabû-bāni-aḫi, son of Nabû-mukīn-apli. Babylon, month of Du'uzu, fifteenth day, first year of Nergal-šarra-uṣur, king of Babylon.

Commentary

7') This line appears on the tablet but was inadvertently left out by Evetts.

21

BM 33562 (Collated)
Published as Evetts, *Ner.* 21

1) 7 GUR 1(PI) 4(BÁN) ZÚ.LUM.MA
2) *šá* ^{Id}EN-DÙ-*uš* A-*šú šá* ^{I}*ra-šil* A LÚ.SIMUG
3) ^{Id}DI.KU$_5$-MU-MU A-*šú šá* ^{I}NUMUN-*ia*
4) A ^{I}*na-ba-a-a ina* UGU ^{Id}EN-DU-NUMUN
5) A-*šú šá* ^{Id}AG-DU-DUMU.UŠ A ^{I}ÈR-^{d}GIR$_4$.KÙ
6) *ina* ITU.APIN ZÚ.LUM.[MA] *gam-ru-tu*
7) *ina* UGU ÍD URU É DU$_{10}$.GA-^{d}EN
8) *ina ma-ši-ḫu šá* 1 *pi ina* UGU [...]
9) *(erasure) i-nam-din*
10) ZÚ.LUM.MA *šá* KASKAL^{II} *šá* ^{I}MU-^{d}AMAR.UD
11) LÚ *mu-kin-nu* ^{Id}AG-*mu-šal-lim*
12) A-*šú šá* ^{Id}AG-*mu-še-ti-iq*-UD.DA
13) A ^{I}ZALÁG-^{d}30 ^{Id}AG-GI
14) A-*šú šá* ^{I}IGI-*ni-ia u* LÚ.ŠID
15) ^{Id}U+GUR-*na-ṣir* A-*šú šá*
16) ^{Id}AG-*mu-še-ti-iq*-UD.DA
17) A ^{I}ZALÁG-^{d}30 TIN.TIR.KI ITU.ŠU UD.17.KAM
18) MU.1.KAM ^{d}U+GUR-LUGAL-ŠEŠ
19) LUGAL TIN.TIR.KI

Translation

(Document concerning) seven *kurru*, one pi, twenty-four qa of dates, property of Bēl-ēpuš, son of Rašil, descendant of Nappāḫu (and) Madānu-šuma-iddina, son of Zērija, descendant of Nabāja (and) charged against Bēl-mukīn-zēri, son of Nabû-mukīn-apli, descendant of Arad-Nergal. He will deliver the full amount of dates at the watercourse of the village of Bīt Ṭābi Bēl in accordance with the measure of one pi [...] in the month of Arahsamnu. The dates (are a portion of) the business capital of Iddina-Marduk. Witnesses (are) Nabû-mušallim, son of Nabû-mušētiq-uddê, descendant of Nūr-Sin, Nabû-ušallim, son of Pānija, and the scribe, Nergal-nāṣir, son of Nabû-mušētiq-uddê, descendant of Nūr-Sin. Babylon, month of Du'uzu, seventeenth day, first year of Nergal-šarra-uṣur, king of Babylon.

22

BM 30551 (Collated)
Published as Evetts, *Ner.* 22

1) ⌜5⌝ GUR 1(PI) 4(BÁN) ZÚ.LUM.MA [...]
2) 3 GUR 1(PI) 4(BÁN) ŠÁM UDU.NITÁ *šá* ^{Id}DI.KU$_5$-MU-[MU]
3) A-*šú šá* ^{I}NUMUN-*ia* A ^{I}*na-ba-a-a*
4) *u* ^{Id}EN-DÙ-*uš* A-*šú šá* ^{I}*ra-šil* A LÚ.SIMUG
5) UGU ^{Id}EN-DÙ A-*šú šá* ^{I}*na-din ina* ITU.APIN
6) ZÚ.LUM.MA *gam-ru-tu ina* UGU ÍD *bar-sip* KI
7) [...] ⌜*xxx*⌝ *pi ina muḫ-*⌜*ḫi*⌝
8) [...] *šá* ^{I}MU-^{d}AMAR.UD
9) [A-*šú šá*] ^{I}BA-*šá-a* A ^{I}ZALÁG-^{d}30
10) [LÚ *mu*]-*kin-nu* ^{I}NUMUN-*ú-tu* A-*šú šá*
11) ^{Id}EN-ŠEŠ.MEŠ-MU A LÚ.GÍR.LÁ
12) ^{Id}AMAR.UD-SU A-*šú šá* ^{I}*na-din*
13) ^{Id}AG-GI A-*šú šá* ^{I}IGI-*ni-ʾa*
14) *u* LÚ.ŠID ^{Id}UTU-SIG$_5$-*iq*
15) A-*šú šá* ^{Id}AG-*mu-še-ti-*<*iq*>-UD.DA
16) A ^{I}ZALÁG-^{d}30 TIN.TIR.KI
17) ITU.ŠU UD.27.KAM
18) MU.1.KAM ^{d}U+GUR-LUGAL-ŠEŠ
19) LUGAL TIN.TIR.KI

Translation

(Document concerning) ⌜five⌝ *kurru*, one pi, twenty-four qa of dates [...] three *kurru*, one pi, twenty-four qa, the equivalent (lit., price) of a ewe, property of Madānu-šuma-[iddina], son of Zērija, descendant of Nabāja, and Bēl-ēpuš, son of Rašil, descendant of Nappāḫu, charged against Bēl-ibni, son of Nādin. [He willl deliver(?)] the full amount of dates at the Borsippa canal in the month of Araḫsamnu [...] charged against [...] Iddina-Marduk, [son of] Iqīša, descendant of Nūr-Sin. {Witn]esses (are) Zērūtu, son of Bēl-aḫḫē-iddina, descendant of Naš paṭri, Marduk-erība, son of Nādin, Nabû-ušallim, descendant of Pānija, and the scribe, Šamaš-udammiq, son of Nabû-mušētiq-uddê , descendant of Nūr-Sin. Babylon, month of Du'uzu, twenty-seventh day, first year of Nergal-šarra-uṣur, king of Babylon.

Commentary

2) Space left at end of line will accomodate [MU] (Madānu-šuma-iddina).

23

BM 30574 (Collated)
Published as Evetts, *Ner.* 23

1) SAL *be-li-li-tum* DUMU-SAL-*su šá* ^{Id}EN-*ú-še-zib*
2) A ^{I}*šá-na-ši-šú ina ḫu-ud lb-bi-šú* ^{I}*ba-zu-zu*
3) LÚ *qal-la-šú a-na 1/2* MA.NA 5 GÍN KÙ.BABBAR
4) *a-na* ŠÁM *gam-ru-tu a-(na)* ^{Id}AG-ŠEŠ.MEŠ-MU
5) *A-šú šá* ^{I}*šu-la-a* A ^{I}*e-gi-bi ta-ad-din pu-ut* LÚ *se-ḫi-i*
6) LÚ *pa-qí-ra-nu* LÚ ÈR.LUGAL-*ú-tu u* LÚ DUMU.DÙ-*ú-tu*
7) *ina* UGU ^{I}*ba-zu-zu il-la-'* ^{I}*e-til-lu*
8) *A-šú šá* ^{I}*ba-laṭ-su* A ^{I}*dan-ni-e-a* DUMU
9) *ša* SAL *be-li-li-tum na-ši*
10) 1-*en pu-ut ša-ni-e na-šu-ú*
11) LÚ *mu-kin-nu* ^{I}*na'-id-*^{d}EN *A-šú šá*
12) ^{Id}UTU-ŠEŠ-MU A ^{Id}AG-*še-me*
13) ^{Id}EN-ŠEŠ.MEŠ-MU *A-šú šá* ^{I}*ta-qiš-*^{d}*gu-la*
14) A ^{I}*ši-gu-ú-a* ^{I}*šá-pik A-šú šá* ^{Id}AMAR.UD-PAP
15) A LÚ.ŠID.DINGIR
16) *u* LÚ.ŠID ^{Id}EN-KÁD *A-šú šá* ^{Id}EN-*ri-man-ni*
17) A ^{I}*ba-bu-tu* TIN.TIR.KI ITU.NE UD.3.KAM
18) MU.1.KAM ^{Id}U+GUR-LUGAL-ŠEŠ LUGAL TIN.TIR.KI

Translation

The lady Bēlilitum, daughter of Bēl-ušēzib, descendant of Šanašišu has, of her own free will, sold (lit., given) Bazuzu, her slave, to Nabû-aḫḫē-iddina, son of Šulâ, descendant of Egibi for the full price of one-half mina, five shekels of silver. Etillu, son of Balāssu, descendant of Dannēa, son of lady Bēlilitum bears the responsibility for claims againt the legality of the sale, claimant, palace service and personal freedom that might arise against Bazuzu. One shall bear the responsibilty for the other. Witnesses are Na'id-Bēl, son of Šamaš-aḫa-iddina, descendant of Nabû-šeme, Bēl-aḫḫē-iddina, son of Taqiš-Gula, descendant of Šigūa, Šāpik, son of Marduk-nāṣir, descendant of Šangû-ili and the scribe, Bēl-kāṣir, son of

Bēl-rīmanni, descendant of Babutu. Babylon, month of Abu, third day, first year of Nergal-šarra-uṣur, king of Babylon.

24

BM 30252
Published as Evetts, *Ner.* 24

1) ⌈*x*⌉ MA.NA KÙ.BABBAR *šá* ^{Id}⌈DI.KU$_5$⌉-MU-MU [A-*šú šá*]
2) ⌈^{I}⌉NUMUN-*ia* A ^{I}*na-ba-a-a ina muḫ-ḫi* ^{Id}⌈EN-MU⌉-GAR-*un*
3) [A]-*šú šá* ^{Id}AMAR.UD-*na-din*-MU A ^{I}*sip-pi-e*
4) É-*su šá* DA É ^{I}*e-til-*⌈*pi*⌉ [A]-⌈*šú*⌉ *šá*
5) ^{Id}AG-KÁD A LÚ.ŠU.I *u* ⌈DA É⌉
6) ^{Id}AG-TIN-*su-iq-bi* A-*šú šá* ^{I}*qar-*⌈*bi*⌉*-e-a*
7) *maš-ka-nu šá* ^{Id}DI.KU$_5$-MU-MU *i-*⌈*di*⌉ ⌈É⌉
8) *ia-a-nu u* HAR.RA KÙ.BABBAR *ia-a-nu a-di* 4 MU.MEŠ É *ina* IGI ^{Id}DI.KU$_5$-MU-MU
9) *ina lìb-bi* 3 MA.NA KÙ.BABBAR *a-na*
10) ⌈*xx*⌉*kam im maš ma ri ša* É *maš-kan*
11) ⌈*ṣab*⌉*-tu* ^{Id}DI.KU$_5$-MU-[MU]
12) [...] ⌈*xx*⌉ 1 MA.NA KÙ.BABBAR
13) *a-na* ^{I}MU-^{d}AMAR.UD A-*šú šá* ^{I}BA-*ša-a*
14) *u* ^{Id}AG-NUMUN--GÁL-*ši* A-*šú šá* ^{I}*e-*⌈*til*⌉*-[pi]*
15) *ra-šu-ú šá* ^{Id}EN-MU-GAR-*un*
16) *iṭ-ṭir* ^{Id}EN-MU-GAR-*un ina lìb-bi*
17) ^{I}*ki-na-a-a-tum it-ti*
18) ^{Id}DI.KU$_5$-MU-MU *im-mar*
19) LÚ *mu-kin-nu* ^{I}*ba-ni-ia* A-*sú šá*
20) ^{I}*šu-la-a* A ^{I}*si-'-a-tum*
21) ^{I}BA-*šá-a* A-*šú šá* ^{I}NÍG.DU A ^{I}ZALÁG-^{d}30
22) ^{Id}AG-DU-NUMUN A-*šú šá* ^{Id}EN-TIN-*iṭ*
23) [...] I *u* LÚ.ŠID ^{Id}AMAR.UD-NUMUN-DÙ
24) A-*šú šá* ^{Id}AG-*mu-še-tiq*-UD.DA A ^{I}DÙ-⌈*eš*⌉-[DINGIR]
25) TIN.TIR.KI ITU.NE UD.15.KAM
26) MU.1.KAM ^{d}U+GUR-LUGAL-ŠEŠ LUGAL
27) TIN.TIR.KI

Translation

(Document concerning) ... minas of silver, property of ⌈Madānu⌉-šuma-iddina, [son of] Zērija, descendant of Nabāja, charged against ⌈Bēl-šuma⸣-iškun, [son] of Marduk-nādin-šumi, descendant of Sippê. His house, which is adjacent to the property of Etilpi, [son] of Nabû-kāṣir, descendant of Galābu and ⸢adjacent to the property⸣ of Nabû-balāssu-iqbi, son of Qarbēa, serves as security for Madānu-šuma-iddina. There will be ⸢no rent on the house⸣ and no interest on the silver. The property is at the disposal of Madānu-šuma-iddina for a period of four years. From that amount, three minas of silver are for [...] ... for which the property was held as pledge. Madānu-šuma-[iddina] [...] and one mina of silver, the assets of Bēl-šuma-iškun, was paid to Iddina-Marduk, son of Iqīša, and Nabû-zēra-ušabši, son of ⸢Etilpi⸣. Bēl-šuma-iškun will witness (the contract) with Madānu-šuma-iddina in the presence of Kinatum. Witnesses (are) Bānija, son of Šulâ, descendant of Si'atum, Iqīša, son of Kudurru, descendant of Nūr Sin, Nabû-mukīn-zēri, son of Bēl-uballiṭ,[...] and the scribe, Marduk-zēra-ibni, son of Nabû-mušētiq-uddê, descendant of Epeš-[ili]. Babylon, month of Abu, fifteenth day, first year of Nergal-šarra-uṣur, king of Babylon.

25

BM 30525 (Collated)
Published as Evetts, *Ner.* 25
Boissier, *Recherches* 37ff, and Marx, BA 4, 13

1) ^{Id}⸢AMAR.UD-LUGAL⸣-ŠEŠ A-*šú šá* ^{Id}AG-SUR
2) *ina ḫu-ud lìb-bi-šú* 5 MA.NA KÙ.BABBAR
3) 2-*ta a-me-lut-tum* 30 *ṣi-e-nu*
4) 2 GUD *u ú-di* É *it-*⸢*ti*⸣
5) SAL *ḫi-ip-ta-a a-na*
6) ⸢*nu*⸣*-dun-nu-ú a-na* ^{Id}AG-DU-NUMUN
7) A-*šú šá* ^{Id}EN-TIN-*iṭ* A ^{I}*dan-ni-e-a*
8) *id-din* ^{Id}AG-DU-NUMUN *nu-dun-nu-ú-šú*
9) ⸢*ina* ŠU^{II}⸣ ^{Id}AMAR.UD-LUGAL-ŠEŠ *e-ṭir*
10) [LÚ *mu-kin-nu*] ^{I}NÍG.DU A-*šú šá*
11) [...] [A] ^{I}*di-ki-i*
12) [^{m}]*mu-še-zib-*^{d}AMAR.UD A-*šú šá* ^{I}A-*a*
13) A LÚ.ŠID ^{d}MAŠ ^{I}*ši-rik-tum*
14) A-*šú šá* ^{I}KI-^{d}AMAR.UD-TIN A nd30-SIG$_{5}$-*iq*
15) *u* LÚ.ŠID ^{Id}AG-NUMUN-GÁL-*ši*
16) A-*šú šá* ^{Id}AG-PAP A ^{Id}EN-A-PAP
17) TIN.TIR.KI ITU.KIN UD.6.KAM
18) MU.1.KAM ^{Id}U+GUR-LUGAL-ŠEŠ

19) LUGAL TIN.TIR.KI

Translation

Marduk-šarra-uṣur, son of Nabû-etir has, of his own free will, given, along with his daughter Ḫiptâ, five minas of silver, two slaves, thirty sheep, two oxen and household utensils to Nabû-mukīn-zēri, son of Bēl-uballiṭ, descendant of Dannēa, as a wedding gift. Nabû-mukīn-zēri was given (lit., paid) his wedding gift ⌈by⌉ Marduk-šarra-uṣur. [Witnesses are] Kudurru, son of [...] [descendant of] Dikî, Mušēzib-Marduk, son of Aplâ, descendant of Šangû-Ninurta, Širiktum, son of Itti-Marduk-balāṭu, descendant of Sin-udammiq and the scribe Nabû-zēra-ušabši, son of Nabû-nāṣir, descendant of Bēl-apla-uṣur. Babylon, month of Ululu, sixth day, first year of Nergal-šarra-uṣur, king of Babylon.

Commentary

2-4) For parallel uses of this phrase, see *Camb.* 193, 4-5; 215, 5-6 and cf. Tallquist, *Schenkungsbriefe*, p. 3ff.

26

BM 30575 (Collated)
Published as Evetts, *Ner.* 26

1) 15 GÍN 4-*ut bit-qa* KÙ.BABBAR
2) *šá* ^{Id}EN-DU-DUMU.UŠ A-*šú šá*
3) ^{I}*ra-šil* A LÚ.SIMUG (erasure)
4) *ina* UGU ^{Id}EN-MU A-*šú šá*
5) ^{Id}AG-ŠEŠ.MEŠ-*bul-liṭ*
6) UD.1.KAM ITU.GAN KÙ.BABBAR
7) *i-nam-din* KÙ.BABBAR
8) [*šá*] KASKAL^{II} *šá* ^{I}MU-^{d}ŠÚ
9) LÚ *mu-kin-nu* ^{I}*si-lim*-^{d}EN
10) ⌈A-*šú šá*⌉ ^{I}MU-DU A LÚ.ŠU.ḪA
11) ^{Id}⌈EN⌉-*šu-zib-an-ni* A-*šú šá*
12) ^{I}⌈MU⌉-DU *u* LÚ.ŠID
13) ^{Id}DI.KU$_5$-MU-MU A-*šú šá*
14) ^{I}NUMUN-*ia* A ^{I}*na-ba-a-a*
15) TIN.TIR.KI ITU.APIN UD.14.KAM
16) MU.1.KAM ^{d}U+GUR-LUGAL-ŠEŠ
17) LUGAL TIN.TIR.KI

Translation

(Document concerning) fifteen and three-eights shekels of silver, property of Bēl-mukīn-apli, son of Rašil, descendant of Nappāḫu, charged against Bēl-iddina, son of Nabû-aḫḫē-bulliṭ. He will deliver the silver on the first day of the month of Kislimu. The silver is [from] the business capital of Iddina-Marduk. Witnesses are Silim-Bēl, son of Šuma-ukīn, descendant of Bā'iru, Bēl-šūzibanni, son of ⌈Šuma⌉-ukīn, and the scribe, Madānu-šuma-iddina, son of Zērija, descendant of Nabāja. Babylon, month of Araḫsamnu, fifteenth day, first year of Nergal-šarra-uṣur, king of Babylon.

27

BM 31558 (Collated)
Published as Evetts, *Ner.* 27

1) *2 2/3* MA.NA *6* GÍN KÙ.BABBAR *šá* [Id]AG-MU-ŠEŠ
2) *A-šú šá* [I]*mar-duk* A [I]DÙ-*eš*-DINGIR *ina* UGU [Id]AG-ŠEŠ.MEŠ-MU
3) *A-šú šá* [I]*šu-la-a* A [I]*e-gi-bi šá* ITU *ina muḫ-*[*ḫi*]
4) *1 ma-ni-e 1* GÍN *6-'* LÁ-ti KÙ.BABBAR [*ina muḫ-ḫi-šú*]
5) *i-rab-bi*
6) LÚ *mu-kin-nu* [Id]AMAR.UD [...]
7) *A-šú šá* [I]*ba-ni-ia* A [Id]AMAR.UD [...]
8) [I]*mu-še-zib*-[d]AMAR.UD *A-šú šá* [I]NÍG.DU A [...]
9) *u* LÚ.ŠID [Id]AG-ŠEŠ.MEŠ-MU *A-šú šá* [I]*su-la-a* A [I]*e-g-bi*
10) TIN.TIR.KI ITU.APIN UD.30.KAM MU.1.KAM
11) [d]U+GUR-LUGAL-ŠEŠ LUGAL TIN.TIR.KI

Translation

(Document concerning) two and two-thirds minas, six shekels of silver, property of Nabû-šuma-uṣur, son of Marduk, descendant of Epeš-ili, charged against Nabû-aḫḫē-iddina, son of Šulâ, descendant of Egibi. Monthly, five-sixths of a shekel of silver [accrues on his account] for each mina (lit., on each mina, five-sixths (shekel) of silver shall increase [against him]). Witnesses (are) Marduk- [...], son of Bānija, descendant of Marduk- [...], Mušēzib-Marduk, son of Kudurru, descendant of [...] and the sribe, Nabû-aḫḫē-iddina, son of Šulâ, descendant of Egibi. Babylon, month of Arahsamnu, thirtieth day, first year of Nergal-šarra-usur, king of Babylon.

28

BM 63834(Collated)
Published as Evetts, *Ner.* 28

1) *ú-*[*ìl-tim*] *šá* ^{Id}EN-*šu-lum-šu-kun*
2) [...] ⌈*nu*⌉ *šá* TA TIN.TIR.KI
3) [...] ^{Id}AG-ŠEŠ.MEŠ-GI
4) [...] ⌈*x*⌉ [...] *a-na* É.BABBAR.RA
5) *id-din-nu* ITU.GAN UD.16.KAM
6) MU.1.KAM ^{d}U+GUR-LUGAL-ŠEŠ LUGAL TIN.TIR.KI
7) 1-*it tap-pal-tum* 1-*en* TÚG.KUR.RA *šá-an-šu*
8) 2-*ta* TÚG ⌈*šir*⌉-'-*a-am* MEŠ *ša* ⌈*x*⌉
9) 2 TÚG *di* ⌈*x*⌉ [...] 2 *ši-pi ša ki-it-ti*
10) 1-*it* TÚG *na-aḫ-lap-tum*
11) 1-*it* TÚG *e-li-ni-tum*
12) 3 *ḫu-ṣa-an-ni-e šá a-mil-tum*
13) 1-*en ša* GIŠ ⌈*x*⌉ 1-*en* TÚG É *ri-še-tum*
14) 1-*it* UD.KA.BAR *mu-šaḫ-ḫi-nu*
15) 3 *mu-kar-ri-šu* MEŠ GAL-*bu-ú-tu*
16) 1-*en ḫa-aṣ-bi* 1-*en ba-šu-ú*
17) 1-*it ka-a-šu šá* UD.KA.BAR
18) 1-*it šá-ši-tum šá* AN.BAR *šá* KASKAL^{II}
19) 1-*it sik-kat-tum šá* GIŠ.APIN
20) 2 GIŠ *maš-šá-nu* MEŠ GAL.MEŠ
21) 2 GIŠ *maš-šá-nu* MEŠ *gal-la-lu-tu*
22) 1-*en* GIŠ *pa-ni pu-ḫa-lu*
23) 2-*ta* GIŠ *ár-bal-lu* MEŠ
24) 3 GIŠ *šu-us-su-lu* MEŠ
25) 1-*it* TÚG *šir-'-a-am šá* GADA *a-mil-tum*
26) 1-*en* GIŠ É *ta-bi-lu*
27) *a-na* 1/2 GÍN KÙ.BABBAR *ina* IGI
28) ^{Id}AG-MU-SI.SÁ
29) 1-*it* GIŠ.NÁ *šá a-da-ri*
30) 1-*en* GIŠ *kan-kan-nu ša ḫi-li-pi*
31) *ina* É NÍG.GA *ina* IGI ^{I}*šu-la-a*
32) *ina lb-bi* 1-*en* GIŠ *maš-šá-nu*

33) *a-na* 1/2 GÍN KÙ.BABBAR *ina* IGI
34) ^{I}*la-a-ba-ši*
35) *ina lìb-bi* 1-*it* TÚG *šir-'-a-am*
36) *[a-na* ^{Id}*ba-'-ti*-DINGIR.MEŠ *i-di-'*]

Translation

Con[tract of] Bēl-šulum-šukun [...] which were delivered (lit., given) to Ebabbar from Babylon [...] Nabû-aḫḫē-šullim [...] . Month of Kislimu, sixteenth day, first year of Nergal-šarra-uṣur, king of Babylon. (The inventory includes) one cover, one blanket of plucked wool, one mens(?) garment,two [...] garments, two containers from the crucible(?), one cloak, one upper garment, three sashes for women, one [...], one garment, one bronze cooking vessel, three large metal bowls, one small pot, one container of earthenware(?), one bronze cup, one iron lantern, one peg for a plow, two large vessels, two small utensils, one container, two sieves, three casks, one linen garment for women, one container--- for one-half shekel of silver placed at the disposal of Nabû-šumu-lišir. One bed of adaru wool, one potstand of willow wood (all from) the storehouse placed at the disposal of Šulâ. From this amount, one utensil was placed at the disposal of Labaši for one-half shekel of silver, (and) from this amount, one garment [...] [was loaned out to Ba'ti-ili].

Commentary

3-4) See Tallqvist ZA 6, 272, who restores (l.3) a-na LÚ.NU.GIŠ.SAR and (l.4) ^{I}ÈR-^{d}*mar-duk*. Collation does not support these restorations, especially the reading of the personal name in line 4.
8) For a discussion of TÚG *šir-'-a-am*, see Oppenheim, JNES 1 (1947). See also JCS 4, 191ff.
18) For *šašitum*, "Laterne," see von Soden, AHw, 1197b.
22) For GIŠ *pāni puḫalu*, see von Soden, AHw 875b.

29

BM 63932 (Collated)

Published as Evetts, *Ner*. 29, translated by Peiser, *Rechtsleben* 3, 17ff

1) É *šá* ^{Id}AG-MU-DU A-*šú šá* ^{Id}UTU-GAR-MU
2) *šá ina* GI.MEŠ *šá* ^{Id}AG-EN-MU.MEŠ *i-pu-uš ina lìb-bi*
3) É TU$_{15}$.KUR.RA É *pa-ni u*(!) (text: *su*) É ŠU^{II} *šá ina tar-ba-ṣu*

4) *a-na* SAL *sik-ku-ti* DUMU.SAL-*su ša* ^{Id}EN-GI
5) *a-na áš-šá*(!) (text: *su*)-*bu-tú a-di ṭup-pi ana ṭup-pi*
6) *a-na* MU.AN.NA 2 GÍN 4-*ut* LÁ-*ti* KÙ.BABBAR
7) *id-din bat-qa ta-ṣab-bat u-ri ta-ša-ni*
8) [*ina*] *ri-eš* MU *a-ḫi i-di* É *mi*-⌜*šil*⌝
9) (erasure) MU *a-ḫi i-di* É *ta*-⌜*nam-din*⌝
10) LÚ *mu-kin-nu* ^{Id}EN-GI A-*šú šá* ^{Id}AG-GÁL-*ši*
11) A ^{Id}IM-*šam-me-e* ^{I}*ri-mut*
12) A-*šú šá* ^{Id}U+GUR-TIN-*iṭ* A LÚ.DUG.QA.BUR
13) *u* LÚ.ŠID ^{I}A-*a* A-*šú šá* ^{Id}AG-MU-GAR-*un*
14) UD.KIB.NUN.KI ITU.AB UD.20.KAM
15) MU.1.KAM ^{d}U+GUR-LUGAL-*ú-ṣur*
16) LUGAL TIN.TIR.KI

Translation

Nabû-šuma-ukīn, son of Šamaš-šākin-šumi rented (lit. gave) (his) house that he built (lit., made) with the reeds belonging to Nabû-bēl-šumi (and) therein a room facing east and a wing opening onto the courtyard to the lady Sikkuti, daughter of Bēl-ušallim in tenancy for the duration of (the period covered by) the lease for an annual (rent) of one and three-fourths shekels of silver. She will repair the damp course of the wall, she will fix the roof (and) she ⌜will pay⌝ (lit., give) one-half of the rent of the house [at the] beginning of the year (and) ⌜one half⌝ of the house-rent (in) the middle of the year. Witnesses are Bēl-ušallim, son of Nabû-ušabši, descendant of Adad-šamê, Rimut, son of Nergal-uballiṭ, descendant of Paḫāru and the scribe, Aplâ, son of Nabû-šuma-iškun. Sippar, month of Ṭebetu, twentieth day, first year of Nergal-šarra-uṣur, king of Babylon.

30

BM 30244 (Collated)
Published as Evetts, *Ner*. 30

1) [*pu-ut*] ⌜*e-ṭè-ru*⌝ *šá* 1/2 MA.NA 5 ⌜GÍN⌝ [KÙ.BABBAR *ra-šu-ti*]
2) *šá* ^{Id}BE-NUMUN-DÙ A-*šú šá* ^{I}*mar-duk* [A ^{I}...]
3) *u* SAL *na-da-a* DAM-*su ša ina* UGU ^{I}*mu* [-*ra-nu* A-*šú šá*]
4) ^{Id}MAS-ŠEŠ-MU A ⌜LÚ.DUG.QA.BUR⌝ *šá* ^{I}MU-^{d}[AMAR.UD]
5) A-*šú šá* ^{I}BA-*šá-a* A ^{I}ZALÁG(!)-^{d}30(!)(text: ^{I}DÙ-*eš*-DINGIR) *ana* ŠU^{II} ^{I}[...]
6) A-*šú šá* ^{Id}EN-*na-din*-A *a-na* UGU ^{I}*mu*-[*ra-nu*]

7) *i-ru-bu* ^{I}MU-^{d}AMAR.UD *na-śi* KÙ.[BABBAR][...]
8) 1/2 MA.NA 5⸢GÍN⸣ ^{I}MU-^{d}AMAR.UD *ul*[...]
9) *ra-ma-ni-šú iṭ-ṭir-ma ú-ìl-tim*
10) *šá* ^{Id}BE-NUMUN-DÙ *u* SAL *na-da-a* [DAM-*su*]
11) [*ina muḫ-ḫi*] $^{[I]}$*mu-ra-nu* ^{I}MU-^{d}[AMAR.UD]
12) [*i*]*-na-áš-šá-am-ma a-na* ^{I}*mu-* ⸢*ra*⸣-[*nu*]
13) *i-nam-din*
14) LU *mu-*⸢*kin*⸣*-nu* ^{Id}AG-⸢*na*⸣*-ṣir* A-*šú šá* ^{I}*šu-*[*la-a*]
15) A LÚ.DÍM ^{I}ZALAG-^{d}30 A-*šú šá* ^{I}*tab-ni-e-a*
16) A ^{I}ZALÁG-^{d}30 ^{I}MU-⸢^{d}AMAR.UD⸣ A-*šú šá* ^{Id}U+GUR-*ú-*[*še-zib*]
17) A ^{Id}ILLAT-I
18) *u* LÚ.ŠID ^{Id}AMAR.UD-⸢NUMUN-DÙ⸣ A-*šú šá* ^{Id}UTU-[MU]
19) A ^{I}DÙ-*eš*-DINGIR TIN.TIR.KI ITU.ZÍZ
20) UD.17.KAM MU.1.KAM ^{Id}U+GUR-LUGAL⸢-ŠEŠ⸣
21) LUGAL TIN.TIR.KI

Translation

Iddina-Marduk bears the [responsibility] ⸢for the payment⸣ of one-half mina, five ⸢shekels⸣ [of silver, the loan] of Ea-zēra-ibni, son of Marduk, [descendant of ...] and Nadâ, his wife, which was charged against Mu[ranu, son of] Ninurta-aḫa-iddina, descendant of ⸢Paḫāru⸣ (silver) which Iddina-[Marduk] son of Iqīša, descendant of Nūr-Sin, obtained from [...] son of Bēl-nādin-apli (and was) charged against Mu[ranu]. Iddina-Marduk...will pay the one-half mina, five shekels of silver himself (and) Iddina-[Marduk] will bring the promissory note [...] in the possession of Ea-zēra-ibni and the lady Nadâ, [his wife] [charged against] Muranu (and) he will give (it) to Mu[ranu]. Witnesses (are) Nabû-nāṣir, son of Šu[lâ], descendant of Itinnu, Nūr-Sin, son of Tabnēa, descendant of Nūr-Sin, Iddina-⸢Marduk,⸣ son of Nergal-u[šēzib] descendant of Illat-na'id, and the scribe, Marduk-zēra-ibni, son of Šamaš-[iddina], descendant of Epeš-ili. Babylon, month of Šabaṭu, seventeenth day, first year of Nergal-šarra-uṣur, king of Babylon.

Commentary

3) The restoration ^{I}*mu-*[*ra-nu* A-*šú šá*] is based on the contents of lines 6 and 11-12.

5) Although collation shows ^{I}DÙ-*eš*-DINGIR to stand, as in Evetts' copy, it is most certainly a scribal error for ^{I}ZALÁG-^{d}30. Cf. citations in Tallquist, NBN, p. 71b and p. 72a.

31

BM 77303 (Collated)

Published as Evetts, *Ner.* 31 and Ungnad, SSS 10, p. 71

1) 10 GUR ZÚ.LUM.MA ZAG.LU
2) *šá* UGU ÍD ^{d}DI.KU$_5$
3) *šá* ^{I}*šu-la-a* A-*šú šá* ^{I}*gi-mil-lu*
4) A ^{I}DÙ-*eš*-DINGIR *ina* UGU ^{I}MU-^{d}AG
5) *A-šú šá* ^{Id}AG-SUR *ina ḫa-*[*ṣa*]*-ri*
6) *i-na ma*(!) (text: *áš*)-*ši-ḫu*
7) *šá* 1 PI ZÚ(!).LUM(!) (text: i ⸢x⸣ *šul*) MA
8) *i-nam-din*
9) LÚ *mu-kin-nu* ^{I}*lu-ṣa-ana*(!) (text: *ši*)-ZÁLAG
10) *A-šú šá* ^{Id}EN-ŠEŠ-GÁL-*ši*
11) A ^{I}*kas-si-dak-ku*
12) LÚ.ŠID ^{I}*mu-še-zib*-^{d}EN
13) *A-šú šá* ^{Id}UTU-KAM ⸢A^{I}⸣ *dam-qu*
14) ÍD ^{d}DI.KU$_5$ ITU.[...]
15) MU.1.KAM ^{d}U+GUR-LUGAL-ŠEŠ
16) LUGAL TIN.TIR.KI
17) 1 *sis-sin-na* NU *e-ṭir*
18) ⸢x x⸣ *lu*
19) ⸢x x⸣ *i-nam-din*

Translation

(Document concerning) ten *kurru* of dates, estimated yield from the Madānu canal, property of Šulâ, son of Gimillu, descendant of Epeš-ilī, charged against Iddina-Nabû, son of Nabû-ēṭir. He will deliver the dates in one delivery [...] at the enclosure in accordance with the measure of one *pi*. Witnesses (are) Lūṣu-ana-nūri, son of Bēl-aḫa-ušabši, descendant of Kassidaku, (and) the scribe, Mušēzib-Bēl, son of Šamaš-ēriš, ⸢descendant of⸣ Damqu. Madānu canal, month of [...] first year of Nergal-šarra-uṣur, king of Babylon. The compensation has not been paid. He will deliver [...].

32

BM 31308 (Collated)
Published as Evetts, *Ner.* 32

1) 10 LIM *gid-dil šá* SUM.SAR
2) 10 GÍN KÙ.BABBAR *šá* ^{I}MU-^{d}AMAR.UD
3) A-*šú šá* ^{I}BA-*šá-a* A ^{I}ZALÁG-^{d}30
4) *ina* UGU ^{I}ŠEŠ-MU A-*šú šá* ^{I}ÈR-*ia*
5) ^{I}*ba-la-ṭu* A-*šú šá* ^{I}*gi-mil-lu*
6) *ina* ITU.GUD *gid-dil ša* SUM.SAR
7) *i-nam-din* KÙ.BABBAR *ḫu-di-i*
8) *i-nam-din*
9) LÚ *mu-kin-nu* ^{I}*ba-la-ṭu*
10) A-*šú šá* ^{Id}UTU-TIN-*iṭ*
11) ^{I}*kal-ba-a* A-*šú šá* ^{I}*gi-mil-lu*
12) A ^{I}*mu-kal*(!) *(text:lul)-lim(!) (text: mu) u* LÚ.ŠID
13) ^{I}ŠEŠ-MU A-*šú šá* ^{I}ÈR-*ia*
14) TIN.TIR.KI ITU.BÁR UD.10.KAM
15) MU.2.KAM ^{d}U+GUR-LUGAL-ŠEŠ
16) LUGAL TIN.TIR.KI

Translation

(Document concerning) ten thousand strings of garlic (and) ten shekels of silver, property of Iddina-Marduk, son of Iqīša, descendant of Nūr-Sin, charged against Aḫa-iddina, son of Ardija, (and) Balāṭu, son of Gimillu. They(!) will deliver the strings of garlic in the month of Ajaru (or) at (their!) option, they(!) will deliver the silver. Witnesses (are) Balāṭu, son of Šamaš-uballiṭ, Kalbâ, son of Gimillu, descendant of Mukallim(!) and the scribe, Aḫa-iddina, son of Ardija. Babylon, nonth of Nisanu, tenth day, second year of Nergal-šarra-uṣur, king of Babylon.

Commentary

12) Although collation shows this line to have been correctly copied by Evetts, one should read, with Tallqvist (NBN86b) *mu-kal-lim*. Cf. Evetts, *Ner.* 43,21 and *Nbn.* 663, 12 where the same person and family name occur.

33

BM 31143 (Collated)
Published as Evetts, *Ner.* 33

1) 55 GUR ŠE.BAR 40 UDU.NITÁ.ME ⸢*xx*⸣
2) 20 *pa*-⸢*rat*⸣-' 10 *ṣi-e-nu* UDU.NITÁ
3) 5 *ka-lu-mu* 5 ÙZ 1 GÚ.UN SÍG.ḪI.A
4) 1/2 MA.NA 7 GÍN ⸢KÙ.⸣BABBAR
5) ša ^{Id}DI.KU$_5$-MU-MU A-*šú šá*
6) ^{I}NUMUN-*ía* A ^{I}*na-ba-a-a*
(remainder broken off)
1') LÚ *mu-kin-nu* [^{Id}EN]-MU A-*šú šá*
2') ^{Id}AG-GI A ^{I}*a-ḫu*-DÙ
3') ^{I}*na-din* A-*šú šá* ^{I}*ba-laṭ-su*
4') A LÚ.GAL.DÙ *u* LÚ.ŠID ^{I}*ba-la-ṭu*
5') A-*šú šá* ^{Id}UTU-*id-din* TIN.TIR.KI
6') ITU.GUD UD.23.KAM
7') MU.2.KAM ^{d}U+GUR-LUGAL-⸢ŠEŠ⸣
8') LUGAL TIN.TIR.[KI]

Translation

(Document concerning) fifty-five *kurru* of barley, forty ... sheep, twenty female lambs, ten sheep, five male lambs, five goats, one talent of wool (and) one-half mina, seven shekels of silver, property of Madānu-šuma-iddina, son of ⸢Zērija,⸣, descendant of Nabāja [...]. Witnesses (are) [Bēl]-iddina, son of Nabû-ušallim, descendant of Aḫu-bāni, Nādin, son of Balāssu, descendant of Rāb-bāni and the scribe, Balāṭu, son of Šamaš-iddina. Babylon, month of Ajaru, twenty-third day, second year of Nergal-šarra-⸢uṣur,⸣ king of Babylon.

Commentary

1) Read 40 instead of 50, as in Evetts' copy.
1') ^{Id}EN is no longer on the tablet.
5') Although collation shows Evetts' copy to be correct here, this is most certainly a scribal error for ^{Id}UTU-TIN-*iṭ*. Cf. Evetts, *Ner.* 32:9 and Strassmaier, *Nbn.* 36:4,17, where the same person and family name occur. See Tallqvist, NBN 20a.

34

BM 30848 (Collated)
Published as Evetts, *Ner.* 34; published in transltieration and translation by Peiser, *Rechtsleben* 3 62 and KB 4 204ff.

1) ⸢É⸣ šá ^{Id}AG-ŠEŠ.MEŠ-MU A-*šú šá* ^{I}*šú-la-a*
2) [A] ^{I}*e-gi-bi ina* ŠU^{II} ^{I}*la-a-ba-ši*
3) *u* ^{I}*kal-ba-a* LÚ.DUMU.MEŠ *šá* ^{Id}AMAR.⸢UD-NUMUN⸣-DÙ
4) *u* ^{I}ŠU-^{d}*gu-la u* ŠEŠ.MEŠ-*šú* LÚ.[DUMU.MEŠ]
5) *šá* ^{I}NUMUN-*ia im-ḫur-ri* SAL *i-lat*
6) DUMU.SAL-*su šá* ^{Id}AG-SUR *a-na*
7) LÚ *mu-kin-nu-tu ina* IM.KIŠIB
8) *šá* ^{Id}AG-ŠEŠ.MEŠ-MU *aṣ-ba-at*
9) LÚ *mu-kin-ni* ^{I}ÈR-*ia* A-*šú šá* ^{I}DU-⸢NUMUN⸣
10) A ^{I}ÈR-^{d}BE ^{I}*ba-ni-ia A-šú šá*
11) ^{I}*ri-mut* A ^{I}DÙ-*eš*-DINGIR ^{I}KI-^{d}UTU-TIN
12) A-*šú šá* ^{Id}AG-NUMUN-SI.SÁ A ^{I}*e-gi-bi*
13) *u* LÚ.ŠID ^{I}MU-DU A-*šú šá* ^{Id}EN-*ri-man-ni*
14) A ^{I}*ba-bu-tu* TIN.TIR.KI ITU.GUD
15) [UD].27.KAM MU.2.KAM ^{Id}U+GUR-LUGAL-ŠEŠ
16) LUGAL TIN.TIR.KI

Translation

⸢The property⸣ belonging to Nabû-aḫḫē-iddina, son of Šulâ, [descendant] of Egibi was received from Labaši and Kalbâ, sons of Marduk-⸢zēra⸣-ibni and Gimil-Gula and his brothers, [sons of] Zērija. The lady Ilat, daughter of Nabû-ēṭir, was present as a witness to the transaction (lit., the seal) involving Nabû-aḫḫē-iddina. Witnesses (are) Ardija, son of Mukīn-zēri, descendant of Arad-Ea, Bānija, son of Rīmūt, descendant of Epeš-ili, Itti-Šamaš-balāṭu, son of Nabû-zēru-lišir, descendant of Egibi, and the scribe, Šuma-ukīn, son of Bēl-rīmanni, descendant of Babutu. Babylon, month of Ajaru, twenty-seventh [day,] second year of Nergal-šarra-uṣur, king of Babylon.

35

BM 31084 (Collated)
Published as Evetts, *Ner.* 35

1) 3 LIM *gid-dil šá* ⸢SUM.SAR⸣ ⸢*x* ⸣GÍN [KÙ.BABBAR]
2) *šá* ^{Id}DI.KU$_5$-MU-MU A-*šú šá* ^{I}NUMUN-*ia*
3) [A] ^{I}*na-ba-a-a u* $^{[I]d}$EN-DÙ-*uš*
4) A-*šú šá* ^{I}*ra-šil-li* A LÚ.SIMUG
5) KASKAL^{II} *šá* ^{I}⸢MU⸣-^{d}AMAR.UD *ina* UGU
6) ^{Id}AG-GI A-*šú šá* ^{I}IGI-*ni-ia*
7) ITU.BÁR *gid-dil u* ⸢KÙ.BABBAR⸣ *a-*⸢*na*⸣ [^{I}MU]-^{d}AMAR.UD *i-nam-din*
8) KÙ.BABBAR *ina* TIN.TIR.KI *i-nam-[din]*
9) *e-lat* ⸢*xx*⸣ KASKAL^{II} 1/2 MA.NA [KÙ.BABBAR]
10) *u* 6 *dan-nu-tu maḫ-ḫu-ru*
11) LÚ *mu-kin-nu* ^{I}NUMUN-*ia* A-*šú šá*
12) ^{I}*nad-na-a* A ^{I}LÚ.GAL.DÙ
13) ^{Id}AG-MU-DÙ A-*šú šá* ^{I}*ri-mut-*^{d}EN
14) A LÚ.EN.NUN.KÁ.⸢GAL⸣ *u* LÚ.ŠID
15) ^{Id}EN-MU A-*šú šá* ^{Id}EN-⸢SU⸣
16) [A ^{I}]*da-bi-bi* TIN.TIR.KI ITU.[SIG$_4$]
17) UD.25.KAM MU.2.KAM
18) ^{d}U+GUR-LUGAL-ŠEŠ
19) LUGAL TIN.TIR.KI

Translation

(Document concerning) three thousand strings ⸢of garlic,⸣ and ... ⸢shekels⸣ [of silver, property of Madānu-šuma-iddina, son of Zērija, [descendant] of Nabāja and Bēl-ēpuš, son of Rašil, descendant of Nappāḫu, business capital belonging to ⸢Iddina⸣-Marduk (and) charged against Nabû-ušallim, son of Pānija. He will deliver the strings (of garlic) and ⸢the silver⸣ to [Iddina]-Marduk in the month of Nisanu and he will repay the silver in Babylon.(This is) apart from ... the business capital (of) one-half mina [of silver] and six vats (which) were received. Witnesses (are) Zērija, son of Nadnâ, descendant of Rāb-bāni, Nabû-šuma-ibni, son of Rīmūt-Bēl, descendant of Maṣṣar-bābi and [the scribe,], Bēl-iddina, son of Bēl-⸢erība,⸣ [descendant] of Dabibi. Babylon, month of [Simanu,] twenty-fifth day, second year of Nergal-šarra-uṣur, king of Babylon.

Commentary

4) Collation shows the name to be written ^{I}*ra-šil-li*. Cf. Nbk 252,4; *EvM*12,3, 18; 20,5; *Ner* 10,10; 21,2; 22,4; 26,2; and 43,15. See also discussion in AOATS 4, 74.

14-17) The signs enclosed in brackets no longer appear on the tablet. The month name was originally read SIG$_4$ by Evetts.

36

BM77825 (Collated)

Published as Evetts, *Ner.* 36; translated by Peiser, *Rechtsleben* 3, 59ff.

1) 1 2/3 MA.NA KÙ.BABBAR *ra-šu-tu šá* ^{Id}EN-BA-*šá* A-*šú šá* ^{Id}AG-*ú-šal-lim*
2) A ^{I}*mu*-SIG$_5$-*iq*-^{d}IM *šá ina* UGU ^{I}NUMUN-TIN.TIR.KI DUMU-*šú*
3) *šá* ^{I}*ra-šil* A ^{I}*e-tel-pi šá* MU.26.KAM ^{Id}AG-NÍG.DU-ŠEŠ
4) LUGAL TIN.TIR.KI *šá i-di É ia-a-ni u* ḪAR.RA KÙ.BABBAR
5) *ia-a-ni É maš-ka-nu ṣab-tu* ^{I}*na-din* DUMU-*šú šá* ^{Id}EN-BA-*šá*
6) 1 2/3 MA.[NA] KÙ.BABBAR-*šú ina* ŠU^{II} ^{Id}AMAR.UD-DUB-NUMUN DUMU-*šú šá* ^{Id}U+GUR-SUR
7) A ^{I}*e-ṭè-ru ma-ḫir ár-ki šá* ^{Id}AMAR.UD-DUB-NUMUN
8) 1 2/3 MA.NA KÙ.BABBAR ⸢*a*⸣-*na* ^{I}*na-din u* SAL *ba-zi-tum* AMA-*šu*
9) *i-ṭi-ru* ^{I}*na-din ú-ìl-tim* MEŠ *la a-ma-ri-e-ti*
10) [...] (*erasure*) *u iš-šá-am-ma it-ti* ^{Id}BE-ŠEŠ.[MEŠ-SUM-*na*]
11) [...] [^{Id}AMAR,UD]-DUB-NUMUN *ul it-ri-ik* [...]
13) [...] ⸢*ri*⸣-*ka-su šá* ^{I}*e-ṭi-ru* [...]
14) [...] ⸢*din*⸣ *ú-kal-lim-ma ú-ìl-tim* MEŠ *šá a-na* [...]
15) [...] *a-na e-ṭi-ri-e-ti i-tur-ra-'* ⸢*x*⸣ [...]
16) [...] *ú-ìl-tim šá ina* UGU ^{Id}AMAR.UD-DUB-NUMUN ⸢*x*⸣ [...]
17) [^{I}*na*]-*di-nu* A-*šú šá* ^{Id}EN-BA-*šá u lu-ú ina qaq-qar šá* [...]
18) [...] *ri-ma-nu šá* ^{Id}BE-ŠEŠ.ME-MU A-*šú šá* ^{Id}U+GUR-SUR A ^{I}*e-ṭi-ru ši-na*
19) [LÚ] *mu-kin* [*nu*] ^{Id}AG-⸢*x*⸣ A-*šú šá* ^{Id}⸢EN⸣-GI A ^{I}*su-ḫa-a-a*
20) ^{I}*za-kir* A-*šú šá* ^{I}⸢*ki*⸣-*na-a* A ^{I}*e-ṭè-ru*
21) [^{Id}EN-A-MU] A-*šú šá* ^{I}I-^{d}AMAR.UD A ^{I}*e-ṭè-ru*
22) ^{I}*la*-[*a-ba*]-*ši* A-*šú šá* ^{I}DI.KU$_5$-^{d}AMAR.UD A LÚ ⸢*x*⸣-*ú*
23) [^{Id}AMAR.UD]-LUGAL-*a-ni* A-*šú šá* ^{Id}EN-MU A ^{I}*e-ṭè-ru*

24) ⌜IdEN⌝-PAP.ME-MU A-*šú šá* IdAMAR.UD-NUMUN-DÙ A I*ú-ṣur-a-mat*-dBE
25) *u* LÚ.ŠID IdUTU-NUMUN-BA-*šá* A-*šú šá* I*ba-la-ṭu* A I[*ši*]-*gu-ú-a*
26) TIN.TIR.KI ITU.ŠU UD.28 KAM MU.[2].KAM IdU+GUR-LUGAL-ŠEŠ
27) LUGAL TIN.TIR.KI

Translation

(Document concerning) one and two-thirds minas of silver, loan of Bēl-iqīša, son of Nabû-ušallim, descendant of Mudammiq-Adad, which was charged against Zēr-Bābili, son of Rašil, descendant of Etilpi in the twenty-sixth year of Nabû-kudurri-uṣur, king of Babylon (and for) which there was no rent on the house and no interest on the silver. The house was held as security. Nādin, the son of Bēl-iqīša, received the one and two-thirds minas of silver from Marduk-šāpik-zēri, son of Nergal-ēṭir, descendant of Eṭēru. After Marduk-šāpik-zēri paid the one and two-thirds minas of silver to Nādin and to the lady Bazitum, his mother, Nādin produced (lit., brought) contracts never before seen and he made a claim (against) [Marduk]-šāpik-zēri and Ea-aḫ[ḫē-iddina], saying, "I have not been paid [the silver] (by) [Marduk]-šāpik-zēri." [...] Eṭēru [...] he produced and the contracts which [were presented(?)] for payment have become paid notes. [...] the contract charged against Marduk-šāpik-zēri [...] [Nā]din, son of Bēl-iqīša or [...] they are the property of Ea-aḫḫē-iddina, son of Nergal-ēṭir, descendant of Eṭēru. [Witnesses] (are) Nabû [...] son of ⌜Bēl⌝-ušallim, descendant of Suḫāja, Zākir, son of Kinâ, descendant of Eṭēru, [Bēl-apla-iddina], son of Na'id-Marduk, descendant of Eṭēru, Labaši, son of Dajān-Marduk, descendant of [...],[Marduk]-šarrāni, son of Bēl-iddina, descendant of Eṭēru, ⌜Bēl⌝-aḫḫē-iddina, son of Marduk-zēra-ibni, descendant of Uṣur-amat-Ea, and the scribe, Šamaš-zēra-iqīša, son of Balāṭu, descendant of Šigūa. Babylon, month of Du'uzu, twenty-eighth day, [second] year of Nergal-šarra-uṣur, king of Babylon.

Commentary

10) For the restoration IdBE-ŠEŠ.[MEŠ-SUM-*na*] see 1.18.
19-27) All bracketed items indicate signs no longer on the tablet. While Evetts' copy indicates the text was datable to the second year of Nergal-šarra-uṣur, the year date no longer appears on the tablet.

37

BM 63933 (Collated)
Published as Evetts, *Ner.* 37

1) 2 *qul-mu-ú* AN.BAR [...]
2) *šá* TA É ^{Id}EN-TIN-*su*-[E][...]
3) *na-šá-'-nu* ^{Id}EN-MU
4) *a-na* É.BABBAR.RA
5) *it-ta-din* ITU.NE
6) UD.11.KAM MU.2.KAM
7) ^{Id}U+GUR-LUGAL-ŠEŠ
8) LUGAL TIN.TIR.KI

Translation

Bēl-iddina has delivered two iron axes [...] which were brought from the house of Bēl-balāssu-[iqbi] [...] to Ebabbar. Month of Abu, eleventh day, second year of Nergal-šarra-uṣur, king of Babylon.

Commentary

2) Collation shows TIN-*su* was not copied by Evetts.

38

BM 31104 (Collated)
Published as Evetts, *Ner.* 38

1) [*x* GÍN 4-*ut*] *bit-qa* KÙ.BABBAR 1 LIM ⌜*x*⌝ ME
2) ⌜*gi*⌝-*di-lu šá* SUM.SAR *šá* ^{I}NUMUN-*ú-tu*
3) A-*šú-šá* ^{Id}EN-SUR A ^{I}*su-ḫa-a-a*
4) *šá* KASKAL *šá* ^{Id}EN-SUR *ina* UGU ^{Id}AG-GI
5) A-*šú šá* ^{I}IGI-*ni-ia*
6) *ina qí-it* ITU.DU$_6$
7) *i-nam-din*
8) LÚ *mu-kin-nu* ^{Id}EN-TIN-*iṭ*
9) A-*šú šá* ^{Id}EN-NUMUN-DÙ A ^{I}GÍR.LÁ
10) ^{Id}AG-TIN-*su-iq-bi* A-*šú šá* ^{I}*šu-zu-bu*
11) A ^{Id}IM-MU-MU
12) *u* LÚ.ŠID ^{Id}AG-DA A-*šú šá* ^{I}ÈR-*a*
13) A ^{I}*ši-gu-ú-a*

14) E.KI ITU.KIN UD.2.KAM
15) MU.2.KAM ^{Id}U+GUR-LUGAL-ŠEŠ
16) LUGAL E.KI

Translation

(Document concerning) ... and three-eighths shekels of silver (and) one thousand ... hundred strings of garlic, property of Zērūtu, son of Bēl-ēṭir, descendant of Suḫāja, from the business capital of Bēl-ēṭir, charged against Nabû-ušallim, son of Pānija. He will deliver (the silver and the strings of garlic) at the end of the month of Du'uzu. Witnesses (are) Bēl-uballiṭ, son of Bēl-zera-ibni, descendant of Naš-paṭri, Nabu-balāssu-iqbi, son of Šūzubu, descendant of Adad-šuma-iddina, and the scribe, Nabû-le'i, son of Ardija, descendant of Šigūa. Babylon, month of Ululu, second day, second year of Nergal-šarra-uṣur, king of Babylon.

39

BM 30443 (Collated)

Published as Evetts, *Ner.* 39, Strassmaier, *Liverpool* 118 and Ungnad, SSS 10, no. 4; published in translation or commentary by Peiser, *Rechtsleben* 3, 31 and Petschow, ZSS 76, 62ff.

1) 12 MA.NA KÙ.BABBAR *šá* LÚ.DUMU.LUGAL
2) *šá* ŠU^{II} ^{Id}AG-*ṣa-bit*-ŠU^{II} LÚ.GAL.É
3) *šá* LÚ.DUMU.LUGAL *ina muḫ-ḫi* ^{I}MU-DU A-*šú šá*
4) ^{I}*mu-šal-lim*-DINGIR *ina* ITU.BÁR KÙ.BABBAR-'
5) 12 MA.NA *ina* SAG.DU-*šú i-nam-din*
6) *mim-ma-šú šá* URU *u* EDIN *ma-la ba-šu-ú*
7) *maš-ka-nu šá* LÚ.DUMU.LUGAL LÚ.TUK-*ú*
8) *šá-nam-ma a-na muḫ-ḫi*
9) *ul i-šal-lat a-di muḫ-ḫi*
10) ^{Id}AG-*ṣa-bit*-ŠU^{II} KÙ.BABBAR
11) *i-šal-lim-mu pu-ut e-ṭir-ru*
12) *šá* KÙ.BABBAR ^{Id}AG-ŠEŠ.MEŠ-MU A-*šú šá*
13) ^{I}*šu-la-a* A ^{I}*e-gi-bi na-a-šú*
14) LÚ *mu-kin-nu* ^{Id}UTU-TIN A-*šú šá*
15) ^{I}BA-*šá-a* ^{I}*kal-ba-a* A-*šú šá* ^{Id}EN-APIN-*eš*
16) LÚ.DUB.SAR ^{Id}EN-ŠEŠ.MEŠ-BA-*šá*
17) A-*šú šá* ^{Id}EN-SUR TIN.TIR.KI ITU.KIN
18) UD.10.KAM MU.2.KAM ^{Id}U+GUR-LUGAL ŠEŠ

19) LUGAL TIN.TIR.KI

Translation

(Document concerning) twelve minas of silver, property of the crown prince, in the possession of Nabû-ṣabit-qāte, the superintendent of the crown prince (and) charged against Šuma-ukīn, son of Mušallim-ili. He will deliver the twelve minas of silver from his capital in the month of Nisanu. All of his possessions in the city and the country (lit., field), everything that he owns, (serves as) the security to be held by the crown prince. No other creditor shall possess any right to (the property of Šuma-ukīn) until Nabû-ṣabit-qāte returns (lit., satisfies) the silver. Nabû-aḫḫē-iddina, son of Šulâ, descendant of Egibi, bears the responsibility for the payment of the silver. Witnesses (are) Šamaš-uballiṭ, son of Iqīša, Kalbâ, son of Bēl-ēriš, (and) the scribe, Bēl-aḫḫē-iqīša, son of Bēl-ēṭir. Babylon, month of Ululu, tenth day, second year of Nergal-šarra-uṣur, king of Babylon.

40

BM65260 (Collated)
Published as Evetts, *Ner.* 40; published in translation by Peiser, *Rechtsleben* 3, 61.

1) ⸢*x*⸣ GÍN KÙ.BABBAR *ul-tu*
2) *qu-up-pu ša* ^{d}*gu-la*
3) *a-na* É.BABBAR.RA *a-na*
4) *dul-lu šá ziq-ru-ra-tum*
5) [*ina*] GUB-*su šá* ^{Id}*mu-še-zib-*^{d}ŠÚ
6) A ^{Id}AG-*ni-ip-šá-ri*
7) ITU.DU$_6$ UD.3.KAM MU.2.KAM
8) ^{Id}⸢U+GUR⸣-LUGAL-ŠEŠ
9) LUGAL TIN.TIR.KI

Translation

(Document concerning) ... shekels of silver, from the cash box of Gula (taken) to Ebabbar for work on the temple tower. [In] the presence of Mušēzib-Marduk, son of Nabû-nipšari. Month of Tašritu, third day, second year of Nergal-šarra-uṣur, king of Babylon.

41

BM 63960 (Collated)
Published as Evetts, *Ner.* 41

1) 4-*ut ḫal-lu-*⸢*ru*⸣
2) *a-na nap-ṭu*
3) *a-na* ^{Id}UTU-TIN-*iṭ*
4) *šá* DUG *qa-bu-tú*
5) SUM-*in*
6) 5 BÁN ŠE.BAR *ina* ŠUK.ḪI.A
7) ^{Id}AMAR.UD-MU-ŠEŠ
8) SUM-*in* ITU.APIN
9) UD.30.KAM MU.2.KAM
10) ^{d}U+GUR-LUGAL-ŠEŠ
11) LUGAL TIN.TIR.KI

Translation

(Document concerning) one-fourth plus one-tenth (shekel of silver) given for naphtha for a bowl to Šamaš-uballiṭ ... (and) thirty qa of barley from the food portion (which) Marduk-šuma-uṣur gave. Month of Araḫsamnu, thirtieth day, second year of Nergal-šarra-uṣur, king of Babylon.

Commentary

1) For similar uses of *ḫalluru*, cf. VAS 6 228, 3; TuM 2-3, 235, 14-15; *Dar.* 119,5 and (with gold) YOS 6 29,1.

42

BM 30454 (Collated)
Published as Evetts, *Ner.*42

1) ^{I}*nu-ur-*^{d}EN-*lu-mur u* SAL ^{d}*na-na-ri-ṣu-ni*
2) DAM-*šú a-me-lut-tum šá* ^{Id}AG-ŠEŠ.MEŠ-MU
3) *A-šú šá* ^{I}*šu-la-a* A ^{I}*e-gi-bi*
4) *ina* ŠU^{II} SAL *be-li-li-tum* DUMU.SAL
5) *šá* ^{Id}EN-*ú-še-zib* AMA *šá* ^{I}NUMUN-*ia*
6) *A-šú šá* ^{I}TIN-*su* A ^{I}*dan-ni-e-a a-na* KÙ.BABBAR
7) *i-bu-ku-ma* ^{I}NUMUN-*ia a-ki*(!)-*i sa-ku-ú-tu*
8) *ú-paq-qí-ru-ma i-bu*(!)-*ku*

9) ^{Id}AG-ŠEŠ.MEŠ-MU *ul uš-ku-ú*
10) [*šá*] ^{I}NUMUN-*ia šu-ú*
11) LÚ *mu-kin-nu* ^{I}*ba-nu-nu A-šú šá* ^{I}*ṣil-la-a*
12) A LÚ.GAL.DÙ ^{I}*ap-la-a A-šú šá* ^{Id}EN-TIN-*iṭ*
13) A ^{I}ŠEŠ-*ba-ni* ^{Id}EN-*ri-man-ni A-šú šá*
14) ^{Id}AG-KAR-ZI.MEŠ A ^{I}ÈR-^{d}GIR$_4$.KÙ
15) LÚ.ŠID ^{I}*mu-šal-lim-* ^{d}AMAR.UD *A-šú šá*
16) ^{I}BA-*šá*-^{d}AMAR.UD A ^{Id}30-PAP
17) TIN.TIR.KI ITU.APIN UD.27.KAM
18) MU.2.KAM ^{Id}U+GUR-LUGAL-ŠEŠ
19) LUGAL TIN.TIR.KI

Translation

(Document concerning) Nūr-Bēl-lummur, and the lady Nanâ-riṣuni, his wife, slaves that Nabû-aḫḫē-iddina, son of Šulâ, descendant of Egibi sold for silver to the lady Belilitu, daughter of Bēl-ušēzib, mother of Zērija, son of Balāssu, descendant of Dannēa. (If) Zērija raises a claim concerning encumberances and (if) he (already) sold (the slaves), then Nabû-aḫḫē-iddina is not responsible. It is the [responsibility] of Zērija. Witnesses (are) Banunu, son of Ṣillâ, descendant of Rāb-bāni, Aplâ, son of Bēl-uballiṭ, descendant of Aḫu-bāni, Bēl-rīmanni, son of Nabû-ēṭir-napšāti, descendant of Arad-Nergal, (and) the scribe, Mušallim-Marduk, son of Iqīša-Marduk, descendant of Sin-nāṣir. Babylon, month of Araḫsamnu, twenty-seventh day, second year of Nergal-šarra-uṣur, king of Babylon.

Commentary

7) Collation shows *sa-ku-ú-tu* (for *zakûtu*, encumberance", "adjustment") to stand, as in Evett's copy. Cf. similar uses of *s* for *z* in *zikru* (*sikru*) in BMS 22:21 and *ziqziqqu* (*siqsi(q)qu*) in JSS 5 121 r. 8, etc.

43

BM 30331 (Collated)
Published as Evetts, *Ner.* 43 and as Strassmaier, *Liverpool*, 119

1) 1 1/2 MA.NA 6 GÍN KÙ.BABBAR 18 GUR ŠE.BAR
2) *šá* ^{I}MU-^{d}AMAR.UD A-*šú šá* ^{I}BA-*šá-a* A ^{I}ZALÁG-^{d}30
3) *ina* UGU ^{I}BA-*šá-a* A-*šú šá* ^{Id}EN-KÁD
4) A LÚ.ŠID.BAR *u* ^{Id}AMAR.UD-SU A-*šú šá*

5) ^{I}*na-din* KÙ.BABBAR ŠE.NUMUN *šá* SUM.SAR
6) *šá* MU.1.KAM *u* MU.2.KAM
7) ^{d}U+GUR-LUGAL-ŠEŠ LUGAL TIN.TIR.KI
8) *ina* ITU.ŠE KÙ.BABBAR SAG.DU-*šú ina ši-kit-ti-šú-nu*
9) *ma-la ba-šu-ú*
10) *ú-šal-li-mu ši-kit-ta-šú-nu*
11) *maš-ka-nu šá* ^{I}MU-^{d}AMAR.UD
12) *ina* ITU.⸢GUD⸣ ŠE.BAR SAG.DU-*šú ina* URU
13) *šá* ^{I}ŠEŠ-MU *i-nam-din-nu*
14) 1-*en pu-ut ša-ni-e na-šu-ú*
15) LÚ *mu-kin-nu* ^{Id}EN-DÙ-*uš* A-*šú šá*
16) ^{I}*ra-šil* A LÚ.SIMUG ^{I}*ri-mut*
17) A-*šú šá* ^{Id}AMAR.UD-SU A ^{Id}30-DINGIR.MEŠ
18) ^{I}*mu-še-zib* A-*šú šá* ^{Id}EN-ŠEŠ.MEŠ-MU
19) A ^{I}*qaq-qa-di-nu* ^{I}MU-DU A-*šú šá*
20) ^{I}*šá*-^{d}AG-*šu-ú u* LÚ.ŠID ^{I}NUMUN-*tú*
21) A-*šú šá* ^{I}A-*a* A ^{I}*mu-kal(!)(text:lul)-lim*
22) URU *šaḫ-ri-nu* ITU.GAN UD.2.KAM
23) MU.2.KAM ^{d}U+GUR-LUGAL-ŠEŠ
24) LUGAL TIN.TIR.KI

Translation

(Document concerning) one and one-half minas, six shekels of silver (and) eighteen *kurrû* of barley, property of Iddina-Marduk, son of Iqīša, descendant of Nūr-Sin, charged against Iqīša, son of Bēl-kāṣir, descendant of Šangû-parakki and Marduk-erība, son of Nādin. The silver and the acreage of garlic(?) (are) from the first and second years of Nergal-šarra-uṣur, king of Babylon. They will satisfy the silver, his capital, from their deposit, as much as they have, in the month of Addaru. Their deposit serves as security for Iddina-Marduk. In the month of ⸢Ajaru,⸣ they will deliver the barley, his capital, in the village of Aḫa-iddina and one shall bear the responsibility for the other. Witnesses (are) Bēl-ēpuš, son of Rašil, descendant of Nappāḫu, Rīmūt, son of Marduk-erība, descendant of Sin-ili, Mušēzib, son of Bēl-aḫḫē-iddina, descendant of Qaqqadinu, Šuma-ukīn, son of Ša-Nabû-šū, and the scribe, Zērūtu, son of Aplâ, descendant of Mukallim. Village of Šaḫrinu, month of Kislimu, second day, second year of Nergal-šarra-uṣur, king of Babylon.

Commentary

20) The personal name NUMUN-*tú* (*Zērūtu*) was miscopied by Evetts.

44

BM 77304 (Collated)
Published as Evetts, *Ner.* 44

1) 2/3 MA.NA KÙ.BABBAR *šá ina* 1 GÍN *bit-*⸢ qa⸣
2) *šá* ^{Id}EN-⸢ŠEŠ.MEŠ-MU⸣ LÚ.SAG.⸢LUGAL⸣
3) *ina* UGU ^{I}⸢ÈR-*ia*⸣ *u* ^{I}*šu-*⸢*la*⸣*-a*
4) [DUMU].MEŠ *šá* ^{I}*gi-*⸢*mil*⸣*-lu* A ^{I}DÙ-⸢*eš*⸣-DINGIR
5) ⸢*x*⸣ *ina* UGU ^{I}*ba-*⸢*ni*⸣-[*ia*] [...]
6) 1 GÍN KÙ.BABBAR [...]
7) *i-rab-bi* [...]
8) KÙ.BABBAR *i-nam-di-nu* 1-*en pu-*[*ut* 2-i]
9) *na-*⸢*šu*⸣*-ú*
10) LÚ *mu-kin-nu* ^{Id}EN-ŠEŠ.⸢MEŠ⸣-MU
11) DUMU-*šú šá* ^{Id}⸢AMAR.⸣UD-MU-DÙ A ^{I}*mar-duk-ú*
12) ^{I}*ki-din-*^{d}AMAR.UD DUMU-*šú šá* ^{Id}AMAR.UD-NUMUN-DÙ
13) A ^{Id}ILLAT-I
14) [*u*] LÚ.ŠID ^{I}*na-di-nu A-šú šá* ^{I}*ri-mu-tu*
15) ⸢A⸣ LÚ.DUG.QA.BUR TIN.TIR.KI ITU.GAN
16) UD.7.KAM MU.2.KAM ^{Id}U+⸢GUR⸣-LUGAL-ŠEŠ
17) LUGAL TIN.TIR.KI

Translation

(Document concerning) two-thirds mina of silver (which has) one-eighth alloy (per shekel), property of Bēl-⸢aḫḫē-iddina,⸣ the ⸢royal⸣ official, charged against ⸢Ardija⸣ and Šulâ, [sons] of Gimillu, descendants of Epeš-ili [...] charged against Bān[ija] [...] one shekel of silver [...] will increase. They will deliver the silver [...] and one shal bear the responsibility [for the other]. Witnesses (are) Bēl-aḫḫē-iddina, son of ⸢Marduk⸣-šuma-ibni, descendant of Marduk, Kidin-Marduk, son of Marduk-zēra-ibni, descendant of Illat-na'id [and] the scribe, Nādin, son of Rīmūt, ⸢descendant⸣ of Paḫāru. Babylon, month of Kislimu, seventh day, second year of ⸢Nergal⸣-šarra-uṣur, king of Babylon.

45

BM 30951 (Collated)
Published as Evetts, *Ner.* 45

1) NA$_4$.UR$_5$ *šá ḫaš-ši-ur u* NA$_4$ *na-áš-ka-bi*
2) *šá* ^{Id}AG-ŠEŠ.MEŠ-MU DUMU-*šú šá*
3) ^{I}*šu-la-a* DUMU ^{I}*e-gi-bi*
4) *ina pa-ni* ^{I}*at-kal-a-na-*^{d}AMAR.UD ŠE.BAR
5) [...]
6) ITU 4-*ta su-ú-tum šá ti-nu*
7) *el-lu a-na* ^{Id}AG-ŠEŠ.MEŠ-MU
8) *i-nam-din*
9) *la*(!)(*text:ha*) *ḫi-pi* NA$_4$(!)(*text:*) *na-áš-ka-bi-ía*
10) *a-na* ^{I}*at-kal-a-na-*^{d}AMAR.UD *na-ši*
11) LÚ *mu-kin-nu* ^{Id}*gu-la*-TIN-*su-iq-bi*
12) A-*šú šá* ^{I}BA-*šá-a* DUMU LÚ.GAL.DÙ
13) ^{I}*e-til-lu* A-*šú šá* ^{I}*ba-laṭ-su*
14) A ^{I}*dan-ni-e-a u* LÚ.ŠID ^{Id}AG-A-MU
15) A-*šú šá* ^{I}ÈR-^{d}EN DUMU ^{I}*e-gi-bi*
16) TIN.TIR.KI ITU.GAN UD.9.KAM
17) MU.2.KAM ^{d}U+GUR-LUGAL-ŠEŠ
18) LUGAL TIN.TIR.KI

Translation

(Document concerning) the cumin mill and its upper stone, property of Nabu-aḫḫē-iddina, son of Šulâ, descendant of Egibi, placed at the disposal of Atkal-ana-Marduk. He will deliver the barley and every month he will give four *sutu* measures of fine grind to Nabû-aḫḫē-iddina. (Furthermore) Atkal-ana-Marduk guarantees not to break the upper millstone. Witnesses (are) Gula-balāssu-iqbi, son of Iqīša, descendant of Rāb-bāni, Etillu, son of Balāssu, descendant of Dannēa and the scribe, Nabû-apla-iddina, son of Arad-Bēl, descendant of Egibi. Babylon, month of Kislimu, ninth day, second year of Nergal-šarra-uṣur, king of Babylon.

Commentary

14) Collation shows Nabû-apla-iddina (A left out by Evetts).

46

BM 72797 (Collated)
Published as Evetts, *Ner.* 46

1) ⌜ZÚ⌝.LUM.MA *gam-mar-ru-tu* [...]
2) *šá* ^{d}UTU *ša* KU *gu-ub-bu a-na* É.[BABBAR.RA]
3) *id-di-nu* ITU.AB UD.4.KAM MU.2.KAM
4) ^{d}U+GUR-LUGAL-ŠEŠ LUGAL TIN.TIR.KI
5) ZÚ.LUM.⌜MA⌝ ŠE.NUMUN *sis-sin-nu*

6) KAR 56 GUR ^{I}ÈR-ŠEŠ.MEŠ-*šú* 1 GUR 2(PI) 3(BÁN) 6(SÌLA)
7) KAR 52 GUR 4(PI) 1(BÁN) ^{Id}AG-*na-ṣir* 1 GUR 2(PI) 3(BÁN) 6(SÌLA)
8) KAR 31 GUR ^{I}*a-gi-ri* 1 GUR 2(PI) 3(BÁN) [...]
9) KAR 47 (GUR) 2(PI) 3(BÁN) ^{Id}UTU-MU 1 GUR [...]
10) KAR 47 (GUR) 4(PI) 1(BÁN) ^{Id}UTU-ŠEŠ-MU [...]
11) [KAR] [...] 2 ME 44 GUR 3(PI) ⌜*xx*⌝ [...]
12) [KAR] [...] GUR 1 (PI) 4(BÁN) ^{I}*ki-na-a* [...]
13) [...] ^{Id}UTU-*kil-la-an-ni* [...]
14) [...] ^{d}UTU-⌜*x*⌝-ŠEŠ ⌜*xxx*⌝ [...]
15) [...] *eri*$_{4}$*-ba* ⌜*x*⌝ [...]
16) [...] ⌜ŠEŠ.MEŠ⌝-MU [...]
17) [...] ⌜*xxx*⌝ [...]
18) [...] ⌜*x*⌝ *ḫar-ri* [...]
19) [...][ZÚ.LUM].MA *gam-ru-tu* [...]
20) [...]KU *gub-bu* [...]

Translation

(Document concerning) dates, complete payment (which) [...] of Šamaš of Šubat gubbu delivered to E[babbar]. Month of Ṭebetu, fourth day, second year of Nergal-šarra-uṣur, king of Babylon.

Dates	Acreage (and) Tax
Payment (of) fifty-six *kurru* by Arad-aḫḫēšu	One *kurru*, two pi, twenty-four(?)qa
Payment (of) fifty-two *kurru*, four pi, six qa (by) Nabû-nāṣir	One *kurru*, two pi, twenty-four(?)qa
Payment (of) thirty-one *kurru*, by Agiri	One *kurru*, two pi, eighteen qa [...]
Payment of forty-seven *kurru*, two pi, eighteen qa (by) Šamaš-iddina	One *kurru* [...]
Payment (of) forty-seven *kurru*, four pi, six qa (by) Šamaš-aḫa-iddina	[...]
[Payment of] two hundred forty-four *kurru*, [...]	[...]
[Payment of] [...] *kurru*, one pi, twenty-four qa (by) Kinâ	[...]
[...] Šamaš-killanni	[...]
[...] Šamaš-...-uṣur	[...]
[...] erība [...]	[...]
[...] ⌜aḫḫē⌝-iddina	[...]
[...]	[...]
[...]	[...]
[...] dates, complete payment	
[...] Šubat gubbu	

47

BM 38135 (Collated)
Published as Evetts, *Ner.* 47

1) ^{Id}UTU-ZÁLAG-*ir* A-*šú šá* ^{I}*di-ḫu-um-mu*
2) [*ina*] ^{d}EN ^{d}AG ^{d}UTU ^{d}U+GUR *u*

3) [*a*]-*di-e šá* ^{d}U+GUR-LUGAL-ŠEŠ
4) LUGAL TIN.TIR.KI *a-na* ^{Id}AG-TIN-KAM
5) LÚ *qí-i-pi šá* É.BABBAR.RA
6) *it-te-me ki-i* ITU.GUD
7) *iq-ta-*⸢*tu*⸣*-ú a-di-i*
8) *a-ḫi* ŠE.BAR-*ka šá ina* ⸢IGI⸣-*ia*
9) *iṭ-ṭir-ru-ka u ri-ḫi-tum*
10) *ina* ITU.DU$_{6}$ *a-gam-mar-ru-ma iṭ-ṭir-ru-ka*
11) LÚ *mu-kin-nu* ^{Id}AG-I A-*šú šá*
12) ^{Id}EN-DÙ-*uš* A ^{I}*mu-še-zib* ^{I}TIN
13) A-*šú šá* ^{I}*eri*$_{4}$*-ba* ^{Id}ḪAR-DÙ A-*šú šá*
14) ^{Id}EN-UŠ(!)(*text: ka*).SA(!)(*text: ia*).DU LÚ.ŠID ^{Id}UTU-PAP
15) A-*šú šá* ^{I}*ši-rik-tum* A LÚ.DUG.QA.BUR
16) *sip-par* KI ITU.AB UD.10.KAM MU.2.KAM
17) ^{d}U+GUR-LUGAL-ŠEŠ LUGAL NUN.KI

Translation

Šamaš-inammir, son of Diḫummu, swore the following to Nabû-balāṭu-ēriš, the overseer of Ebabbar before Bēl, Nabû, Šamaš, Nergal and the majesty of Nergal-šarra-uṣur, king of Babylon: "I will pay you your barley, which (was) placed at my disposal, by the end of the month of Ajaru, and the remainder (i.e., whatever is left that I owe you) I will pay you in full in the month of Tašritu." Witnesses (are) Nabû-na'id, son of Bēl-ēpuš, descendant of Mušēzib, Balāṭu, son of Erība, Bunene-ibni, son of Bēl-iti(!) (and) the scribe, Šamaš-nāṣir, son of Širiktu, descendant of Paḫāru. Sippar, month of Ṭebetu, , tenth day, second year of Nergal-šarra-uṣur, king of Babylon.

Commentary

14) Although collation shows the signs *ka ia* to stand, as in Evetts' copy, the personal name, in all probability, should be read *Bēl-iti* (UŠ.SA.DU). The same individual appears in *Lab.* 1, 24 where the signs DU SA were written by the scribe composing the tablet. Cf. usages of *itu* in personal names in other periods in Meissner, BAP 110, 20 and 23, CBS 10743 ii 10 (Clay PN 69) and see Stamm, *Namengebung*, 212 (against Tallqvist, NBN 51a).

48

BM 63830 (Collated)
Published as Evetts, *Ner.* 48

1) [...] [GUR] ⸢ZÚ⸣ LUM.[MA] ⸢*šá*⸣ ŠUK.ḪI.A
2) [...] [ŠE].GIŠ.[Ì] 6 GUR ŠUK.ḪI.A
3) [ITU].ZÍZ ITU.ŠE MU.2.[KAM]
4) [ITU].BÁR u ITU.GUD MU.3.KAM
5) *šá* 3 LÚ.MUŠEN.DÙ.MEŠ
6) *u* LÚ *mu-*⸢*šá-kil*⸣ *iṣ-ṣur*
7) *a-na* ⸢*x*⸣ *su ud dur* ⸢*x*⸣
8) SUM-*in* ITU.AB UD.20.1.[LÁ.KAM]
9) MU.2.KAM ^{d}U+GUR-LUGAL-ŠEŠ
10) LUGAL TIN.TIR.KI
11) ZÚ.LUM.⸢MA⸣ TA É ŠU^{II} ⸢*ub*⸣ [...]

Translation

(Document concerning) ... [*kurru* of dates] sustenance, (and)[...] ⸢of sesame oil⸣, six *kurru*, sustenance [for the month] of Šabaṭu (and) the month of Addaru, second year, (and) [the month] of Nisanu and the month of Ajaru, third year, for three fowlers and bird feeders given for [...]. Month of Ṭebetu, nineteenth day, second year of Nergal-šarra-uṣur, king of Babylon. The dates are from the storehouse of [...].

Commentary

1-4, 8) Signs indicated in brackets are no longer on the tablet.

49

BM75778 (Collated)
Published as Evetts, *Ner.* 49

1) 6 GÍN KÙ.GI *na-al-tar*
2) *la pi-it-qu šá* ^{I}GI-^{d}⸢AMAR.UD⸣
3) A-*šú šá* ^{Id}UTU-MU-*ú-kin* A LÚ.⸢ŠID⸣ UD.KIB.NUN.KI
4) [*ina*] *muḫ-ḫi* ^{I}*li-ši-ru* A-*šú šá*
5) ^{I}KI(!)(*text: ki-din*)-^{d}UTU-TIN LÚ.ŠÀ.TAM É ^{d}⸢NIN.GAL⸣
6) *ina* ITU.BÁR *i-nam-din*

7) KÙ.BABBAR *ša a-na dul-lu šá ka-a-ri*
8) *šá* ⌜*e*⌝*-bi-ir i-lu(!)(text:kin)* SUM-*na*
9) LÚ *mu-*⌜*kin*⌝*-nu* ^{Id}AG-*na-ṣir*
10) A-*šú šá* ^{I}É.BABBAR.RA-*šá-du-nu*
11) ⌜A⌝ LÚ.ŠID UD.KIB.NUN.KI ^{Id}AG-MU-ŠEŠ
12) [A]-*šú šá* ^{Id}U+GUR-MU A ^{I}*na-bu-un-na-a-a*
13) [^{Id}]AG-NUMUN-MU A-*šú šá* ^{Id}UTU-SU *u* LÚ.ŠID
14) [^{Id}]30-A-MU A-*šú šá* ^{I}*ki-din* UD.KIB.NUN.KI
15) ⌜ITU⌝ ZÍZ UD.11.KAM MU.2.KAM
16) ^{Id}U+GUR-LUGAL-ŠEŠ LUGAL TIN.TIR.KI

Translation

(Document concerning) six shekels of *naltar* gold that has not been melted down, property of Mušallim-⌜Marduk,⌝ son of Šamaš-šuma-ukīn, descendant of Šangû Sippar, charged against Itti-Šamaš-balāṭu(!), the administrator of the temple of ⌜Ningal⌝. He will deliver (the gold) in the month of Nisanu. (This is apart from) the silver given for work on the embankment which is on the (other?) side (of the river). Witnesses (are) Nabû-nāṣir, son of Ebabbar-šadûnu, descendant of Šangû Sippar, Nabû-šuma-uṣur, [son] of Nergal-iddina, descendant of Nabunāja, Nabû-zēra-iddina, son of Šamaš-erība and the scribe, Sin-apla-iddina, son of Kidin. Sippar, month of Šabaṭu, eleventh day, second year of Nergal-šarra-uṣur, king of Babylon.

Commentary

1-2) *na-al-tar la pi-it-qu*. For other uses of *naltar* gold, cf. GCCI 1:324, 2; 391, 3 and GCCI 2:39, 20; 75, 1 and 7; 141,2. See also YOS 6 112, 19 (list of equivalencies). For a discussion of the smelting of metals, see Oppenheim, JNES 6 117ff.

5) The reading of the personal name in this line represents a problem that is not so easily solved. Collation shows ^{I}*ki-din*-^{d}UTU-TIN to stand, as in Evett's copy (against Tallqvist, NBN 97a, who reads ^{I}*ki-din*-^{d}EN) and it is possible that it is a scribal error either for ^{I}*ki-din*-^{d}UTU or for ^{I}KI-^{d}UTU-TIN (i.e., *Itti-Šamaš-balāṭu*). Since no text is presently known or published containing the name of this person, one can only, therefore, make an intelligent guess as to what the scribe originally intended to write.

5) For a discussion of the functions of the *šatammu*, cf. San Nicolò, *Prosopographie*, pp. 17, 19-20 and see AOATS 4 pp. 97-8.

8) For parallel uses of this phrase, cf. VAS 4 23, 11ff.(il-li) and *Nbn* 993, 6.

50

BM 30526 (Collated)
Published as Evetts, *Ner.* 50 and as Strassmaier, *Liverpool*, no. 120

1) ⌈10 GÍN⌉ KÙ.BABBAR 500 *gi-dil*
2) *šá* ^{I}*ki*-^{d}EN-⌈*ki*⌉-*nu ina muh-hi*
3) ^{Id}AG-GI A-*šú šá* ^{I}IGI-*ni-iá*
4) *ina* GIŠ.MÁ-*šú ḫi-ru-up-tum*
5) *i-nam-din* LÚ *mu-kin-nu*
6) ^{Id}AG-⌈MU⌉-GAR-*un* A-*šú šá* ^{Id}AG-NUMUN-[DÙ]
7) A ^{I}ZALÁG-^{d}30 ^{I}*na-din*
8) A-*šú šá* ^{I}MU-DU A LÚ.⌈NAGAR⌉
9) *u* LÚ.ŠID ^{Id}AG-A-MU A-*šú šá*
10) ^{Id}AMAR.UD-MU-DÙ TIN.TIR.KI
11) ITU.ZÍZ UD.20.1.LÁ.KAM
12) MU.2.KAM ^{Id}U+GUR-LUGAL-ŠEŠ
13) LUGAL E.KI

Translation

(Document concerning) ten shekels of silver (and) five hundred strings (of garlic), property of Itti-Bēl-kīnu, (and) charged against Nabû-ušallim, son of Pānija. He will deliver the (silver and the garlic) at the early sailing of his boat. Witnesses (are) Nabû-šuma-iškun, son of Nabû-zēra-[ibni], descendant of Nūr-Sin, Nādin, son of Šuma-ukīn, descendant of ⌈Naggāru,⌉ and the scribe, Nabû-apla-iddina, son of Marduk-šuma-ibni. Babylon, month of Šabaṭu, nineteenth day, second year of Nergal-šarra-uṣur, king of Babylon.

51

BM 63931 (Collated)
Published as Evetts, *Ner.* 51

1) 1 GUR ZÚ.LUM.MA ⌈ŠUK⌉.[ḪI].A
2) ITU.GUD ⌈MU⌉.3.KAM ^{I}*ina*-GIŠ.[GE$_{6}$]-*a-a*
3) 2 GUR ⌈TA⌉ ITU.ZÍZ *a*-[*di*] ⌈ITU.⌉ GUD [MU.3.KAM]
4) ^{Id}UTU-⌈AMA-*šu-kun*⌉

5) 1 GUR 3(PI) 2(BÁN) *ki-is-*⌈*ki*⌉*-ir-ri*
6) *šá* LÚ.[MÁ].LAḪ$_4$-*ú-tu* ^{Id}ŠÚ-[MU]
7) [1] ⌈GUR⌉ ŠE.BAR 1 GUR ZÚ.LUM.[MA]
8) [ŠUK].ḪI.A ITU.ZÍZ u ITU.ŠE
9) MU.2.KAM ^{Id}AMAR.UD-[MU ...]
10) PAP 5 GUR 3(PI) 2(BÁN) ZÚ].[LUM.MA]
11) 1 GUR ŠE.BAR TA É ŠU^{II} [...]
12) *šá* KÁ SUM-*in* ITU.ŠE
13) UD.22.KAM MU.2.KAM
14) ^{d}U+GUR-LUGAL-ŠEŠ LUGAL TIN.TIR.KI

Translation

(Document concerning) one *kurru* of dates, ⌈sustenance⌉ (for) the month of Ajaru, third ⌈year⌉ at the disposal of Ina-⌈Ṣillâ⌉ two *kurru* (placed at the disposal of) Šamaš-rīmi-šukun ⌈from⌉ the month of Šabaṭu ⌈until⌉ the ⌈month⌉ of Ajaru, [third year]. One *kurru*, three pi, twelve qa (are for) payment of the ⌈boatman⌉ Marduk-[iddina], [one] *kurru* of barley (and) one *kurru* of dates, [sustenance] for the months of Šabaṭu and Addaru, second year, (are for) Marduk-[iddina] [...]. Total (of) five *kurru*, three pi, twelve qa ⌈of dates⌉ (and) one *kurru* of barley (are) delivered from the storehouse [...] of the gate. Month of Addaru, twenty-second day, second year of Nergal-šarra-uṣur, king of Babylon.

Commentary

1-8) Bracketed items indicate signs no longer on the tablet.
3, 9) Restoration of the year and personal name are based on the contents on lines 2 and 6, respectively.

52

BM 31209(Collated)
Published as Evetts, *Ner.* 52 and Strassmaier, *Liverpool*, no. 121 and Ungnad, SSS 10, no. 33. Published in translation by Peiser, *Rechtsleben* 3, 40.

1) *i-di-e šá ul-tu* UD.1.KAM ITU.ŠU
2) MU.2.KAM ^{d}U+GUR-LUGAL-ŠEŠ LUGAL.TIN.⌈TIR⌉.KI
3) *a-di* UD.1.KAM *šá* ITU.ŠU MU.3.KAM
4) ^{d}U+GUR-LUGAL-ŠEŠ LUGAL TIN.TIR.KI
5) ^{Id}EN-GI *ina* ŠU^{II} ^{I}MU-A *e-ṭir*

6) 10 GÍN 1/2 *ḫum-mu-šú* KÙ.BABBAR
7) *ina ri-e-šú* MU.AN.NA-*šú*
8) *šá ul-tu* UD.1.KAM *šá* ITU.ŠU
9) MU.3.KAM ^{d}U+GUR-LUGAL-ŠEŠ
10) LUGAL TIN.TIR.[KI] ^{Id}EN-GI
11) *ina* ŠU^{II} ^{I}MU-A ⌜*ma-ḫir*⌝
12) LÚ *mu-kin-nu* ^{I}⌜*šul-lu*⌝-*mu* A-*šú šá*
13) ^{I}*bul-lu-ṭu* A ^{I}ZALÁG-^{d}30
14) ^{I}*ṣil-la-a* A-*šú šá* ^{I}*ina*-SÙḪ-SUR
15) A ^{I}*ši-gu-ú-a u* LÚ.ŠID ^{I}KAR-^{d}EN
16) A-*šú šá* ^{Id}AMAR.UD-NUMUN A ^{Id}IM-MU-KAM
17) E.KI ITU.GUD UD.25.KAM
18) MU.3.KAM ^{d}U+GUR-LUGAL-ŠEŠ
19) LUGAL TIN.TIR.KI

Translation

Bēl-ušallim was paid the rent for (the period extending) from the first day of the month of Du'uzu, second year of Nergal-šarra-uṣur, king of Babylon to the first day of the month of Du'uzu, third year of Nergal-šarra-uṣur, king of Babylon by Nādin-apli. (Furthermore) ten and seven-tenths shekels of silver were received (by) Bēl-ušallim from Nādin-apli at the beginning of his (rental) year extending from the first day of the month of Du'uzu, third year of Nergal-šarra-uṣur, king of Babylon. Witnesses (are) Šullumu, son of Bulluṭu, descendant of Nūr-Sin, Ṣillâ, son of Ina-tēši-ēṭir, descendant of Šigûa and the scribe, Mušēzib-Bēl, son of Marduk-zēri, descendant of Adad-šuma-ēriš. Babylon, month of Ajaru, twenty-fifth day, third year of Nergal-šarra-uṣur, king of Babylon.

53

BM 63842 (Collated)
Published as Evetts, *Ner.* 53

1) [*ḫum*]-*mu-šú a-na*
2) ^{Id}AG-MU-SI.SÁ-*ir*
3) MAR.ZA SUM-*in*
4) ITU.SIG$_4$ UD.2.KAM
5) MU.3.KAM
6) $^{[d]}$U+GUR-LUGAL-ŠEŠ
7) LUGAL TIN.TIR.KI

Translation

(Document concerning) one-fifth (shekel of silver?) given to Nabû-šumu-lišir (for) cultic use(?) Month of Simanu, second day, third year of Nergal-šarra-uṣur, king of Babylon.

Commentary

2) Read ^{Id}AG-MU-SI.SÁ (SÁ left out by Evetts).
3) Given the shortness of this document, an exact determination of the meaning of MAR.ZA cannot be made. For the equation MAR.ZA=*par-su*, see Deimel, SL II2, p. 527, 68 and VR 2, 38d. For suggested meanings see von Soden, AHw 835 bff and Landsberger, AK 2, 64ff ("*(kult) Brauch*,") etc.

54

BM 63843 (Collated)
Published as Evetts, *Ner.* 54

1) 40 GUR ŠE.BAR 20 GUR ZÚ.LUM.MA
2) PAP 60 GUR ŠE.BAR *u* ZÚ.LUM.MA *eš-ru-ú*
3) [...] ^{d}UTU *ul-tu hu-us-si-e-ti*
4) [...] *al si ka ab lul hu-uṣ-ṣi-e-ti*
5) [...] ⸢*la mi*⸣ *hu-[uṣ]-ṣi-e-ti*
6) *šá* ^{Id}GAŠAN-*iq-bi hu-uṣ-ṣi-e-ti*
7) *šá* ^{I}*id-du-ú-tum hu-uṣ-ṣi-e-tú ša* ^{I}TIN-*su*
8) ⸢*e*⸣-*li-ni-ti* URU BAD ^{d}UTU
9) *a-di-i* URU *kal-bi-nu*
10) [*ina*] *muḫ-ḫi* ^{I}⸢*bul*⸣-*ṭa-a* A-*šú šá* ^{Id}AG-NUMUN-GÁL-*ši*
11) A ^{I}*dan-ni-e-a* ŠE.BAR *u* ZÚ.LUM.MA
12) *eš-ru-tu ina ma-ši-ḫi šá* 1 PI
13) *ina* ⸢*sip-par*⸣ KI *ina* É NÍG.GA *i-nam-din*
14) *e-*[*lat*] [ŠE.GIŠ].Ì *u ka-*⸢*si*⸣-*ia*
15) LÚ ⸢*mu-kin-nu*⸣ ^{I}*ba-[la]-ṭu*
16) [A-šú] *šá* ^{I}*zi-*⸢*ka-ri*⸣ ⸢A⸣ LÚ.PA.ŠE.KI
17) ^{Id}AG-⸢*ni-ip*⸣-*ša-ri* A-*šú šá* ^{I}DU-NUMUN
18) [A] ^{Id}ILLAT-I ^{Id}⸢AG⸣-NUMUN-DU
19) ⸢A-*šú šá*⸣ ^{Id}UTU-MU-DÙ A ^{I}*dan-*⸢*ni*⸣-*e-a*
20) ⸢LÚ.ŠID⸣ ^{I}I-^{d}AMAR.UD A-*šú šá* ^{I}*šu-la-a*
21) A ^{I}MU-^{d}AMAR.UD UD.KIB.NUN.KI ITU.SIG$_4$

22) UD.18.KAM MU.3.KAM ^{d}U+GUR-LUGAL-ŠEŠ
23) LUGAL TIN.TIR.KI

Translation

(Document concerning) forty *kurru* of barley (and) twenty *kurru* of dates, total of sixty *kurru* of barley and dates, tithe [...] Šamaš from the rural settlement [...] the settlement [...] (of), the settlement of Bēlit-iqbi, the settlement of Iddutum (and) the settlement of Balāssu, (all lying) above the village of Dūr Šamaš as far as the village of Kalbinu, charged against Bulṭâ, son of Nabû-zēra-ušabši, descendant of Dannēa. He will deliver the barley and dates, the tithe, in accordance with the measure of one pi, at the treasury (of the temple of Šamaš) in Sippar. (This is) apart from the sesame oil and spice. Witnesses (are) Balāṭu, [son] of ⌜Zikari,⌝ ⌜descendant⌝ of the Isinite, Nabû-⌜nipšari,⌝ son of Mukīn-zēri, [descendant] of Illat-na'id, ⌜Nabû⌝-zēra-ukīn, ⌜son of⌝ Šamaš-šuma-ibni, descendant of Dannēa, (and) the ⌜scribe,⌝ Na'id-Marduk, son of Šulâ, descendant of Iddina-Marduk. Sippar, month of Simanu, eighteenth day, third year of Nergal-šarra-uṣur, king of Babylon.

Commentary

7) Read ^{I}TIN-*su*.
17) Read ^{I}DU-NUMUN (*Mukīn-zēri*).
8-20) The text is in much poorer condition than when Evetts copied it. Restorations based on space on tablet and Evetts' original copy.

55

BM 31009 (Collated)

Published as Evetts, *Ner.* 55 and with translation and/or commentary by Peiser, *Rechtsleben* 3 61 ff. and Ebeling, ZA 50 212 ff.

1) UD.10.KAM *šá* ITU.ŠU ^{Id}AMAR.UD-MU-MU
2) A-*šú šá* ^{Id}AMAR.UD-LUGAL-*a-ni u* ^{Id}AG-NUMUN-DÙ
3) A-*šú šá* ^{Id}AG-*tuk-te-e-eri*$_4$*-ba* ^{I}*kal-ba-a*
4) A-*šú šá* ^{Id}AG-*tuk-te-e-eri*$_4$*-ba u* ^{I}*kal-ba-a*
5) A-*šú šá* ^{I}*gab-bi-ia a-na* KÁ É DUMU.⌜LUGAL⌝
6) *ib-ba-ku-nim-ma* NÍG.ŠID *šá ṣal-la-a-nu*
7) *u du-še-e* ^{I}*ki-na-a* LÚ.SAG.⌜LUGAL⌝
8) *it-ti-šú-nu ip-pu-uš-ma*

9) *ṣal-la-a-nu u du-še-e [ša]*
10 *ina* UGU-*šú-nu il-la-'* ^{Id}⌈AMAR⌉.[UD-MU-MU]
11) *u* ^{Id}AG-NUMUN-DÙ *iš-ši-⌈ri⌉ i la* [...]
12) *a-⌈ki⌉-i ni-'-a-ri ša* ^{I}*ki-na-a ṣal-[la-a-nu]*
13) *u* KUŠ *du-še-e iṭ-ṭi-ri*
14) LÚ *mu-kin-nu* ^{I}*ba-nu-nu* DUMU-*šú ša* ^{I}*⌈ṣil-la-a⌉*
15) DUMU LÚ.GAL.DÙ ^{I}EN-*šú-nu* ⌈A-*šú šá*⌉ ^{Id}⌈AG-NUMUN⌉-[GÁL]-*ši*
16) ⌈DUMU⌉ LÚ.PA.ŠE.KI *u* LÚ.ŠID ^{Id}AG-ŠEŠ.MEŠ-⌈MU⌉
17) A-*šú šá* ^{I}*šu-la-a* DUMU ^{I}*e-gì-bi* TIN.TIR.KI
18) ITU.ŠU UD.9.KAM MU.3.KAM
19) ^{d}U+GUR-LUGAL-ŠEŠ LUGAL TIN.TIR.KI

Translation

(On) the tenth day of the month of Du'uzu, Marduk-šuma-iddina, son of Marduk-šarrāni, Nabû-zēra-ibni, son of Nabû-tuktê-erība, Kalbâ, son of Nabû-tuktê-erība, and Kalbâ, son of Gabbija, will appear at the gate of the house of the ⌈crown⌉ prince and (there) Kinâ, the royal official, will settle with them the account concerning the tanned hides and dyed leather. Marduk-šuma-iddina and Nabû-zēra-ibni will deliver (lit., pay) the tanned hides and dyed leather with [which] they have been debited [...] They will deliver the tanned hides and d[yed] leather in accordance with (the terms of) a papyrus document (in the possession of) Kinâ. Witnesses (are) Banunu, son of Ṣillâ, descendant of Rāb bāni, Bēlšunu, son of ⌈Nabû-zēra-ušabši⌉, descendant of the Isinite and the scribe, Nabû-aḫḫē-⌈iddina⌉, son of Šulâ, descendant of Egibi. Babylon, month of Du'uzu, ninth day, third year of Nergal-šarra-uṣur, king of Babylon.

Commentary

12) *akî ni'ari*. It is known that Assyrian scribes used "papyrus" when writing Aramaic and that even garments could be manufactured from it. See AfO 8 (1932-33), 20 r ix 15). It was imported from the west in rolls called *kirku* (cf. ABL 568 r. 19). For further discussion and references, see Oppenheim, JCS 21 (1967) 245ff and 249.

56

BM 64956 (Collated)
Published as Evetts, *Ner.* 56

1) 30 GUR 3 (BÁN) 2 SÌLA *ri-ḫi-tum* ŠE.BAR
2) *šá* URU *ku-um-an-da-ar a-na*
3) *tar-ḫu a-na* ^{I}ÈR-^{d}EN SUM-*in*
4) ITU.ŠU UD.25.KAM MU.3.[KAM]
5) ^{Id}U+GUR-LUGAL-ŠEŠ
6) LUGAL TIN.[TIR.KI]
7) 3 ME *ma-ši-*[*ḫi*] [...]
8) *u* EGIR [...]
9) [...] *ku* [...]
10) 1 LIM 2 ME 75 GUD [...]

Translation

(Document concerning) thirty *kurru*, twenty qa, the remainder of the barley from the village of Kumandar, delivered to Arad-Bēl for fodder. Month of Du'uzu, twenty-fifth day, third year of Nergal-šarra-uṣur, king of Babylon. Three hundred measures [...] twelve hundred seventy-five oxen [...]

57

BM 63841 (Collated)
Published as Evetts, *Ner.* 57

1) [...] [GUD] ⸢*um*⸣*-man-nu* ⸢*šá a-na*⸣
2) [...] ⸢*xx*⸣ MEŠ ⸢*x*⸣ *ka*
3) [...] [É] *ú-ru-ú*
4) ⸢*xx*⸣ [...] IGI [...]
5) ⸢*xx*⸣ *ri* [...]
6) ⸢*xx*⸣ GUD ⸢*x*⸣ [...]
7) ⸢*xx*⸣ IGI ^{Id}EN [...]
8) A ^{I}*ba-ku-ú-a* [...]
9) 1 GUD *la*-IGI ^{Id}UTU-ZALÁG-*ir* A-*šú*
10) *šá* ^{I}ÈR-*a* PAP 4 GUD *a-na*
11) GIŠ.APIN *a-na* ^{Id}UTU-TIN-*iṭ*
12) A-*šú šá* ^{I}ÈR-*a* SUM-*in*
13) ITU.ŠU UD.27.KAM MU.3.KAM

14) ^{d}U+GUR-LUGAL-ŠEŠ LUGAL TIN.TIR.KI
15) GUD *a-na* ^{Id}UTU-[TIN-*ịt*]
16) [...] SUM-*in*

Translation

(Document concerning) [...] trained [oxen] ⌜which, for⌝ [...] cattle shed [...] at the disposal of Bēl[...] descendant of Bakūa, (and) one bull [at the] disposal of Šamaš-inammir, son of Ardija--- total of four oxen for the plow, given to Šamaš-uballiṭ, son of Ardija. Month of Du'uzu, twenty-seventh day, third year of Nergal-šarra-uṣur, king of Babylon. The oxen [...] were given to Šamaš-[uballiṭ].

58

BM 31858 (Collated)
Published as Evetts, *Ner.* 58 and Strassmaier, Liverpool no. 122

1) *a-di qí-it šá* ITU.KIN ^{I}*ni-qu-du*
2) A-*šú šá* ^{I}*ri-mut-*^{d}*gu-la* ^{Id}*É*(!)(*text:a*)-*a*(!)(*text:É*)-MU
3) A-*šú šá* ^{Id}U+GUR-MU A ^{I}ÈR-^{d}BE
4) ^{I}*na-di-nu* A-*šú šá* ^{Id}AG-NUMUN-DÙ ^{I}A-*a*
5) A-*šú šá* ^{I}BE-*ia* A ^{I}*da-mi-qu*
6) *a-na pa-ni* ^{Id}AG-*ṣa-bit*-ŠU^{II} LÚ.SAG.LUGAL
7) [...] ⌜ŠE.BAR⌝ ⌜*xx*⌝ *ina* IGI
(remainder broken off)
1') [...] 1-*en pu-ut* 2-*ú* ⌜*na*⌝-[*šu-ú*]
2') ^{I}A-*a* A-*šú šá* ^{I}BE-*ia pu-ut uk*-[*tin*]-⌜*nu*⌝
3') *na-ši* LÚ *mu-kin-nu* ^{I}⌜*ba*⌝-*nu-nu* A-*šú šá*
4') ^{I}*sil-la-a* A LÚ.GAL.DÙ <<A LÚ.GAL.DÙ>>
5') ^{Id}EN-ŠEŠ.MEŠ-MU A-*šú šá* ^{Id}AMAR.UD-NUMUN-DÙ
6') A ^{I}*e-gi-bi u* LÚ.ŠID ^{Id}AG-ŠEŠ.[MEŠ]-MU
7') A-*šú šá* ^{I}*šu-la-a* A ^{I}*e-gi-bi* TIN.TIR.KI
8') ITU.NE UD.20.1.LÁ.KAM MU.3.KAM
9') ^{d}U+GUR-LUGAL-ŠEŠ LUGAL TIN.TIR.KI
10') [...]*a a* ^{I}*ni-qu-du*
11') [...] *mu u* ^{I}*na-din i-tab-ku*
12') [...] ⌜*x*⌝ *šu*

Translation

Until the end of the month of Ululu, Niqudu, son of Rīmūt-Gula, Ea-iddina, son of Nergal-iddina, descendant of Arad-Ea, Nādin, son of Nabû-zēra-ibni, and Aplâ, son of Kābtija, descendant of Damiqu, (will be) at the disposal of Nabû-ṣabit-qāte, the royal official [...] at the disposal [...] one shall bear the responsibility for the other. Aplâ, son of Kābtija, bears the responsibility for certifying (the above arrangements). Witnesses (are) Banunu, son of Ṣillâ, descendant of Rāb bāni, Bēl-aḫḫē-iddina, son of Marduk-zēra-ibni, descendant of Egibi, and the scribe, Nabû-aḫḫē-iddina, son of Šulâ, descendant of Egibi. Babylon, month of Abu, nineteenth day, third year of Nergal-šarra-uṣur, king of Babylon.[...] Niqudu [...] Nādin will come [...].

59

BM 30871 (Collated)
Published as Evetts, *Ner.* 59. Published in translation by Peiser, *Rechtsleben* 3, 36

1) *a-di-i* ITU.BÁR [*šá*] MU.4.KAM ^{d}U+GUR-LUGAL-ŠEŠ
2) LUGAL TIN.TIR.KI SAL *nu-up-ta-a*
3) DUMU.SAL-*su šá* ^{Id}AMAR.UD-MU-DÙ A LÚ.DUG.QA-BUR
4) 1 1/3 MA.NA KÙ.BABBAR ŠÁM [SAL] ^{d}DÙ-*tum-gu-uz-zu*
5) SAL *ši-i-lu-da-ra-at u* ^{Id}AG-AMA-*šu-kun*
6) LÚ.UN.MEŠ É-*šú tu-ta-ri-'-ma a-na*
7) ^{I}*na-din* A-*šú šá* ^{I}*šu-la-a* A ^{I}LÚ-*ú ta-nam-din*
8) *ki-i a-di-i* ITU.BÁR SAL *nu-up-ta-a*
9) KÙ.BABBAR *la tu-te-ru-ma a-na* ^{I}*na-din la ta-ad-dan-nu*
10) ^{I}*na-din ina ú-ìl-tim-šú šá* ŠÁM *ḫa-ri-*⸢*iṣ*⸣
11) *šá a-me-lut-tum ú-šu-uz-zu*
12) *ki-i a-di-i* ITU.BÁR LÚ *a-me-lut-tum*
13) *pa-ni* ^{I}*na-din la ta-an-da-ḫar*
14) SAL *nu-up-ta-a* KÙ.BABBAR *tu-ta-ri-'-ma a-na*
15) ^{I}*na-din ta-nam-din-nu* LÚ *mu-kin-nu*
16) ^{Id}AG-ŠEŠ.MEŠ-MU A-*šú šá* ^{I}*šu-la-a*
17) A ^{I}*e-gi-bi* ^{Id}EN-*na-din*-A <<A>> A-*šú šá*
18) <<A>> ^{Id}AG-GÁL-*ši* A ^{I}*e-gi-bi*
19) <<A ^{I}*ir-a-an*>> *u* LÚ.ŠID ^{Id}UTU-ZÁLAG-*ir*
20) A-*šú šá* ^{I}*ri-mut-*^{d}EN A ^{I}*e-gi-bi*
21) TIN.TIR.KI ITU.KIN UD.5.KAM

22) MU.3.KAM ^{d}U+GUR-LUGAL-ŠEŠ
23) LUGAL TIN.TIR.KI
24) *ul-tu* UD.1.KAM *šá* ITU.ŠU *a-di* [...]
25) ^{I}*na-din* [...] ⌜*xxx*⌝
26) ^{I}*li-ši-ru*
27) A-*šú šá* ^{Id}AG-SUR
28) A ^{I}*e-gi-bi*

Translation

By the month of Nisanu [of] the fourth year of Nergal-šarra-uṣur, king of Babylon, the lady Nuptâ, daughter of Marduk-šuma-ibni, descendant of Paḫāru, will turn over the lady Banitum-guzzu, the lady Šīlu-darat and Nabû-rīmu-šukun, servants (in) her house, to Nādin, son of Šulâ, descendant of Amēlu, (and) she will sell (lit., give) (them to him for) the price of one and one-third minas of silver.If, by the month of Nisanu, the lady Nuptâ does not return the silver and does not give (it) to Nādin, then she (i.e., the slave girl) is inscribed (lit., placed) on Nādin's document at the exact price of a slave girl (i.e., she is considered sold). If,(however), she does not place the slave at the disposal of Nādin in the month of Nisanu, then the lady Nuptâ will return the silver and she(!) will give it to Nādin. Witnesses (are) Nabû-aḫḫē-iddina, son of Šulâ, descendant of Egibi, Bēl-nādin-apli, son of Nabû-ušabši, descendant of Egibi and the scribe, Šamaš-inammir, son of Rīmūt-Bēl, descendant of Egibi. Babylon, month of Kislimu,fifth day, third year of Nergal-šarra-uṣur, king of Babylon. From the first day of the month of Du'uzu to the [...] Nādin [...] Liširu, son of Nabû-ēṭir, descendant of Egibi.

Commentary

19) In view of the obvious confusion in the writing of the genealogy of the witness *Bēl-nādin-apli*, one should probably view the writing of the family name as a scribal error here. Cf. lines 17 and 18.

60

BM 31151(Collated)
Published as Evetts, *Ner.* 60. Published in translation by Peiser, *Rechtsleben* 3 12ff.

1) *ú-ìl-tim šá* 1 MA.NA 10 GÍN KÙ.BABBAR *šá* SAL(!) (*text*:I) *gu-gu-ú-a*

2) DUMU.SAL-*su šá* ^{I}*za-kir* A ^{I}LÚ.PA.ŠE.KI *šá ina la a-šá-bi*
3) *šá* ^{Id}É-*a*-NUMUN-DÙ <<DUMU-*šú*>> DUMU-*šú šá* ^{Id}EN-NUMUN-SI.SÁ
4) A ^{I}*e-gi-bi* KÙ.BABBAR *ŠÁM* GI.MEŠ *nu-dun-nu-šú*
5) *pu-ut* ḪA.LA *šá* ^{Id}É-<a>-NUMUN-DÙ *šá it-ti*
6) ŠEŠ.MEŠ-*šú pa-ni-šú tu-šad-gi-lu* KÙ.BABBAR-' 1 MA.NA 10 GÍN
7) [...] ^{I}*tab-ni-e-a A-šú šá* ^{Id}AG-GI A ^{Id}30-*šá-du-nu*
8) [...] ⌜*xx*⌝ *a-ḫi* É-*sú ku-um* 1/2 MA.NA 5 GÍN KÙ.BABBAR
9) [...] [*ta*]-*aṣ-ṣa-bat ina* MU.AN.NA 5 GÍN ḪAR.RA
10) [...] *i-nam-da'-aš-šú a-di muḫ-ḫi* [...]
11) [...] ^{Id}É-*a*-NUMUN-DÙ *ú-il-tim* [...]
12) [...] ^{Id}AG-ŠEŠ.MEŠ-MU A-*šú šá* ^{I}*šu*-[*la-a*]
13) [A ^{I}*e-gi*]-*bi pa-aq-da-at*
14) [...] MA.NA 10 GÍN KÙ.BABBAR ^{Id}AG-ŠEŠ.MEŠ-MU
15) [...] ⌜*x*⌝ *gu-ú-a*
16) [...][^{Id}]É-*a*-NUMUN-DÙ DUMU-*šú ki-i ú-šam-ṭe-ir*
17) *ta-ad-di*
18) LÚ *mu-kin-nu* ^{I}EN-*šú-nu* A-*šú šá* ^{Id}AG-NUMUN-GÁL-*ši*
19) A LÚ.PA.ŠE.KI ^{I}*tab-ni-e-a* A-*šú šá* ^{Id}AG-GI
20) A ^{Id}30-*šá-du-nu* ^{I}*ina*-SÙḪ-SUR A-*šú šá* ^{Id}AG-NUMUN-SI.SÁ
21) A ^{I}*e-gi-bi u* LÚ.ŠID ^{Id}AMAR.UD-KAR-*ir* A-*šú šá*
22) ^{Id}U+GUR-TIN-*iṭ* A ^{Id}EN-*e-ṭè-ru* TIN.TIR.KI
23) ITU.KIN UD.6.KAM MU.3.KAM ^{d}U+GUR-LUGAL-ŠEŠ
24) LUGAL TIN.TIR.KI ^{Id}AG-ŠEŠ.MEŠ-TIN-*iṭ*
25) DUMU-*šú šá* ^{Id}AG-NUMUN-SI.SÁ DUMU ^{I}*e-gi-bi*

Translation

(Document concerning) the contract for one mina, ten shekels of silver, silver (that is) the equivalent (lit., price) of the property (lit., the reeds), the dowry of the lady Gugūa, the daughter of Zākir, the descendant of the Isinite, which (she sold) without the permission of Ea-zēra-ibni, son of Bēl-zēru-lišir, descendant of Egibi. She will hand over to him the jointly held property to which Ea-zēra-ibni has title and of which his brothers are co-owners (without title). The silver, namely one mina, ten shekels [...] Tabnēa, son of Nabû-ušallim, descendant of Sin-šadûnu [...] She will hold his house in place of one-half mina, five shekels of silver. Each year he will give him five shekels of silver in interest [...] until [...] Ea-zēra-ibni. The contract [...] Nabû-aḫḫē-iddina, [son of Šulâ, descendant of Egibi] is entrusted. One mina, ten shekels of silver [...] Nabû-aḫḫē-iddina. [...] Ea-zēra-ibni [...] if he prepares a written document she will .... Witnesses (are) Bēlšunu, son of Nabû-zēra-ušabši, descendant of the Isinite, Tabnēa, son of Nabû-ušallim, descendant of Sin-šadûnu, Ina-tēšî-ēṭir, son of Nabû-zēru-lišir, descendant of Egibi, and the scribe, Marduk-ēṭir, son of Nergal-uballiṭ, descendant of Bēl-ēṭir. Babylon, month of Ululu, sixth day, third year of Nergal-šarra-uṣur, king of Babylon. Nabû-aḫḫē-bulliṭ, son of Nabû-zēru-lišir, descendant of Egibi (was present as a witness).

61

BM 54259 (Collated)
Published as Evetts, *Ner.* 61

1) [ZÚ.LUM].MA ZAG.LU [*la*] ⸢*gam*⸣-[*ma*]-*ru-ú-tu*
2) [*šá* LÚ.NU].GIŠ.ŠAR.MEŠ *šá* ^{d}[...] ⸢*xxx*⸣ LÚ.ŠU ⸢*xx*⸣
3) [ITU].KIN UD.13.KAM MU.3.KAM ^{d}U+GUR-LUGAL-ŠEŠ LUGAL TIN.[TIR.KI]
4) 7 GUR ^{Id}AG-*ú-še-zib*
5) 38 GUR ^{Id}EN-ŠEŠ.MEŠ-MU
6) 7 GUR ^{Id}UTU-DÙ
7) 21 GUR É ⸢*x*⸣ *šá* ^{Id}UTU-BA-*šá* ^{Id}UTU-DÙ
8) 18 GUR [...] *šá* ^{Id}UTU-*ana-kit-ti-šú* ^{Id}⸢*xxx*⸣
9) [...] ⸢*xxxxx*⸣ [...]

(remainder of obverse broken off)

1') 12 ⸢*xx*⸣ [...] ^{d}[...]
2') ^{Id}AG-I [...]
3') ⸢PAP⸣ [...] ZÚ].LUM.MA šá GU ÍD [...]
4') [...]
5') [...] GUR ^{I}*ki-na-a* LÚ] *za-qip-pa-nu*
15) ⸢x⸣ GUR 1 (PI) 3 (BÁN) 4 *qa* ZÍD ^{Id}UTU-*ana*-É-*šú*

Translation

(Document concerning) dates (constituting) the [in]complete estimated yield [of the gar]deners of [...] month of Ululu, thirteenth day, third year of Nergal-šarra-uṣur, king of Babylon. Seven *kurru* (are from) Nabû-ušēzib, thirty-eight *kurru* (are from) Bēl-aḫḫē-iddina, seven *kurru* (are from) Šamaš-ibni, twenty-one *kurru* (are from) ... of Šamaš-iqīša from Šamaš-ibni, eighteen *kurru* [...] of Šamaš-ana-kittišu [...] twelve [...] Nabû-na'id [...] Total of [...] of dates from the watercourse [...] *kurru* (are from) Kinâ, the caretaker of the garden [...] *kurru*, one pi, twenty-two qa of flour (are from) Šamaš-ana-kittišu.

62

BM 54244 (Collated)
Published as Evetts, *Ner.* 62

1) ZÚ.LUM.MA ZAG.LU *la gam-ru-tu*
2) *šá* LÚ.NU.GIŠ.ŠAR.MEŠ ÍD *gub-bu*
3) ITU.KIN UD.15.KAM MU.3.KAM
4) [^{d}U+GUR-LUGAL]-ŠEŠ LUGAL TIN.TIR.KI
5) [...] GUR ^{I}ÈR-ŠEŠ.MEŠ-*šú*
6) [...] ⌈*x*⌉ *na-ṣir*
(remainder of obverse broken off)
1') [...]
2') [...] MU
3') [...] ⌈*x*⌉ A
4') [...] *dul-la-an-ni*
5') [...] 1 GUR ^{Id}UTU-⌈DÙ⌉-ŠEŠ
6') 7 GUR ^{Id}UTU-SU
7') 6 GUR ^{Id}UTU-ŠEŠ.MEŠ-MU
8') PAP.PAP 8 ME 15 GUR [...]

Translation

(Document concerning) dates, a portion of (lit., the incomplete) the estimated yield of the gardeners of the Gubbu watercourse, month of Ululu, fifteenth day, third year of [Nergal-šarra]-uṣur, king of Babylon. [...] *kurru* (are from) Arad-aḫḫēšu [...] nāṣir. [...] iddina [...] apli [...] dullanni (?) [...] one *kurru* (is from) Šamaš-⌈bāni⌉-aḫi, seven *kurru* (are from) Šamaš-erība, six *kurru* (are from) Šamaš-aḫḫē-iddina--- total of eight hundred fifteen *kurru* (of dates) [...].

63

BM 31207 (Collated)
Published as Evetts, *Ner.* 63

1) ⌈*x*⌉ GUR 1 PI ZÚ].LUM.MA ⌈*šá*⌉
2) ^{I}ÈR-^{d}EN A-*šú šá* ^{I}BE-*ia*
3) A ^{I}*pap-pa-a-a ina muḫ-ḫi* ^{I}*na*-⌈*din*⌉-A

4) A-*šú šá* ^{Id}AG-EN-*šú-nu* A ^{I}DÙ-[*eš*]-DINGIR
5) *ina* ITU.APIN ZÚ.LUM.MA-'
6) 2 GUR 1 PI *ina ma-ši-*[*ḫu*]
7) *šá* ^{I}ÈR-^{d}EN *ina muḫ-*[*ḫi*]
8) [*i*]*-nam-din*
9) ⌜LÚ⌝ ⌜*mu-kin*⌝*-nu* ^{Id}AG-*qa* ⌜*xx*⌝
10) A-*šú šá* ^{I}BA-*šá-a* A ^{I}[...]
11) ^{Id}EN-SU A-*šú šá* ^{I}[...]
12) A ⌜LÚ *x*⌝ *u* LÚ.ŠID ⌜*xxx*⌝ [...]
13) A-*šú šá* ^{Id}EN-KÁD A ⌜*xxx*⌝
14) [ÍD] *eš-šú* ITU.KIN UD.13.KAM
15) [MU].3.KAM ^{Id}U+GUR-LUGAL-[ŠEŠ]
16) LUGAL ⌜TIN.TIR.⌝KI

Translation

(Document concerning) ⌜two⌝ *kurru*, one pi of dates, ⌜property⌝ of Arad-Bēl, son of Kābtija, descendant of Pappāja, charged against Nādin-apli, son of Nabû-bēlšunu, descendant of Epeš-ili. He will deliver the dated charged against (him), the two *kurru*, one pi, in the month of Araḫsamnu in accordance with the measure of Arad-Bēl. Witnesses (are) Nabû [...] son of Iqīša, descendant of [...] Bēl-erība, son of [...] and the scribe [...] son of Bēl-kāṣir, descendant of [...]. New [canal], month of Ululu, thirteenth day, third [year] of Nergal-šarra-[uṣur], king of ⌜Babylon⌝.

Commentary

1) Reading of 2 GUR is based on the contents of line 6.
3) Read personal name ^{I}*na-din*-A.
9-10) Collation of these lines shows Evetts' copy to be accurate (against Tallqvist, NBN 119b and ZA 7 272).
14) Read UD.13.KAM.

64

BM 64969
Published as Evetts, *Ner.* 64

1) [...]
1) ⌜6 *la*⌝ ⌜*x*⌝ *su*
3) PAP ⌜14 GADA⌝ *ina* IGI ^{I}⌜*pa-ni-*^{d}AG⌝
4) LÚ *ša-*⌜*bu-ú*⌝ ITU.KIN UD.⌜24⌝.KAM

5) MU.3.KAM ^{d}U+GUR-LUGAL-⸢ŠEŠ⸣
6) LUGAL TIN.TIR.KI

Translation

(Document concerning) [...] six [...] total of ⸢fourteen pieces⸣ of linen at the disposal of ⸢Pāni-Nabû,⸣ the dyer. Month of Ululu, ⸢twenty-fourth⸣ day, third year of Nergal-šarra-⸢uṣur,⸣ king of Babylon.

65

BM 55712 (Collated)
Published as Evetts, *Ner.* 65

1) ⸢1⸣ 2/3 MA.NA 3 GÍN GADA
2) *a-na gú-ḫal-ṣa-ṭum*
3) *šá* ⸢^{d}UTU⸣ *u* ^{d}A-*a* ^{d}*bu*-⸢*ne*⸣-*ne*
4) [...] *lu* [...] ⸢*x*⸣ ⸢UD.KIB⸣.NUN.KI
5) [...] *šá* UD.15.KAM
6) [...] ^{I}*ba-ku-ú-a*
7) LÚ *qal-la šá* ^{I}[...] MU-*šú*
8) LÚ.ŠID ^{d}⸢AMAR.UD⸣
9) 2 UDU.NITÁ *ba-la-ṭum* 16 UDU.[NITÁ]
10) *ina* UDU.NITA *sul-lu-un*-⸢*ḫu-ú*⸣
11) *šá ina* IGI ^{I}ZALÁG-^{d}UTU <<^{I}ZALÁG-^{d}UTU>>
12) *a*-[*na*] ⸢É⸣.BABBAR.RA ⸢*it-ta-din*⸣
13) ⸢UDU.NITÁ⸣ *a-na* SAT.⸢TUK⸣ *ina pa-ni*
14) [^{Id}]UTU-TIN-*it* ITU.APIN
15) UD.12.KAM MU.3.KAM
16) ^{d}U+GUR-LUGAL-ŠEŠ
17) LUGAL ⸢TIN⸣.TIR.KI

Translation

(Document concerning) ⸢one⸣ and two-thirds minas, three shekels of linen, for a scarf for ⸢Šamaš⸣, for Aja and for Bunene [...] Sippar [...] for the fifteenth day [...] Bakua, slave of [...] the priest of ⸢Marduk.⸣ Nūr-Šamaš ⸢delivered⸣ to the Ebabbar two live sheep and sixteen sheep (that were) from the sheep placed at the disposal of Nūr-Šamaš. The ⸢sheep⸣ were placed at the disposal of Šamaš-uballiṭ (and are) for the ⸢regular offering⸣. Month of Araḫsamnu, twelfth day, third year of Nergal-šarra-uṣur, king of Babylon.

Commentary

10) For the translation of *su-lum-ḫu* (*zu-lum-ḫu, suluḫḫu, sulunḫu*) = "*Edelschaf*," see von Soden, AHw 1056b and 1057a.

66

BM 30577 (Collated)
Published as Evetts, *Ner.* 66

1) 17 LIM *gid-dil šá* SUM.SAR ^{I}MU-^{d}AMAR.UD
2) <*A-šú*> *šá* ^{I}BA-*šá-a* A ^{I}ZALÁG-^{d}30 *ina* UGU
3) ^{I}ŠEŠ-*i-tab-ši A-šú šá* ^{Id}AG-*ma-lik*
4) ^{Id}AG-NUMUN-MU *A-šú šá* ^{Id}AG-*ki-i*-DINGIR.MEŠ
5) ^{I}BE-*ia A-šú šá* ^{I}*i-di-in* ^{Id}AG-NUMUN-MU
6) *A-šú šá* ^{I}*ba-ri-qi* ^{Id}AG-ŠEŠ-MU
7) *A-šú šá* ^{I}DINGIR.MEŠ-*a-di-nu* ^{I}SUM-*nu-nu*
8) *A-šú šá* ^{I}ŠEŠ-*li-kin*$_7$ ^{Id}EN-SIG$_5$
9) *A-šú šá* ^{Id}UTU-A-MU(!) (text: A)*ina* ITU.GUD *gid-dil*
10) *šá* SUM.SAR *bab-ba-nu-ú ina* UGU ÍD *bar*(!) (text: *me*)-*sip*
11) *e* ⸢x⸣ *lu i-nam-din-nu-' 1-en pu(!)-ut(!)*(text: MU)
12) *2-i na-šu-u pu-ut e-ṭè-ru*
13) *šá gid-dil* ^{I}ŠEŠ(-*i*)-*tab-ši na-ši*
14) *e-lat ú-íl-tim.*MEŠ *maḫ-(ri-tu)šá ina* UGU ^{I}ŠEŠ(-*i*)-*tab-ši*
15) *a-na e-lat-ti-šú* LÚ *mu-kin-nu* ^{Id}EN-MU
16) *A-šú šá* ^{Id}AG-GI A ^{I}ŠEŠ-*ú-ba-ni-i*
17) ^{I}MU-^{d}AG *A-šú šá* ^{Id}AG-*mu-še-ti-iq*-UD.DA
18) A ^{I}*nu-ḫa-šú u* LÚ.ŠID ^{Id}EN-MU
19) *A-šú šá* ^{Id}EN-NIGIN-*ir* A ^{I}*da-bi-bi a-mat gi*⸢xx⸣
20) TIN.TIR.KI ITU.ZÍZ UD.5.KAM MU.3.KAM
21) ^{d}U+GUR-LUGAL-ŠEŠ LUGAL TIN.TIR.KI
22) *ina* IGI ^{I}ÈR-*ia A-šú šá*⸢xx⸣ [...]
23) [...] ⸢x⸣ LÚ.SIPA *i* ⸢xxxx⸣
24) ⸢xxx⸣ [...]

Translation

(Document concerning) seventeen thousand strings of garlic, (property of) Iddina-Marduk, son of Iqīša, descendant of Nūr-Sin, charged against Aḫa-ittabši, son of Nabû-mālik, Nabû-zēra-iddina, son of Nabû-kī-ilāni, Kābtija, son of Idin, Nabû-zēra-iddina, son of Bariqu, Nabû-aḫa-iddina, son of Ili-a-di-nu, Iddinunu, son of Ahu-likin, (and) Bēl-udammiq, son of Šamaš-apla-iddina. They will deliver the strings of good quality garlic at the Borsippa canal ... in the mouth of Ajaru, and one shall bear the responsibilty for the other. Aḫa-ittabši bears the responsibility for payment of the strings (of garlic). (This is) apart from the earlier contracts which are exclusively debited to Aḫa-ittabši. Witnesses (are) Bēl-iddina, son of Nabû-ušallim, descendant of Aḫu-bāni, Iddina-Nabû, son of Nabû-mušētiq-uddê, descendant of Nuḫašu, and the scribe Bēl-iddina, son of Bēl-upaḫḫir, descendant of Dabibi ... Babylon, month of Šabaṭu, fifth day, third year of Nergal-šarra-uṣur, king of Babylon. At the disposal of Ardija, son of [...] Rē'û[...].

67

BM 31044 (Collated)
Published as Evetts, *Ner.* 67

1) 7 GUR 2(PI) 3(BÁN) ŠE.BAR *šá* ^{Id}DI.KU$_5$-MU-MU
2) A-*šú šá* ^{I}NUMUN-*ia* A ^{I}*na-ba-a-a*
3) *ina* UGU ^{I}*gi-mil-lu* A-*šú šá*
4) ^{I}*lu-ut-tu-ú-a ina* ITU.GUD
5) ŠE.BAR *ga-mir-tum ina* UGU ÍD *bar-sip* KI
6) *ina* URU *šá* ^{I}ŠEŠ-MU A-*šú šá* ^{I}ÈR-*ia*
7) [*i*]-*nam-din e-lat ú-ìl-tim* MEŠ
8) [...] *u* ŠE.BAR
9) [ŠE.BAR] *šá* KASKAL^{II} *šá* ^{I}MU-^{d}AMAR.UD
10) *(erasure)* A-*šú šá* ^{I}BA-*šá-a*
11) LÚ *mu-kin-nu* ^{Id}AG-*di-i-ni-e-pu-uš*
12) A-*šú šá* ^{I}*ki-ne-nu-na-a-a*
13) ^{I}MU-DU A-*šú šá* ^{I}NUMUN-*ia*
14) *u* LÚ.ŠID *(erasure)* ^{Id}EN-MU
15) A-*šú šá* ^{Id}EN-NIGIN-*ir* A ^{I}*da-bi-bi*
16) URU *šaḫ-ri-nu* ITU.ŠE
17) UD.12.KAM MU.3.KAM
18) ^{d}U+GUR-LUGAL-ŠEŠ LUGAL
19) TIN.TIR.KI

Translation

(Document concerning) seven *kurru*, two pi, eighteen qa of barley, property of Madānu-šuma-iddina, son of Zērija, descendant of Nabāja, charged against Gimillu, son of Luttūa. He will deliver the barley in (its) entirety at the Borsippa canal in the village of Aḫa-iddina, son of Ardija, in the month of Ajaru. (This is) apart from contracts [...] and barley. [The barley] is from the business capital of Iddina-Marduk, son of Iqīša. Witnesses (are) Nabû-dīni-ēpuš, son of Kinenâ, Šuma-ukīn, son of Zērija, and the scribe, Bēl-iddina, son of Bēl-upaḫḫir, descendant of Dabibi. City of Šaḫrinu, month of Addaru, twelfth day, third year of Nergal-šarra-uṣur, king of Babylon.

68

BM 41401 (Collated)
Published as Evetts, *Ner.*68

1) 1 LIM 2 ME *gid-dil šá* SUM.SAR
2) *šá* ^{Id}DI.KU$_5$-MU-MU A-*šú šá* ^{I}NUMUN-*ia*
3) A ^{I}*na-ba-a-a u* ^{Id}AG-GI
4) A-*šú šá* ^{I}IGI-*ni-ia ina muḫ-ḫi*
5) ^{Id}AG-DÙ-ŠEŠ A-*šú šá* ^{Id}AG-*ma-lik*
6) *ina* ITU.GUD *gid-dil šá* SUM.SAR
7) *bab-ba-nu-ú ina* SAG.DU-*šú*
8) *i-nam-din*
9) LÚ *mu-kin-nu* ^{I}ŠEŠ-*it-tab-ši*
10) ⌜A⌝-*šú šá* ^{Id}AG-*ma-lik*
11) ^{I}*e-rib-šú* A-*šú šá* ^{Id}AG-*ma-lik*
12) ^{I}*gi-mil*-^{d}UTU A-*šú šá* ^{Id}AG-NUMUN-MU
13) *u* LÚ.ŠID ^{Id}UTU-ŠEŠ-MU
14) A-*šú šá* ^{I}*ra-šil* URU *šaḫ-ri-ni*
15) ITU.BÁR UD.2.KAM MU.4.KAM
16) ^{Id}U+GUR-LUGAL-ŠEŠ LUGAL TIN.TIR.KI

Translation

(Document concerning) one thousand two hundred strings of garlic, property of Madānu-šuma-iddina, son of Zērija, descendant of Nabāja, and Nabû-ušallim, son of Pānija, charged against Nabû-bāni-aḫi, son of Nabû-mālik. He will deliver the strings of good qualtiy garlic from his capital in the month of Ajaru. Witnesses (are) Aḫa-ittabši, ⌜son⌝ of Nabû-mālik, Eribšu, son of Nabû-mālik, Gimil-Šamaš, son of Nabû-zēra-iddina, and the scribe, Šamaš-aḫa-iddina, son of Rašil. City of Šaḫrinu, month of Nisanu, second day, fourth year of Nergal-šarra-uṣur, king of Babylon.

69

BM 30334(Collated)
Published as Evetts, *Ner.* 69 and Ungnad, SSS 10 no. 6

1) 1/2 MA.NA KÙ.BABBAR ŠÁM SUM.SAR
2) *šá* ^{I}ŠEŠ-<*it*>*-tab-ši* A-*šú šá* ^{Id}AG-*ma-lik*
3) *ina muḫ-ḫi* ^{Id}DI.KU$_5$-MU-MU A-*šú šá*
4) ^{I}NUMUN-*ia* A ^{I}*na-ba-a-a*
5) *u* ^{Id}AG-GI A-*šú šá* ^{I}IGI-*ni-ia*
6) *ina* ITU.BÁR KÙ.BABBAR *šá ina* 1 GÍN *bit-qa*
7) *ina* SAG.DU-*šú-*<*nu*> *i-nam-din-nu-'*
8) ⌈1-*en*⌉ *pu-ut* 2-*i na-šu-ú*
9) [LÚ] *mu-kin-nu* ^{I}*ka-ṣir*
10) [A-*šú šá*] ^{I}BA-*šá-a* A ^{I}ZALÁG-^{d}30
11) [^{I}*e*]-*ri-šú* A-*šú šá* ^{Id}AG-*ma-lik*
12) ^{I}*gi-mil-*^{d}UTU A-*šú šá* ^{Id}AG-NUMUN-MU
13) ^{I}*ri-mut* A-*šú šá* ^{Id}AG-*ma-lik*
14) *u* LÚ.ŠID ^{Id}UTU-ŠEŠ-MU A-*šú*
15) *šá* ^{I}*ra-šil* URU *šaḫ-ri-ni*
16) ITU.BÁR UD.2.KAM MU.4.KAM
17) ^{Id}U+GUR-LUGAL-ŠEŠ LUGAL TIN.TIR.KI

Translation

(Document concerning) one-half mina of silver, the price of garlic belonging to Aḫa-ittabši, son of Nabû-mālik, charged against Madānu-šuma-iddina, son of Zērija, descendant of Nabāja and Nabû-ušallim, son of Pānija. They will deliver the silver which has one-eighth alloy (per shekel), from their(!) capital in the month of Nisanu, and ⌈one⌉ shall bear the responsibility for the other. Witnesses (are) Kāṣir, [son of] Iqīša, descendant of Nūr-Sin, Erišu, son of Nabû-mālik, Gimil-Šamaš, son of Nabû-zēra-iddina, Rīmūt, son of Nabû-mālik, and the scribe, Šamaš-aḫa-iddina, son of Rašil. Village of Šaḫrinu, month of Nisanu, second day, fourth year of Nergal-šarra-uṣur, king of Babylon.

Commentary

12) Read ^{Id}AG-NUMUN-MU (miscopied by Evetts). Compare *Ner.* 68, 12 where the same witnesses and personnel occur.

70

BM 63831 (Collated)
Published as Evetts, *Ner.* 70

1) [...] ⸢*x*⸣ MEŠ *u* ⸢*x*⸣ [...]
2) [...] [^{d}U+GUR]-LUGAL-ŠEŠ LUGAL TIN.TIR.KI
3) [*a-na* É.BABBAR].RA SUM-*na*
4) 7 ME ŠE.BAR GIŠ.BAR LÚ.APIN.MEŠ *ina* ŠU^{II} ^{Id}UTU-MU [*ma-ḫi-ir*]
5) 2 ME ŠE.BAR GIŠ.BAR *ša* ^{Id}UTU-MU
6) 1 ME 33 GUR ^{I}*ap-pa-ni*
7) 80 GUR ^{Id}UTU-*a-na*-É-*šú*
8) 1 ME 70 GUR ^{I}*li-ši-ru*
9) 1 ME 80 GUR ^{Id}UTU-ZALÁG-*ir*
10) 45 GUR ^{Id}UTU-TIN-*iṭ šá* ÍD *pal-lu-uk-kat-[tum]*
11) 5 ME 60 GUR ^{Id}UTU-EN-DINGIR *šá* URU *gi-lu-šú*
12) 4 ME 50 GUR ^{I}*šu-la-a ša* URU *ḫal-la-a*
13) 23 GUR ^{Id}UTU-⸢MU⸣ *ša* URU ^{d}EN-SUR
14) 1 ME 30 GUR ^{Id}UTU-ZALÁG-*ir šá* ÍD *su-man-ban-dù*
15) 20 GUR ^{Id}EN-TIN-*iṭ šá bir-tum šá* ^{I}[...]
16) 80 GUR *ina* ŠE.BAR *ri-ḫa-ni šá* [...]
17) *ina* ŠU^{II} ^{Id}UTU [...]
18) 1 ME *ina* ŠU^{II} ^{Id}⸢*x*⸣ [...]
19) 1 ME *ina* ŠU^{II} ^{I}BA-[*šá-a*] [...]
20) 4 ME *ina* ŠU^{II} ^{I}*mu-še-zib*-^{d}EN [...]
21) 25 GUR *ina* ŠU^{II} ^{I}MU-DU *a* ^{I}[...]
22) 2 ME 24 [...] ⸢*x*⸣ [...]
23) PAP 3 LIM 7 ME 20 [GUR ŠE.BAR]
24) *ina* [*lìb*]-*bi* 1 LIM ŠE.BAR *ša* [...]
25) 4 MU.AN.NA *a-na* [LÚ.BAPPIR.MEŠ] ⸢SUM⸣-*in*
26) 1 LIM ŠE.BAR [...] 1 MU.AN.NA LÚ.MU.MEŠ
27) 7 ME ŠE.BAR ⸢*xx*⸣ GUD.MEŠ ⸢*xxxx*⸣
28) MUŠEN.ḪI.A *šá* ⸢*xxx*⸣ [...]
29) [...] LÚ ŠEŠ *šá* ⸢*x*⸣ *iq* ⸢*x*⸣
30) [...] *a-na* [...] ⸢*x*⸣ *ka* É ⸢*xx*⸣ *šu*
31) [...] ^{d}UTU-TIN-iṭ LÚ ⸢*xxx*⸣ [...] ŠEŠ-*ia*
32) [...] ^{Id}AG-MU-MU ⸢*xx*⸣ LÚ ⸢KAB.SAR⸣
33) [...] GUR *a-na* [...]
34) [...] ŠUK.ḪI.A LÚ.BAPPIR.MEŠ 4 UD [...]

Translation

(Document concerning) [...] and [...] delivered [to Ebabbar] [...] of [Nergal]-šarra-uṣur, king of Babylon. Seven hundred (*kurru*) constitute the rent of the plowmen (and) [were received] from Šamaš-iddina, two hundred (*kurru*) of barley (constitute) the rent of Šamaš-iddina, one hundred thirty-three (*kurru*) (are from) Appani, eighty (*kurru*) (are from) Šamaš-ana-kittišu, one hundred seventy *kurru* (are from) Liširu, one hundred eighty *kurru* (are from) Šamaš-inammir, forty-five *kurru* (are from) Šamaš-uballiṭ from the Pallu[katum] watercourse, five hundred sixty (*kurru*) (are from) Šamaš-bēl-ili from the village of Gilušu, four hundred fifty *kurru* (are from) Šulâ from the village of Ḫallâ, twenty-three *kurru* (are from) Šamaš-iddina of the village of Bēl-ēṭir, one hundred thirty *kurru* (are from) Šamaš-inammir from the watercourse of Sumanbandu(?), twenty *kurru* twenty *kurru* (are from) Bēl-uballiṭ from the outlying district of [...] eighty *kurru* (are) a portion of the remaining barley [...] from Šamaš [...] one hundred (are from) [...] one hundred (*kurru*) (are from) Iq[īša] four hundred (*kurru*) are from Mušēzib-Bēl [...] twenty-five *kurru* are from Šuma-ukīn, son of [...] two hundred twenty-four (*kurru*) {...] --- total of three thousand seven hundred twenty [*kurru* of barley]. From this [amount], one thousand (*kurru*) of barley [...] four years were given to the [brewers], one thousand (*kurru*) of barley (are for) the bakers for one year, seven hundred (*kurru*) of barley [...] oxen [...] birds [...] for [...] Šamaš-uballiṭ [...] Nabû-šuma-iddina, ⸢the jeweler⸣, [...] *kurru* for [...] sustenance for the brewers, four [...].

71

BM 30713 (Collated)
Published as Evetts, *Ner.* 71

1) ⸢*x*⸣ GÚ.UN 1 MA.NA KÙ.BABBAR *u ki* ⸢*x*⸣ [...]
2) *šá* ^{I}MU-^{d}AMAR.UD A-*šú šá* ^{I}BA-*šá-a* A ^{I}ZALÁG-[^{d}30]
3) *šá ina* GÚ.UN *ina* UGU ^{Id}AMAR.UD-SU A-*šú šá* ^{I}[...]
4) ê ^{I}BA-*ša-a* A-*šú šá* ^{Id}EN-⸢*ka*⸣-[*ṣir*]
5) *i-'-i-li u* ^{Id}AMAR.UD-SU *u* ^{I}⸢BA⸣-[*šá-a*]
6) 1-*en pu-ut* 2-*i na-šú-ú* ^{Id}[AMAR.UD-SU]
7) *u* ^{I}BA-*šá-a ina* ŠU^{II} ^{I}MU-^{d}AMAR.UD *e-ṭir*
8) 2 MA.NA KÙ.BABBAR *e-lat ú-ìl-tim maḫ*-⸢*ru*⸣-[*tu*]
9) ^{I}MU-^{d}AMAR.UD *a-di-i qí-it* MU.AN.NA

10) ⸢*si*⸣*-bu-tum šá* ^{Id}AMAR.UD-SU *u* ^{I}BA-*šá-a*
11) *i-na-áš-ši*
12) LÚ *mu-kin-nu* ^{I}ÈR-*ia* A-*šú šá*
13) ^{Id}EN-ŠEŠ.MEŠ-MU A ^{I}LÚ.SIPA-*i*
14) ^{Id}AG-GI A-*šú šá* ^{I}IGI-*ni-ia* [...]
15) [LÚ.SID ^{Id}EN]-MU A-*šú šá* ^{Id}[...]
16) [...] [TIN.TIR].KI ITU.[...]
17) [...] ^{d}U+GUR-[LUGAL-ŠEŠ]
18) [LUGAL TIN.TIR].KI

Translation

(Document concerning) ... ⸢talents, one mina⸣ of silver and [...] a portion of the talents concerning which Iddina-Marduk, son of Iqīša, descendant of Nūr [Sin] made a binding agreement to the debit of Marduk-erība, son of [...] and Iqīša, son of Bēl-⸢kāṣir⸣ and (concerning which) Marduk-erība and ⸢Iqīša⸣ bear the responsibility for each other. Two minas of silver were paid by Iddina-Marduk (to) [Marduk-erība] and Iqīša. (This is) apart from the ⸢former⸣ contract charged against Iddina-Marduk. Until the end of the year he will act under power of disposition for Marduk-erība and Iqīša. Witnesses (are) Ardija, son of Bēl-aḫḫē-iddina, descendant of Rē'û, Nabû-ušallim, son of Pānija [...] [and the scribe Bēl]-iddina, son of [...] [Baby]lon, month of [...] Nergal-[šarra-uṣur], [king of Babyl]on.

Commentary

4) For the restoration ^{Id}EN-*ka*-[*ṣir*], cf. Ner. 10:3; 43:3, etc.
14-18) Bracketed signs indicate condition of tablet and restoration based on parallel texts as well as Evetts' original copy.

72

BM 64935 (Collated)
Published as Evetts, *Ner.* 72

1) É *ša* ^{I}*sag-gil-lu* A-*sú šá* ^{I}SUM-ŠEŠ
2) [A] ^{Id}EN-*e-ṭè-ru šá* ^{I}*muk-ki-e-a*
3) A-*šú šá* ^{Id}UTU-*ru-ṣu-ú-a ina lìb-bi áš-bi*
4) *bat-qa i-ṣab-bat ú-ri i-šá-an-ni*
5) ITU *bit-qa* ⸢KÙ.BABBAR⸣ *i-di* É *a-na* [^{I}*sag-gil-lu*]
6) *i*-⸢*nam*⸣*-din* UD-*mu i-na* [...]

7) ITU *bit-qa* ⌜*šá*⌝ [...]
8) ⌜LÚ *mu-kin*⌝-*[nu]* [...]
9) [...] *gal šá* LÚ.⌜ŠID⌝ [...]
10) [*u*] LÚ.ŠID ^{I}*ri-mut-*⌜^{d}EN⌝
11) [A-*šú*] *šá* ^{Id}LUGAL ⌜*xxxx*⌝ [...]
12) [...] ⌜TIN-*su*⌝ ^{d}[...] UD.KIB.NUN.KI
13) [ITU].ŠE.DIRI.GUR$_{10}$ ⌜UD⌝[...].⌜KAM⌝ [MU] [...]
14) ^{Id}U+GUR-LUGAL-ŠEŠ LUGAL [TIN.TIR.KI]

Translation

(Document concerning) the house of Saggilu, son of Nādin-aḫi, descendant of Bēl-ēṭir, which Mukkēa, son of Šamaš-riṣūa is renting (lit., lives in). He will repair the damp course of the wall, he will repair the roof (and) monthly, one-eighth shekel ⌜of silver⌝, the rent of the house, he will give to [Saggilu]. Whenever [...] monthly one-eighth shekel [...]. ⌜Witnesses⌝ (are) [...] of the ⌜scribe⌝ [...] [and] the scribe, Rīmūt-⌜Bēl,⌝ [son of] [...]⌜balāssu⌝. Sippar, [month] of Addaru, [...] ⌜day,⌝ [...] [year] of Nergal-šarra-uṣur, king of [Babylon].

Commentary

9-14) Signs enclosed in brackets are no longer on the tablet.

73

BM 54179 (Collated)
(=Bertin no. 1183)

1) ⌜*x*⌝ *qa* ŠE.NUMUN A [...]
2) [...] ⌜*x*⌝ DAGRIN *qa* ⌜*x*⌝ [...] ⌜TIN.TIR.KI⌝
3) *šá* ^{Id}AG-⌜MU⌝-ŠEŠ A-*šú šá* [^{Id}AG]-GI A ^{I}*dul-lu-[pu]*
4) *ina* [UGU] [^{I}*ri*]-*mu-ú-tu-*⌜^{d}EN⌝ *ul-tu* UGU [...]
5) ⌜*ma-kal*⌝-[*lu*]-*ú* ŠE.NUMUN *zaq-pi* A.ŠÀ ŠE.NUMUN *šá* 1 *pi* [...]
6) *u* ^{I}ÈR ⌜^{d}*gu-la*⌝ *ina* ŠU^{II} ^{Id}AG-MU-ŠEŠ *im-*⌜*maḫ*⌝-[*ḫu-ru*]
7) ^{Id}AG-MU-ŠEŠ [A-*sú šá*] ^{Id}AG-GI A ^{I}*dul-lu-pu*
8) ^{I}ÈR-[^{d}*gu*]-⌜*la*⌝ A-*šú šá* ^{I}*ki-rib-tu* A ^{I}*dul-lu-*[*pu*]
9) *a-ki-*[*i*] KI.LAM.MEŠ *maḫ-ri-ti šá ina* ŠU^{II}
10) ^{Id}[AG-MU]-ŠEŠ *i-pu-šú* KI.LAM
11) [*im-bi*]-*e-ma i-šá-am a-na* ŠÁM
12) ⌜*gam-ru*⌝-*tu ma-ḫi-ir a* ⌜*xxx*⌝

13) [...] ⸢*xxxx*⸣
14) [LÚ] *mu-kin-[nu]* [...] *ki a*
15) ^{I}*mu-ra-nu* [A]-*šú šá* [...] *kal-lim*
16) ^{I}*ar-ra-bi* A-*šú [šá]* [...] *na-a-a*
17) [^{I}]SUM-*na*-^{d}AG DUB.SAR A-*šú* [*šá*] [...] A LÚ [...]
18) [TIN].⸢TIR.KI ITU⸣.GAN UD.14.KAM
19) MU.⸢*x*⸣.KAM ^{Id}U+GUR-LUGAL-⸢ŠEŠ⸣
20) LUGAL TIN.⸢TIR.⸣KI

Translation

(Document concerning) a field of ... qa [...] in the district of [...] ⸢Babylon,⸣ ⸢belonging to⸣ Nabû-⸢šuma⸣-uṣur, son of [Nabû]-ušallim, descendant of Dullupu, ⸢adjacent to⸣ (the property of) Rīmūt-⸢Bēl,⸣ from [...] the ⸢mooring place,⸣ a field planted (with date palms), areable land of one ⸢pi⸣ [...] and which Arad-⸢Gula,⸣ ⸢received⸣ from Nabû-šuma-uṣur. Arad-[Gula], son of Kiribtu, descendant of Dullu[pu], bought (the property) from Nabû-šuma-uṣur, [son of] Nabû-ušallim, decsendant of Dullupu.[He declared] (lit., named) the price and he paid (it). It was received for the [full] price.[...] Witnesses (are) [...], Muranu, [son] of [...] Arabi, son [of] [...] Iddina-Nabû, the scribe, son [of] [...] descendant of [...]. ⸢Babylon,⸣ month of Kislimu, fourteenth day, ... year of Nergal-šarra-⸢uṣur,⸣ king of Babylon.

74

BM 54180(Collated)
(=Bertin no. 1184)

1) LÚ *mu-kin-ni-*⸢*e ša*⸣ *ina pa-ni-šú-nu*
2) ⸢^{Id}EN⸣-[MU]-GAR-*un* A-*šú šá* ^{Id}⸢*x*⸣ [...]
3) A LÚ Ì ⸢*xx e x*⸣
4) [...] NUMUN *šá* ^{I}ÈR-^{d}AG
5) [...] ^{Id}AG-*na-din*-ŠEŠ *im-ḫu-ru*
6) [...] SU-*ba iq-bu-ú*
7) *um-ma a-ḫi šá bi* ⸢*xxxx*⸣ *a*
8) ⸢*xxx*⸣ *a-hi šá bi* ⸢*x*⸣ *ša* ^{I}⸢*xxx*⸣
9) ^{I}*ṣil-la-a* A-*šú šá* ^{I}*la-a-ba-ši*
10) A ^{Id}UTU-*da-a-ri* ^{I}ŠEŠ-⸢*x*⸣
11) A-*šú šá* ^{I}*ba-la-ṭu* A ^{I}*na-bu-un-na-a-a*
12) ^{I}*ba-la-ṭu* A-*šú šá* ^{Id}EN-ŠEŠ.MEŠ-MU

13) A ^{I}*dul-lu-pu* ^{Id}AG-EN-*šú-nu*
14) A-*šú šá* ^{Id}EN-GI A ^{I}AD-NU-ZU
15) TIN.TIR.KI ITU.ZÍZ UD.6.KAM
16) MU.1.KAM ^{d}U+GUR-LUGAL-ŠEŠ
17) LUGAL TIN.TIR.KI

Translation

(The following are) the witnesses before whom ⌜Bēl⌝-[šuma]-iškun, son of [...] descendant of [...] field(?) which Arad-Nabû, [...] Nabû-nādin-aḫi received [...] erība spoke as follows: [...] which [...] which [...]-- Ṣillâ, son of Labaši, descendant of Šamaš-dari, Aḫa-[...], son of Balāṭu, descendant of Nabunāja, Balāṭu, son of Bēl-aḫḫē-iddina, descendant of Dullupu, Nabû-bēlšunu, son of Bēl-ušallim, descendant of Abi-ul-idi. Babylon, month of Šabaṭu, sixth day, first year of Nergal-šarra-uṣur, king of Babylon.

75

BM 75968(Collated)
(=Bertin no. 1202)

1) [...] GÍN KÙ.BABBAR *šá* ^{I}GI-^{d}AMAR.UD A-*šú šá*
2) ^{Id}UTU-MU-DU A LÚ.ŠID UD.KIB.NUN.KI
3) *ina* UGU ^{I}*at-kal-ana-*^{d}EN A-*šú šá* ^{I}*ri-mut*
4) A ^{I}ÈR-^{d}AMAR.UD *šá* MU.AN.NA *ina* UGU *ma-ni-e*
5) [...] GÍN KÙ.BABBAR *ina muḫ-ḫi-šú i-rab-bi*
6) [...] ŠE.NUMUN-*šú* GIŠ.SAR GIŠ.GIŠIMMAR *zaq-pu*
7) [...] URU EDIN ⌜*ú*⌝ A.GÀR URU *šá-dir-tum*
8) [...] DU DUMU.MEŠ LÚ *qal-*[*la*] *maš-ka-nu*
9) [...] [^{I}GI]-^{d}AMAR.UD LÚ.TUK-*ú šá-nam-ma*
10) [...] *ul i-šal-lat a* [...]
11) [...] *ma* [...] *lim*
12) [...] ⌜*xx*⌝ ^{I}ÈR-^{d}EN
13) [...] GI A-*šú šá* ^{Id}AMAR.UD-NUMUN-DÙ
14) [...] ⌜*x*⌝ A-*šú šá* [...] ^{I}*ri-mut* A-*šú šá*
15) [...] ⌜*x*⌝ MU A ^{I}*na-din* A ^{I}*dan-na-a-a*
16) ^{I}MU-^{d}EN A-*šú šá* ^{Id}AMAR.UD-LUGAL-*a-ni* A LÚ.ŠID.BÁR
17) LÚ.[ŠID] ^{Id}AG-MU-SI.SÁ A-*šú šá* ^{I}TIN-*su*
18) A LÚ.ŠID ^{d}INNIN TIN.TIR.KI URU *šá-dir-tum*
19) [...] UD.28.KAM MU.1.KAM

20) ^{d}U+GUR-LUGAL-ŠEŠ LUGAL TIN.TI.RKI

Translation

(Document concerning) [...] shekels of silver, property of Mušallim-Marduk, son of Šamaš-šuma-ukīn, descendant of Šangû Sippar, charged against Atkal-ana-Bēl, son of Rīmūt, descendant of Arad-Marduk and on which annually [...] shekels of silver per mina increase against him (i.e., there is an interest charge of [...] shekels of silver per mina annually).[...] his acreage (and) garden planted with date palms [...] the village (or) open country ⌜and⌝ along the irrigation ditch of the village of Šadirtum [...] the slave(?) (was taken) as pledge [...].[Mušallim] Marduk. No other creditor [...] shall have the right to dispose of [...] . Arad-Bēl [...] ušallim, the son of Marduk-zēra-ibni, [...] Rīmūt, son of [...] iddina (?), son of Nādin, descendant of Dannēa, Iddina-Bēl, son of Marduk-šarrāni, descendant of Šangû parakki (and) the[scribe], Nabû-šumu-lišir, son of Balāssu, descendant of Šangû Ištar Bābili. Village of Šadirtum [...] eighteenth day, first year of Nergal-šarra-uṣur, king of Babylon.

76

BM 74511 (Collated)
(=Bertin no. 1206)

1) 2 GUR ŠE.BAR SAL *bu-sa-sa*
2) DUMU.SAL-*su šá* ^{I}*ḫu-un-da-ri*
3) *ina* UGU ^{Id}UTU-MU-GIŠ A-*šú šá*
4) ^{Id}UTU-*na-ṣir* A LÚ.ŠID *sip-par* KI
5) *ina* ITU.DU$_6$ *ina* ⌜*x*⌝ [...]
(remainder broken away)
1') A-*šú šá* ^{I}[...] ⌜*xx*⌝ [...]
2') ^{Id}UTU-SIG$_5$-*iq* A-*šú šá* ^{I}*lib-luṭ*
3') A LÚ.SIPA.ANŠE.KUR.RA *u* LÚ.ŠID
4') ^{Id}UTU-DÙ-ŠEŠ A-*šú šá* ^{I}ŠU-^{d}ŠÚ
5') A LÚ.ŠID ^{d}INNIN TIN.TIR.KI *sip-par* KI
6') ITU.DU$_6$ UD.6.KAM MU.1.KAM
7') ^{Id}U+GUR-LUGAL-ŠEŠ LUGAL E.KI

Translation

(Document concerning) two *kurru* of barley, (belonging to) the lady Busasa, daughter of Ḫundari, charged against Šamaš-šumu-lišir, son of

Šamaš-nāṣir, descendant of Šangû Sippar. In the month of Tašritu [...] son of [...] Šamaš-udammiq, son of Libluṭ, descendant of Rē'û sisi and the scribe, Šamaš-bāni-aḫi, son of Gimil-Marduk, descendant of Šangû Ištar Bābili. Sippar, month of Tašritu, sixth day, first year of Nergal-šarra-uṣur, king of Babylon.

77

BM 74495 (Collated)
(=Bertin no. 1209)

1) 7 GUR 3(PI) 2(BÁN) ŠE.BAR *šá* Id[...]
2) A-*šú šá* IdAMAR.UD-ŠEŠ.ME [...]
3) A I*ši-gu-ú-a ina muḫ-ḫi*[...]
4) IdAG-NUMUN-SI.SÁ A-*šú šá*
5) I*ba-la-ṭu* A LÚ.PA.ŠE.KI
6) *ina lìb-bi* 4 GUR ŠE.BAR *ina* ITU.GUD
7) *i-nam-din* 3 GUR 3(PI) 2(BÁN) ŠE.BAR [...]
8) *ina* ITU.SIG$_4$ *ina* UGU ⌈*xx*⌉ [...]
9) *i-nam-din* [...]
10) *ú-ìl-tim* [...]
11) LÚ *mu-kin-nu* I[...]
12) A-*šú šá* IdEN-TIN-*iṭ* A LÚ.PA.ŠE.KI
13) IdAMAR.UD-SU A-*šú šá* IdAG [...]
14) A LÚ.PA.ŠE.KI LÚ.ŠID IdAG-NUMUN-[SI.SÁ]
15) A-*šú šá* ITIN A LÚ.PA.ŠE.KI
16) *sip-par* KI ITU.ZÍZ UD.28.KAM
17) MU.2.KAM IdU+GUR-LUGAL-ŠEŠ
18) LUGAL TIN.TIR.⌈KI⌉

Translation

(Document concerning) seven *kurru*, three pi, twelve qa of barley, property of [...] son of Marduk-aḫḫē-[...] descendant of Šiguā, charged against [...] Nabû-zēru-lišir, son of Balāṭu, descendant of the Isinite. Of this amount, he will deliver four *kurru* of barley in the month of Ajaru. He will deliver (the remaining) three *kurru*, three pi, twelve qa of barley in the month of Simanu at the [...]. The contract [...]. Witnesses (are) [...] son of Bēl-uballiṭ, descendant of the Isinite, Marduk-erība, son of Nabû-[...] descendant of the Isinite (and) the scribe, Nabû-zēru-[lišir,] son of Balāṭu, descendant of the Isinite. Sippar, month of Šabaṭu, twenty-eighth day,second year of Nergal-šarra-uṣur, king of Babylon.

78

BM 77626 (Collated
(=Bertin 1213)

1) *ú-ìl-tim šá a-na muḫ-ḫi*
2) *ṭup-pi ki-i-nu šá nu-dun-nu-ú šá* ^{I}*šu-*⌈*la*⌉*-a*
3) A-*šú šá* ^{I}*gi-mil-lu* A ^{I}DÙ-*eš*-DINGIR
4) ⌈*xxxx*⌉ A-*šú šá* ^{I}*ri-mut*
5) [...] ⌈*xxx*⌉ GÍN KÙ.BABBAR
6) [...] *ma i-na-áš-šú-nu*
7) [...] *ḫi-pa-a-tú*
8) [...] *rit ma a-ḫi*
9) [...] *i-šal-lim*
10) [...] *maḫ-rit-ma*
11) [...] *a-ḫi-šú i-šal-lim*
12) LÚ *mu-kin-nu* ^{Id}AMAR.UD-EN-*šú-nu*
13) A-*šú šá* ^{Id}AG-SUR A ^{Id}30-*šá-du-nu*
14) ^{Id}U+GUR-GI A-*šú šá* ^{I}⌈*x*⌉ *qar*
15) A ^{Id}30-*šá-du-nu*
16) LÚ.ŠID ^{I}*tab-ni-e-a*
17) A-*šú šá* ^{I}*ri-mut* A ^{Id}EN-*e-ṭè-ru*
18) ⌈TIN.TIR.KI⌉ ITU.GAN UD.19.KAM
19) MU.SAG.NAM.LUGAL.LA ^{Id}U+GUR-LUGAL-PAP
20) [LUGAL TIN].TIR.KI

Translation

Contract with respect to the unalterable document concerning the dowry of Šulâ, son of Gimillu, descendant of Epeš-ili [...] son of Rīmūt [...] shekels of silver [...] he will bring them [...] is invalidated [...] he will satisfy [...] was received [...] he will satisfy. Witnesses (are) Marduk-bēlšunu, son of Nabû-ēṭir, descendant of Sin-šadûnu, Nergal-ušallim, son of [...] descendant of Sin-šadûnu, (and) the scribe, Tabnēa, son of Rīmūt, descendant of Bēl-ēṭir. ⌈Babylon,⌉ month of Kislimu, nineteenth day, accession year of Nergal-šarra-uṣur, [king of Ba]bylon.

79

BM 77637 (Collated)
(=Bertin no 1214)

1) [...] 4-*ut* KÙ.BABBAR *šá ina* 1 GÍN *bit-qa*
2). [...] ^{d}AMAR.UD A-*šú šá* ^{Id}BE-MU
3) [...] *bi bi ina* UGU ^{I}*la-a-ba-ši*
4) [...] A ^{I}É.SAG.ÍL-*a-a*
5) [...] *i-nam-din*
6) [...] A-*šú šá* ^{I}*tab-ni-e-a*
7) [...] ^{Id}EN-MU-A
8) [...] A LÚ.SIPA ANŠE.[KUR.RA]
9) [...] *šá* A-*šú šá* ^{I}MU-DU
10) [...]^{d}BE LÚ.ŠID ^{Id}AG-A-MU
11) [A-*šú šá*] ^{Id}AG-MU-MU A ^{I}ŠEŠ-DÙ-*i*
12) [TIN.TIR].KI ITU.NE UD.21.KAM
13) [MU.x].KAM ^{Id}U+GUR-LUGAL-ŠEŠ
14) LUGAL TIN.TIR.KI

Translation

(Document concerning) [...] one-fourth shekel of silver which has one-eighth alloy (per shekel) [...] Marduk, son of Ea-iddina, [...] charged against Labaši, [...] descendant of Esagilâ. He will deliver [...]. son of Tabnēa, [...] Bēl-nādin-apli, [...] descendant of Rē'û [sīsi], [...] son of Šuma-ukīn, [...] Ea (and) the scribe, Nabû-apla-iddina, [son of] Nabû-šuma-iddina, descendant of Aḫu-bāni. [Babylon], month of Abu, twenty-first day, [... year] of Nergal-šarra-uṣur, king of Babylon.

80

BM 41399
VR 67, I (Collated)

1) 24 GUR ŠE.NUMUN A.ŠÀ EDIN GIŠ.GIŠIMMAR.MEŠ *za-aq-pu*
2) *mi-ri-šú tap-tu-ú e-liš šap-liš šá* ÍD *eš-šu*
3) *mi-iḫ-ra-at* KÁ.GAL ^{d}EN.LÍL *pi-ḫa-at* TIN.TIR.KI
4) UŠ.AN.TA IM.MAR.TU UŠ.SA.DU ^{I}*si-li-im-*^{d}EN

5) DUMU-*šú šá* ^{I}ÈR-^{d}U+GUR DUMU ^{I}*ib-ni*-DINGIR ^{Id}AMAR.UD-NUMUN-*ú-ṣur*
6) DUMU-*šú šá* ^{I}SUM-*nu-nu* DUMU ^{Id}EN-*e-ṭè-ru* ^{Id}AG-DUMU.NITA-SUM-*na*
7) DUMU-*šú šá* ^{Id}AMAR.UD-LUGAL-*a-ni* DUMU LÚ.DÍM
8) ^{I}*kal-ba-a* DUMU-*šú šá* ^{I}*za-ki-ru* DUMU ^{Id}EN-*e-ṭè-ru*
9) UŠ.KI.TA IM.KUR.RA UŠ.SA.DU ^{Id}AG-*e-ri-iš*
10) DUMU-*šú šá* ^{I}*šu-la-a* DUMU ^{Id}30-*na-din-šu-mi*
11) SAG AN.TA IM.SI.SÁ UŠ.SA.DU A.ŠÀ *pi-ḫa-at* LUGAL
12) SAG.KI.TA IM.U$_{x}$.LU UŠ.SA.DU *ma-kal-lu-ú ša* 50.MEŠ-*e*
13) ŠU.NIGIN *24* GUR ŠE.NUMUN A.ŠÀ *šu-a-tim i -na lìb-bi*
14) 2 GUR ŠE.NUMUN A-ŠÀ GIŠ.GIŠIMMAR.MEŠ GAL.MEŠ *ki-i 6 1/3* NINDA.ḪI.A ŠE.NUMUN
15) *a-na* 1 GÍN KÙ.BABBAR 9 MA.NA KÙ.BABBAR KI.LÁ.BI 1 GUR *4* BÁN *3* SILÀ ŠE.NUMUN
16) GIŠ *ta-la-a-ni ki-i 2* SILÀ ŠE.NUMUN *a-na* 1 GÍN KÙ.BABBAR
17) *2 1/3* MA.NA *7* GÍN KÙ.BABBAR KI.LÁ.BI *u 20* GUR 5(BÁN) 2 SILÀ ŠE.NUMUN
18) A.ŠÀ *mi-ri-šú ù tap-tu-ú ki-i* 1(BÁN) ŠE.NUMUN *a-na* 1 GÍN KÙ.BABBAR
19) *10* MA.NA *4 1/3* GÍN KÙ.BABBAR KI.LÁ.BI
20) *it-ti* ^{Id}AMAR.UD-GAR-MU ^{I}BA-*šá*-^{d}AMAR.UD
21) *ù* ^{Id}AG-KAR-ZI.MEŠ DUMU.MEŠ *šá* ^{Id}AMAR.UD-*e-ṭi-ir*
22) DUMU ^{I}*e-ṭi-ru* ^{Id}AG-ŠEŠ.MEŠ-SUM-*na* DUMU-*šú šá* ^{I}*šu-la-a*
23) DUMU ^{I}*e-gi-bi ma-ḫi-ri im-bi-e-ma*
24) *21* MA.NA *51 1/3* GÍN KÙ.BABBAR *i-šá-am a-na ši-mi-šú ga-am-ru-tu*
25) *ù 1/3* MA.NA *8 2/3* GÍN KÙ.BABBAR *ki-i a-ta-ar id-din-su-nu-ti*
26) ŠU.NIGIN *22 1/3* MA.NA KÙ.BABBAR KÙ.PAD.DU *i-na qa-at*
27) ^{Id}AG-ŠEŠ.MEŠ-SUM-*na* DUMU-*šú šá* ^{I}*šu-la-a* DUMU ^{I}*e-gi-bi*
28) ^{Id}AMAR.UD-GAR-MU ^{I}BA-*šá*-^{d}AMAR.UD ^{Id}AG-DÙ-ŠEŠ *ù* ^{Id}AG-KAR-ZI.MEŠ
29) DUMU.MEŠ *šá* ^{Id}AMAR.UD-*e-ṭi-ir* DUMU ^{I}*e-ṭi-ru*
30) *ši-i-mi* A.ŠÀ-*šu-nu* KÙ.BABBAR *ga-mi-ir-tim ma-aḫ-ru*
31) *ap-lu ru-gu-um-ma-a ul i-šu-ú ul i-tur-ru-ma*
32) *a-na a-ḫa-mi-iš ul i-ra-ag-gu-mu*
33) *ma-ti-ma i-na* ŠEŠ.MEŠ DUMU.MEŠ *ki-im-ti*

34) *ni-su-tu ù sa-la-ta*
35) *šá* DUMU.MEŠ ^{I}*e-ṭi-ru šá i-rag-gu-mu um-ma*
36) A.ŠÀ *šu-a-tim ul na-din-ma* KÙ.BABBAR *ul ma-ḫi-ir*
37) *pa-qí-ir-a-ni* KÙ.BABBAR *im-ḫu-ru a-*⌜*di*⌝ 12 *ta-àm*
38) *i-ta-nap-pal* KÙ.BABBAR ŠÁM ⌜A⌝.ŠÀ *šu-a-tim*
39) *i-na* GUD.MEŠ NÍG.GA ^{d}AMAR.UD *šu-ul-lu-un-du*
40) *šá* UGU ^{Id}AMAR.UD-GAR-MU *ú* ŠEŠ.MEŠ-*šú* DUMU.MEŠ
41) *šá* ^{Id}AMAR.UD-KAR-*ir* DUMU ^{I}*e-ṭi-ru*
42) *a-na ma-ak-ku-ru* ^{d}AMAR.UD *a-na* É.SAG.ÍL *šu-ru-ub*
43) *i-na ka-na-ku* [IM].KIŠIB *šu-a-tim*
44) IGI ^{I}*mu-še-zib*-^{d}EN LÚ.GAR.UMUŠ TIN.TIR.[KI] [DUMU] ^{I}*e-li*-DINGIR.MEŠ-*ra-bi*-^{d}AMAR.UD
45) ^{I}*ri-mut*-^{d}EN-DINGIR.MEŠ DI.KU$_5$ DUMU ^{I}ŠEŠ-*ba-ni*
46) ^{Id}U+GUR-*ina*-SÙḪ-KAR-*ir* DI.KU$_5$ DUMU LÚ.GAL.DÙ
47) ^{Id}AMAR.UD-GAR-MU DI.KU$_5$ DUMU LÚ.AD.KID
48) ^{Id}AMAR.UD-GAR-MU DI.KU$_5$ DUMU ^{Id}ŠEŠ.DU-MA.AN.SUM
49) ^{I}ÈR-^{d}*gu-la* DI.KU$_5$ DUMU ^{Id}IM-*šam-me-e*
50) ^{I}*gi-mil*-^{d}*gu-la* DI.KU$_5$ DUMU ^{I}*ir-an-ni*-^{d}AMAR.UD
51) ^{Id}AG-SUM-*na* DI.KU$_5$ DUMU ^{I}*mu-dam-mi-iq*-^{d}IM
52) ^{Id}AG-*mu-tir-gi-mil* DUB.SAR DUMU ^{I}*ga-ḫúl*-^{d}TU(!).TU
53) ^{I}*šu-uš-ra-an-ni*-^{d}AMAR.UD DUB.SAR DUMU LÚ.É.MAŠ-^{d}*gu-la*
54) ^{I}*kab-ti*-DINGIR.MEŠ-^{d}AMAR.UD DUB.SAR DUMU ^{I}*su-ha-a-a*
55) ^{Id}AG-NUMUN-SI.SÁ DUB.SAR DUMU ^{I}*na-bu-un-na-a-a*
56) KÁ.DINGIR.RA.KI ITU.ZÍZ.A.ÀM UD.8.KAM MU.SAG.NAM.LUGAL.E
57) ^{Id}U+GUR-LUGAL-*ú-ṣu-ur* LUGAL KÁ.DINGIR.RA.KI
58) *ṣu-up-ru* ^{Id}AMAR.UD-GAR-MU ^{I}BA-*šá*-^{d}AMAR.UD ^{Id}AG-DÙ-ŠEŠ
59) *ù* ^{Id}AG-KAR-ZI.MEŠ *na-di-ni-e* A.ŠÀ *ki-ma* NA$_4$.KIŠIB-*šú-nu*

Seals

1) ⌜NA$_4$.KIŠIB⌝ ^{Id}AMAR.UD-GAR-⌜MU⌝ DI.KU$_5$
2) NA$_4$.KIŠIB ^{Id}AMAR.UD-GAR-MU DI.KU$_5$
3) NA$_4$.KIŠIB ^{I}ÈR-^{d}*gu-la* DI.KU$_5$
4) NA$_4$.KIŠIB ^{I}*gi-mil*-^{d}*gu-la* DI.KU$_5$
5) NA$_4$.KIŠIB ^{Id}AG-SUM-*na* DI.KU$_5$

6) NA$_4$.KIŠIB ^{Id}AG-*mu-ṭir-gi-mil* DUB.SAR
7) NA$_4$.KIŠIB ^{I}*šu-uš-ra-an-ni-*^{d}AMAR.UD DUB.SAR
8) NA$_4$.KIŠIB ^{I}*mu-še-zib-*^{d}EN LÚ.GAR.UMUŠ TIN.TIR.KI
9) NA$_4$.KIŠIB ^{I}*ri-mut*-EN-DINGIR.MEŠ DI.KU$_5$
10) NA$_4$.KIŠIB ^{Id}U+GUR-*ina*-SÙḪ-KAR-*ir* DI.KU$_5$

Translation

(Document concerning) 24 *kurru* of outlying territory, planted with date palms, planted territory, as well as newly broken ground, upstream and downstream along the new canal, opposite the gate of Enlil in the district of Babylon. The upper west side adjoins (the property of) Silim-Bēl, son of Arad-Nergal, descendant of Ibni-ili, Marduk-zēra-uṣur, son of Iddinunu, descendant of Bēl-ēṭir, Nabû-apla-iddina, son of Marduk-šarrāni, descendant of Itinnu, and (that of) Kalbâ, son of Zakir, descendant of Bēl-ēṭir. The lower east side adjoins the property of Nabû-ēriš, son of Šulâ, descendant of Sin-nādin-šumi. The upper northern length adjoins the field of the royal district (and) the lower southern length adjoins the (locality called) the Harbor of the Fifty. A total of 24 *kurru* of acreage (constitutes) that field. Of this amount, two *kurru* of arable land, a field (with) mature date palm trees, with (lit., according to which) 6 1/3 *ninda* of land (equal) to one shekel of silver, (has) a market value (lit., weight) of 9 minas of silver. One *kurru*, 27 qa of acreage (planted with) young date trees, with two qa of land (equal) to one shekel of silver, (has) a market value of 2 1/3 minas, 7 shekels of silver, and 20 *kurru*, 32 qa of acreage, planted territory as well as newly broken ground, with 6 qa of land (equal) to one shekel of silver, (has) a market value of 10 minas, 4 1/3 shekels of silver. Nabû-aḫḫē-iddina, son of Šulâ, descendant of Egibi, calculated the market value with Marduk-šākin-šumi, Iqīša-Marduk, Nabû-bāni-aḫi, and Nabû-ēṭir-napšāti, the sons of Marduk-ēṭir, descendant of Eṭēru, and he bought (the property) for the full price of 21 minas, 51 1/3 shekels of silver, and he paid (lit., gave) them (i.e., the sons of Marduk-ēṭir) an additional payment of 1/3 mina, 8 2/3 shekels of silver. A total of 22 1/3 minas of silver in pieces, the full price of their field (in) silver, was received (by) Marduk-šākin-šumi, Iqīša-Marduk, Nabû-bāni-aḫi and Nabû-ēṭir-napšāti, sons of Marduk-ēṭir, descendant of Eṭēru, from Nabû-aḫḫē-iddina, son of Šulâ, descendant of Egibi. They will not have a claim (to the property), they will not reopen suit against one another, and (if) in the future among the brothers, the sons, the family, the relatives, and the kin of the sons of Eṭēru there is someone who raises a claim and (asserts) that the field was not sold, the silver was not received, the claimant will pay twelvefold the amount of silver which he had received. (The obligation concerning) the silver, the price of that field, was realized (lit., satisfied) in connection with (lit., from) the oxen, property of Marduk, charged against Marduk-šākin-šumi and his brothers, sons of Marduk-ēṭir, descendant of Eṭēru, (and) brought to the Esagila to the treasury of Marduk.

Present at the sealing of this tablet (were) Mušēzib-Bēl, the prefect of the city of Babylon, [son of] Eli-ilāni-rābi-Marduk, Rīmūt-bēl-ili, judge, son of Aḫu-bāni, Nergal-ina-tēšî-ēṭir, judge, son of Rāb-bāni, Marduk-šākin-šumi, judge, son of Atkuppu, Marduk-šākin-šumi, judge, son of Nusku-iddina, Arad-Gula, judge, son of Adad-šamê, Gimil-Gula, judge, son of Iranni-Marduk, Nabû-iddina, judge, son of Mudammiq-Adad, Nabû-muṭir-gimil, scribe, son of Gaḫul-Marduk, Šušranni-Marduk, scribe, son of Šangû-Gula, Kābti-ilāni-Marduk, scribe, son of Suḫāja, Nabû-zēru-lišir, scribe, son of Nabunnaja. Babylon, month of Šabaṭu, eighth day, accession year of Nergal-šarra-uṣur, king of Babylon. Fingernail(marks) of Marduk-šākin-šumi, Iqīša-Marduk, Nabû-bāni-aḫi, and Nabû-ēṭir-napšāti, (signifying) the handing over of the field in the same manner as with their seals. ⌜Seal of Marduk⌝ - šākin-⌜šumi⌝, judge, seal of Marduk-šākin-šumi, judge, seal of Arad-Gula, judge, seal of Gimil-Gula, judge, seal of Nabû-iddina, judge, seal of Nabû-muṭir-gimil, scribe, seal of Šušranni-Marduk, scribe, seal of Mušēzib-Bēl, the prefect of the city of Babylon, seal of Rīmūt-bēl-ili, judge, seal of Nergal-ina-tēšî-ēṭir, judge.

Commentary

16) For a discussion of GIŠ *ta-la-a-ni*, see Landsberger, *Date Palm*, p. 1, note no. 1 and p. 2., 1.291.

23-4) For *maḫiru ... išam*, see AOATS4, note to text 22.

81

BM 30315 (Collated)
Published as VR 67 no.2

1) ^{Id}EN-TIN-*iṭ* A-*šú šá* ^{Id}AG-*ga-mil*
2) A ^{I} *e-gi-bi ina ḫu-ud lìb-bi-šú*
3) ^{f}*še-pít-su-aṣ-bat u* ^{f}*taš-li-mu*
4) LÚ.SAL *la-ta-ni-šú a-na* 1 MA.NA 3 GÍN KÙ.BABBAR
5) *a-na* ŠÁM *ḫa-ri-iṣ a-na* ^{Id}U+GUR-GI
6) A-*šú šá* ^{I}MU-MU A ^{I}DA-^{d}AMAR.UD *id-din*
7) *pu-ut si-ḫu-ú u pa-qí-ra-nu ša ina* UGU
8) ^{f}*še-pít-su-aṣ-bat u* ^{f}*taš-li-mu*

9) *il-la-a* ^{Id}EN-TIN-*iṭ na-ši*
10) LÚ *mu-kin-nu* ^{I}*ba-nu-nu* A-*šú šá* ^{I}*ṣil-la-a*
11) A LÚ.GAL.DÙ ^{I}DUB-NUMUN A-*šú šá* ^{I}*mu-še-zib*-^{d}AMAR.UD
12) A ^{I}*su-ḫa-a-a* ^{I}*mu-še-zib*-^{d}AMAR.UD
13) A-*šú šá* ^{I}ZALÁG-*e-a* A ^{Id}BE-*qa-a-lu-i-šem-me*
14) *u* LÚ.ŠID ^{I}MU-^{d}AG A-*šú šá* ^{Id}UTU-NUMUN-BA-*šá*
15) A ^{I}KAL-^{d}IM TIN.TIR.KI ITU.ZÍZ
16) UD.18.KAM MU.1.KAM
17) ^{Id}U+GUR-LUGAL-ŠEŠ LUGAL TIN.TIR.KI

Translation

Bēl-uballiṭ, son of Nabû-gamil, has, of his own free will, sold (lit., given) his slaves Šepissu-aṣbat and Tašlimu to Nergal-ušallim, son of Nādin-šumi, descendant of Ili'-Marduk, for the full price of one mina, three shekels of silver. Bēl-uballiṭ bears the responsibility (for) claims against the legality of the sale that might arise against the (slaves) Šepissu-aṣbat and Tašlimu. Witnesses (are) Banunu, son of Ṣillâ, descendant of Rāb bāni, Šāpik-zēri, son of Mušēzib-Marduk, son of Suḫāja, Mušēzib-Marduk, son of Nūrea, descendant of Ea-qalu-išemme, and the scribe, Iddina-Nabû, son of Šamaš-zēra-iqīša, descendant of Dannu-Adad. Babylon, month of Šabaṭu, eighteenth day, first year of Nergal-šarra-uṣur, king of Babylon.

82

BM 30297 (Collated)

Published as VR 67 no. 3. Published in translation by Stevenson, ABC no. 29 and de Vogué, CIS 2/1 p.63ff no. 62.

1) *a-di-i* UD-*mu šá* ^{I}*pa-ni*-^{d}AG-*ṭè-e-mu*
2) ŠEŠ-*šú šá* ^{I}DINGIR.MEŠ-*qa-nu-ú-a*
3) TA *a-ḫu-la-' ib-bi-ir*
4) SAL *bu-ra-šú pu-ut še-e-pi*
5) *šá* ^{I}DINGIR.MEŠ-*qa-nu-ú-a* DAM-*šú*
6) *ina* ŠU^{II} ^{I}*pa-ni*-^{d}AG-*ṭè-e-mu na-šá-a-tú*
7) UD-*mu šá* ^{I}*pa-ni*-^{d}AG-*tè-e-mu*
8) *i-te-bi-ir* ^{I}DINGIR.MEŠ-*qa-nu-ú-a*
9) *ta-bak-kam-ma a-na* ^{I}*pa-ni*-^{d}AG-*ṭè-e-mu*
10) *ta-nam-din*
11) LÚ *mu-kin-nu* ^{I}*šá-lam-ma-nu*
12) A-*šú šá* ^{I}*bal-tú-mu-'* LÚ.DAM.QAR LUGAL

13) ^{Id}EN-SUR A-*šú šá* ^{Id}IGI.DU-AD-ŠEŠ
14) ^{Id}IGI.DU-LUGAL-ŠEŠ A-*šú šá* ^{I}*šá-lam-ma-nu*
15) *u* LÚ.ŠID ^{Id}AG-NUMUN-MU A-*šú šá* ^{Id}IM-KAM
16) ÚḪ.KI ITU.KIN UD.2.KAM
17) MU.2.KAM ^{Id}U+GUR-LUGAL-ŠEŠ
18) LUGAL TIN.TIR.KI

Translation

Until Pāni-Nabû-ṭēmu, the brother of Ili-qanūa, crosses over from the other side, the lady Burašu, the wife of Ili-qanūa, assumes guaranty (for her husband) with respect to Pāni-Nabû-ṭēmu. When Pāni-Nabû-ṭēmu crosses over, she will bring Ili-qanūa (her husband) and she will hand him over to Pāni-Nabû-ṭēmu. Witnesses (are) Šalammanu, son of Baltumu', the royal merchant, Bēl-ēṭir, son of Nergal-aba-uṣur, Nergal-šarra-uṣur, son of Šalammanu, and the scribe, Nabû-zēra-iddina, son of Adad-ēriš.Akšak, month of Ululu, second day, second year of Nergal-šarra-uṣur, king of Babylon.

83

BM 30599 (Collated)
Published as VR 67, no. 4

1) 5 LIM *gi-dil šá* SUM.SAR
2) 7 GUR 2(PI) 3(BÁN) ŠE.BAR *šá* ^{I}MU-^{d}AMAR.UD
3) A-*šú šá* ^{I}BA-*šá-a* A ^{I}ZALÁG-^{d}30 *ina muḫ-ḫi*
4) ^{I}ŠEŠ-*it-tab-ši* A-*šú šá* ^{Id}AG-*ma-lik*
5) *ina* ITU.GUD *gi-dil u* ŠE.BAR *ina muḫ-ḫi*
6) ÍD *bar-sip* KI *ina muḫ-ḫi* ÍD
7) *i-nam-din e-lat ú-ìl-tim*
8) IGI-*tum šá gi-dil u* ŠE.BAR
9) LÚ *mu-kin-nu* ^{Id}EN-SUR A-*šú šá* ^{I}*ina*-SÙḪ-SUR
10) A ^{I}*dam-qa* ^{I}MU-^{d}AG A-*šú šá*
11) ^{Id}AG-*mu-še-ti-iq*-UD.DA
12) A ^{I}*nu-ḫa-šú u* LÚ.ŠID
13) ^{I}É.SAG.-ÍL-MU-DÙ A-*šú šá*
14) ^{I}DI.KU$_5$-^{d}AMAR.UD A ^{I}*mu-še-zib*
15) TIN.TIR.KI ITU.GAN UD.23.KAM
16) MU.3.KAM ^{d}U+GUR-LUGAL-ŠEŠ
17) LUGAL TIN.TIR.KI

Translation

(Document concerning) five thousand strings of garlic (and) seven *kurru*, two pi, eighteen qa of barley, property of Iddina-Marduk, son of Iqīša, descendant of Nūr-Sin, charged against Aḫa-ittabši, son of Nabû-mālik. He will deliver the strings (of garlic) and the barley on the bank of the Borsippa canal in the month of Ajaru. (This is) apart from the former contract concerning strings (of garlic) and barley. Witnesses (are) Bēl-ēṭir, son of Ina-tēši-eṭir, descendant of Damqa, Iddina-Nabû, son of Nabû-mušētiq-uddê, descendant of Nuḫašu, and the scribe, Esagila-šuma-ibni, son of Dajān-Marduk, descendant of Mušēzib. Babylon, month of Kislimu, twenty-third day, third year of Nergal-šarra-uṣur, king of Babylon.

84

BM 74937 (Collated)
Published by Winckler, ZA 2 168

1) *ul* GUR-*ma* ^{Id}AG-DU-IGI A-*šú šá*
2) ^{I}DINGIR.MEŠ-MU *a-na* UGU *u-di-šú*
3) *ma-la ba-šu-ú it-ti* ^{Id}EN-MU
4) A-*šú šá* ^{Id}U+GUR-*ú-še-zib ul i-dab-bu-ub*
5) u ^{Id}EN-MU *ša* UGU *ra-šu-ti-šú*
6) *it-ti* ^{Id}AG-DU-IGI *ul i-dab-bu-ub*
7) *ta-a-ri u da-ba-bi*
8) *ia-a-nu*
9) LÚ *mu-kin-ni* ^{Id}AG-MUG-*e-lip*
10) A-*šú šá* ^{I}*mu-šib-ši* A ^{I}Á.GÁL-*e-a*
11) ^{Id}UTU-DU-A A-*šú šá* ^{I}*ba-la-ṭu*
12) A ^{Id}AG-*ú-še-zib* LÚ *qal-la šá* LÚ TIL.LA.GID.DA
13) *šá é-sag-gil* LÚ.ŠID
14) ^{I}ÈR-^{d}EN A-*šú šá* ^{Id}EN-GI
15) A ^{Id}IM-*šam-me-e sip-par* KI
16) ITU.AB UD.3.KAM MU.1.KAM
17) ^{d}U+GUR-LUGAL-ŠEŠ LUGAL TIN.TIR.KI

Translation

Nabû-ālik-pāni, son of Ili-iddina, will not renew litigation with Bēl-iddina, son of Nergal-ušēzib, concerning his possessions, as much as he owns, and Bēl-iddina will not litigate with Nabû-ālik-pāni concerning his property.

There will be no renewal of litigation (between them). Witnesses (are) Nabû-mukku-elip,son of Mušēzib, descendant of Li'ea, Šamaš-mukīn-apli, son of Balāṭu, descendant of Nabû-ušēzib, the slave of the overseer of Esagila, (and) the scribe, Arad-Bēl, son of Bēl-ušallim, descendant of Adad-šamê.Sippar, month of Ṭebetu, third day, first year of Nergal-šarra-uṣur, king of Babylon.

85

BM 33350

1) 1/2 MA.NA ⸢x⸣ GÍN KÙ.BABBAR *šá* ^{I}KI-^{d}AG-[TIN]
2) A-*šú šá* ^{I}MU-MU A ^{I}*maš-tuk ina* UGU ^{Id}AMAR.UD-⸢EN⸣-⸢NUMUN⸣
3) A-*šú šá* ^{I}*mu-še-zib*-^{d}AMAR.UD A ^{I}*maš-tuk* SAL *ta-ap-lu-šu*
4) SAL *la-*[*ta-ni*]*-su maš-ka-nu šá* ^{I}KI-^{d}AG-TIN *a-di* 2-*ta* MU.MEŠ
5) *i-di a-me-lut-tum ia-a-nu u* ḪAR.RA KÙ.BABBAR
6) *ia-a-nu ina* UD-*mu a-na a-šar šá-nam-ma*
7) ⸢*ta*⸣*-at-*⸢*ta*⸣*-al-ka* UD-*mu* 3 *qa* ŠE.BAR
8) ^{Id}⸢AMAR⸣.[UD-EN]-NUMUN *i-nam-din* KÙ.BABBAR *ša*
9) ⸢*x*⸣ GÍN [...] *i-nam-din ina a-šá-bi*
10) *šá* SAL *be-lit* DUMU.⸢SAL⸣ [...] *ni šá* ^{Id}AMAR.UD-EN-[NUMUN] [...]
11) *šá* ^{I}*mun-na-bit-ti* AMA *šá*
12) ^{Id}AMAR.UD-EN-⸢NUMUN⸣
13) LÚ *mu-kin-nu* ^{I}A-*a* A-*šú šá* ^{I}NÍG.DU
14) ⸢A ^{I}ZALÁG⸣-^{d}30 ^{Id}AG-MU-ŠEŠ A-*šú šá* ^{Id}⸢*xxx*⸣
15) A ^{I}*e-g-bi* ^{Id}U+GUR-TIN-*iṭ* A-*šú šá*
16) ^{I}KI-^{d}EN-*lum-mir* A ^{I}*ba-si-ía*
17) ^{Id}AMAR.UD-LUGAL-*a-ni* A-*šú šá* ^{Id}AMAR.UD-SUR
18) [A] LÚ.A.ZU *u* LÚ.ŠID ^{Id}AMAR.UD-EN-NUMUN
19) A-*šú šá* ^{I}*mu-še-zib*-^{d}AMAR.UD A ^{I}*maš-tuk*
20) TIN.TIR.KI ITU.GUD UD.15.KAM
21) MU.2.KAM ^{d}U+GUR-LUGAL-ŠEŠ
22) ⸢LUGAL⸣ TIN.TIR.KI

Translation

(Document concerning) one-half mina, ... ⸢shekels⸣ of silver, property of Itti-Nabû-[balāṭu], son of Šuma-iddina, descendant of Maštuk, charged against Marduk-⸢bēl-zēri,⸣, son of Mušēzib-Marduk, descendant of Maštuk. The lady Taplušu, his slave, (serves as) security for Itti-Nabû-balāṭu. For two years there will be no wages (to pay) for the slave and no interest on the silver. Whenever she goes elsewhere, ⸢Marduk⸣-[bēl]-zēri will deliver (i.e., pay) three qa of barley daily. The silver, namely ... shekels [...] he will deliver. In the presence of the lady Bēlit, daughter of Marduk-bēl-[zēri] [...] descendant of Munnabitti, mother of Marduk-bēl-[zēri]. Witnesses°(are) Aplâ, son of Kudurru, ⸢descendant of Nūr⸣ Sin, Nabû-šuma-uṣur, son of [...] descendant of Egibi, Nergal-uballiṭ, son of Itti-Bēl-lummir, descendant of Basija, Marduk-šarrāni, son of Marduk-ēṭir, [descendant of] Asû and the scribe, Marduk-bēl-zēri, son of Mušēzib-Marduk, descendant of Maštuk. Babylon, month of Ajaru, fifteenth day, second year of Nergal-šarra-uṣur, king of Babylon.

Commentary

1) Restoration of the personal name is based on the contents of l. 4.

2,8,12) Restoration of the personal name is based on the contents of l. 18.

86

BM 32602

1) [...] LÚ] *qal-la šá* ^{Id}AG-ŠEŠ.MEŠ-*id-din*
2) [A-*šú šá* ^{I}*šu-la-a*] A ^{I}*e-gi-bi*
3) [...] ŠU^{II} ^{Id}U+GUR-TIN-*iṭ*
4) [...] DU A ^{Id}BE-DINGIR-*ṭi*-DÙ
5) [...] *ip-ta-a* DAM-*šú*
6) [...] *ú-ìl-tim a-na šu-mu*
7) [...] *ni* LÚ.SAG.LUGAL
8) [...] *ša* ^{Id}AG-ŠEŠ.MEŠ-MU
9) [...] *mu* É ŠU^{II}
10) [...] *qal-la ia-a-nu*
11) [...] BA-*šá-an-ni* A-*šú šá* ^{I}DÙ-*ia*
12) A ^{Id}ILLAT-I ^{I}EN-*šú-nu* A-*šú šá* ^{Id}AG-NUMUN-GÁL-*ši*
13) A LÚ.PA.ŠE.KI u LÚ.ŠID ^{Id}EN-BA-*šá*
14) A-*šú šá* ^{Id}U+GUR-GI A ^{Id}30-SIZKUR.SIZKUR-ŠE.GA
15) [TIN].TIR.KI ITU.ŠE UD 9.KAM MU.1.KAM
16) [^{d}U+]GUR-LUGAL-ŠEŠ LUGAL TIN.TIR.KI

Translation

[...] the slave of Nabû-aḫḫē-iddina, [son of Šulâ], descendant of Egibi [...] by Nergal-uballiṭ, [...] ukin, descendant of Ea-ilūtu-ibni, [Ḫi]ptâ(?), his wife. [...] the contract in the name [...] the royal official [...] of Nabû-aḫḫē-iddina [...] the storehouse [...] the slave [...] Iqīšanni(?), son of Bānija, descendant of Illat-na'id, Bēlšunu, son of Nabû-zēra-ušabši, descendant of the Isinite, and the scribe, Bēl-iqīša, son of Nergal-ušallim, descendant of Sin-karābi-išemme. [Baby]lon, month of Addaru, ninth day, first year of [Ne]rgal-šarra-uṣur, king of Babylon.

87

BM 75509

1) 6 [...] ⸢*xx*⸣ *ú šá qí-rib* UD.KIB.NUN.KI
2) [*šá* ^{I}] ⸢*na*⸣-'-*id*-⸢^{d}⸣ [AMAR.UD DUMU-*šú šá* ^{I}*šu*]-*la-a* DUMU ^{I}MU-^{d}AMAR.UD
3) *ina* ŠU^{II} ^{Id}AG-APIN-*eš* [...] DUMU ^{Id}30-ZAG.[LU]
4) *a-na* 1 MA.NA 5 GÍN KÙ.BABBAR *a-na* ŠÁM *gam-ru-tu im-ḫu-ru*
5) ⸢*xxx*⸣ *šá* É ⸢*xx*⸣ *šá* ⸢*xx*⸣ *mu šú ik-nu-ku*
6) [...] *ma-na-a-ti šá* ^{I}GI-^{d}AMAR.UD DUMU-*šú šá* ^{Id}UTU-MU-*ú-kin*
7) [DUMU] LÚ.É.MAŠ UD.KIB.NUN.KI É *im-ta-ḫar* [...]
8) [1 MA].NA 5 ⸢GÍN⸣ [KÙ.BABBAR] ⸢*a*⸣-*na* ŠÁM É *šu-a-tim* SUM.NA
9) [...] GABA.RI IM.KIŠIB
10) [...] ⸢*ri*⸣ *ri-ka-su šá* KI.LAM *pa-nu-ú*
11) ⸢*šá*⸣ É *šu-a-tim šá a-na* ⸢MU⸣ ^{I}I-^{d}⸢AMAR.UD⸣ DUMU-*šú*
12) [*šá*] ^{I}*šu-la-a* ⸢*la*⸣-IGI $^{[I]}$*tab-ni-e-a* DUMU-*šú*
13) *šá* ^{I}*ki-rib-ti iš-šá-am-ma a-na* ^{I}GI-^{d}AMAR.UD
14) *id-di-nu a-šar il-ku-nu šá* ^{I}GI-^{d}AMAR.UD
15) LÚ *mu-kin-nu* ^{I}*ba-la-ṭu* A-*šú šá* ^{I}*zi-ka-ri* A LÚ.PA.ŠE.KI
16) ^{I}*mu-še-zib*-^{d}AMAR.UD A-*šú šá* ^{Id}UTU-NUMUN-DÙ A LÚ.ŠID ^{d}INNIN TIN.TIR.KI
17) ^{Id}AG-MU-DU A-*šú šá* ^{Id}AMAR.UD-MU-DÙ A ^{I}*dan-ni-e-a*
18) ^{I}ÈR-^{d}EN A-*šú šá* ^{Id}AG-ŠEŠ.MEŠ-MU A LÚ.PA.ŠE.KI
19) ^{I}*tab-ni-e-a* A-*šú šá* ^{I}*ki-rib-ti* A ^{I}ÈR-^{d}GIR$_4$.KÙ
20) ^{Id}UTU-SIG$_5$-*iq* A-*šú šá* ^{I}*bul-lu-ṭu* A LÚ.PA.ŠE.KI
21) *u* ^{I}*na-'-id*-^{d}AMAR.UD LÚ.DUB.SAR A-*šú šá* ^{I}*šu-la-a*
22) A ^{I}MU-^{d}AMAR.UD UD.KIB.NUN.KI ITU.NE UD.20.KAM

23) MU.2.KAM ^{d}U+GUR-LUGAL-ŠEŠ LUGAL TIN.TIR.KI

Translation

(Document concerning) six [...] in the midst of Sippar [which] ⌜Na'id⌝-[Marduk, son of Šul]â, descendant of Iddina-Marduk, bought (lit., received) from Nabû-ēriš, [...] descendant of Sin-imit[ti], for one mina, five shekels of silver as the full price [...] of the house [...] which [...] he sealed [...] the accounting of Mušallim-Marduk, son of Šamaš-šuma-ukīn, [descendant] of Šangû Sippar; he bought (lit., received) the property [...]. He paid (lit., gave) [one mi]na, five ⌜shekels⌝ [of silver] as the (full) price of that house. [...]. He will bring the corresponding document of sale [...] the earlier contract for the sale ⌜of⌝ that house which was in the ⌜name⌝ of ⌜Na'id-Marduk,⌝ son [of] Šulâ (and) which was assigned to Tabnēa, son of Kiribti and he will give(!) (them) to Mušallim-Marduk. Wherever they (i.e, the contracts of sale) are found, they are the property of Mušallim-Marduk. Witnesses (are) Balāṭu, son of Zikari, descendant of the Isinite, Mušēzib-Marduk, son of Šamaš-zēra-ibni, descendant of Šangû Ištar Bābili, Nabû-šuma-ukīn, son of Marduk-šuma-ibni, descendant of Dannēa, Arad-Bēl, son of Nabû-aḫḫē-iddina, descendant of the Isinite, Tabnēa, son of Kiribti, descendant of Arad-Nergal, Šamas-udammiq, son of Bulluṭu, descendant of the Isinite, and Na'id-Marduk, the scribe, son of Šulâ, descendant of Iddina-Marduk. Sippar, month of Abu, twentieth day, second year of Nergal-šarra-uṣur, king of Babylon.

Commentary

2) The restoration is based on the contents of lines 21-22.

88

BM 75757

1) 2 GÍN KÙ.BABBAR *šá ina* 1 GÍN *bit-qa šá*
2) $^{[I]d}$AG-*na-ṣir* A-*šú šá* ^{I}*é-kur-ra-*⌜*ta*⌝
3) A LÚ ŠID UD.KIB.NUN.KI *ina muḫ-ḫi*
4) ^{Id}*hum-hum-ia*-ŠEŠ-MU A-*šú šá*
5) ^{I}*bi-ri-qu-' ina* ITU.ŠE *i*-[*nam*]-*din*
6) *e-lat* ŠE.BAR LÚ *mu-kin-ni*
7) ^{Id}AMAR.UD-MU-DÙ A-*šú šá* ^{Id}U+GUR-TIN-⌜*iṭ*⌝
8) A ^{I}ZÁLAG-^{d}30 ^{I}*tab-ni-e-a*
9) A-*šú šá* ^{I}*ki-rib-tú*

10) A ^{I}ÈR-^{d}GIR$_{4}$.KÙ
11) *u* LÚ.ŠID ^{Id}⸢*x*⸣-⸢GI⸣ A-*šú šá* ^{I}NUMUN-*tú*
12) A ^{I}*mi-ṣir-a-a* UD.KIB.NUN.KI
13) ITU.DU$_{6}$ UD.⸢*x*⸣.KAM
14) MU.SAG.[NAM].LUGAL.LA
15) [^{Id}]U+GUR-[LUGAL]-⸢ŠEŠ⸣ LUGAL TIN.[TIR.KI]

Translation

(Document concerning) two shekels of silver which have one-eighth alloy (per shekel), property of Nabû-nāṣir, son of Ekurrata, descendant of Šangû Sippar, charged against Ḫumḫumija(?)-aḫa-iddina, son of Biriqu. He will deliver (the silver) in the month of Addaru. (This is) apart from the barley (owed). Witnesses (are) Marduk-šuma-ibni, son of Nergal-uballiṭ, descendant of Nūr Sin, Tabnēa, son of Kiribtu, descendant of Arad-Nergal and the scribe, ... ⸢ušallim,⸣ son of Zērūtu, descendant of Miṣirāja. Sippar, month of Tašritu, ... day, acc[ess]ion year of Nergal-[šarra]-⸢uṣur,⸣ king of Ba[bylon].

89

BM 33796

1) 37 GUR ZÚ.LUM.MA ZAG.LU *šá* ^{Id}UTU-MU-GIŠ
2) A-*šú šá* ^{Id}AG-NUMUN-GÁL-*ši u* SAL *ni-din-tum*-^{d}*be-lit*
3) DUMU.SAL-*su šá* ^{Id}UTU-MU-DU ⸢*xxx*⸣ *tu*
4) *u* ^{I}*nu-ur-e-a* DUMU.⸢MEŠ⸣ *šá* ^{I}ŠEŠ.MEŠ-*ša-a* A ^{I}[...]
5) ZÚ.LUM.MA *gam-ru-tu ina ma-ši-*⸢*ḫu*⸣ *šá* ^{Id}UTU-MU-DU
6) *ina* 1-*it rit-tú ina ha-ṣa-ri gim-ri*
7) *šá a-di* UGU ÍD *i-na-ad-di-nu-'*
8) *ina* UGU 1 GUR *tu-ḫal-la lìb-bi-lìb-bi*
9) *man-ga-ga gi-pu-ú* ⸢*bil*⸣-*tú*
10) *ša hu-šá-bi* ⸢*xx*⸣ [...]
11) *i-na-ad-di-nu*
12) LÚ *mu-kin-nu* ^{I}*mu-šal-lim*-^{d}AMAR.⸢UD⸣ [A-*šú šá*]
13) ^{Id}AMAR.UD-MU-MU A ^{I}*ši*-⸢*gu-ú*⸣-*a*
14) ^{Id}AG-MU(!)(text:ME)-GIŠ A-*šú šá* ^{Id}AG-[*e*]-*ṭir*
15) A ^{Id}BE-DINGIR-*tú*-DÙ [*u*] LÚ.ŠID(!)
16) ^{Id}EN-A-MU A-*šú šá* ^{Id}[...] ⸢*x*⸣
17) TIN.TIR.KI ITU.KIN ⸢UD.x.KAM⸣ MU.2.KAM
18) [^{d}]U+GUR-LUGAL-⸢ŠEŠ⸣ [LUGAL TIN.TIR].KI

Translation

(Document concerning) thirty-seven *kurru* of dates, (estimated) yield of Šamaš-šumu-lišir, son of Nabû-zēra-ušabši, and the lady Nidintum-bēlit, daughter of Šamaš-šuma-ukīn, [...] and Nūrea, sons of Aḫḫēšâ, descendant of [...]. They will deliver the entire amount of dates at the enclosure on the bank of the watercourse in one delivery in accordance with the measure of Šamaš-šuma-ukīn. They will deliver with every *kurru* the baskets, leaves, fibers, baskets and a load of poles [...]. Witnesses (are) Mušallim-Marduk, [son of] Marduk-šuma-iddina, descendant of Ši⌈gū⌉a, Nabû-šumu(!)-lišir, son of Nabû-[ē]ṭir, descendant of Ea-ilūtu-ibni [and] the scribe(!) Bēl-apla-iddina, son of [...]. Babylon, month of Ululu, ⌈... day⌉, second year of Nergal-šarra-⌈uṣur,⌉ [king of Babylon].

90

BM 79569

1) ⌈ŠE.BAR⌉ *ri-ḫa-ni šá* MU.SAG.NAM. ⌈LUGAL. ⌉LA
2) MU.1.KAM LÚ- ^{d}AMAR.UD LUGAL TIN.TIR. ⌈KI ⌉
3) *šá ina* IGI ^{I}*mar-duk*
4) ŠE.BAR ZÚ.LUM.MA
5) KU 34 GUR 4 BÁN *šá*
MU.SAG.NAM.LUGAL.LA
6) LÚ-[^{d}AMAR.UD]
7) 1 ME 20 20 *šá* MU.1.KAM LÚ-^{d}AMAR.UD
8) [...] 1 ME 80 GUR ŠE.BAR ⌈53⌉ [...]
9) *ri-ḫa-nu šá eš-ru-*[*ú*] [...]
10) MU.SAG.NAM.LUGAL.LA
11) LÚ-^{d}⌈AMAR.UD⌉ ⌈LUGAL⌉ [TIN.TIR.KI]
12) *ina* IGI ^{I}*mar-duk*
13) ITU.BÁR UD.⌈28⌉.KAM [MU] [...]
14) ^{d}U+GUR-LUGAL-⌈ŠEŠ⌉ [LUGAL TIN.TIR.KI]

Translation

(Document concerning) ⌈barley⌉ and remaining (commodities) for the accession year and first year of Amēl-Marduk, king of Babylon which (were) placed at the disposal of Marduk.

Sixty (*kurru*) of barley, thirty-four *kurru*, twenty-four qa of dates for the accession year of Amēl-Marduk, one hundred twenty (*kurru*) of barley, twenty (*kurru*) of dates for the first year of Amēl-[Marduk. [...] one hundred eighty *kurru* of barley (and) ⸢fifty-three⸣ [...] remainder of the tithe [...] accession year of Amēl-⸢Marduk,⸣ ⸢king⸣ [of Babylon] placed at the disposal of Marduk [...] Month of Nisanu, ⸢twenty-eighth⸣ day, [...] [year] of Nergal-šarra-⸢uṣur,⸣ [king of Babylon].

91

BM 75489

1) 4-*ut* ⸢*xx*⸣ ⸢GÍN⸣ KÙ.BABBAR *a-na dar na*
2) ŠUK.ḪI.A *šá* ⸢LÚ *qí-i*⸣*-pi a-na*
3) [...] *um-man-nu šá* TA TIN.TIR.KI
4) [...] *li da nu* ⸢*xxx*⸣
5) [...] *a-na* ⸢ *a nu tum* ⸣ *a-na*
6) ⸢*xxxx*⸣ 4-*ut* KÙ.BABBAR
7) *a-na* ^{Id}UTU-ŠEŠ-MU *ma-ḫir*
8) ITU.GUD [UD].⸢4.⸣KAM
9) MU.SAG.NAM.LUGAL.LA
10) ^{Id}U+GUR-LUGAL-ŠEŠ
11) LUGAL E.KI

Translation

(Document concerning) ... ⸢shekels⸣ of silver for ... provisions which the ⸢overseer⸣ brought(?) for [...] craftsmen from Babylon [...] for [...] for [...] of silver was received for Šamaš-aḫa-iddina. Month of Ajaru, ⸢fourth⸣ [day], accession year of Nergal-šarra-uṣur, king of Babylon.

92

BM 74953

1) 20 GUR 1 (PI) 1 (BÁN) 3 *qa* ŠE.BAR *eš*-⸢*ru*⸣*-ú*
2) GÁ.DUB *šá* ^{I}BA-*šá-a* A-*šú šá* ^{I}*šá*-^{d}AG-*šu*-[*ú*]
3) *a-na* É.BABBAR.RA *it-ta-din*
4) ITU.NE UD.24.KAM
5) MU.SAG.NAM.LUGAL.LA
6) ^{Id}U+GUR-LUGAL-ŠEŠ ⸢LUGAL⸣ TIN.TIR.KI
7) ŠE.BAR *ina* ⸢*x*⸣ [...]

Translation

(Document concerning) twenty *kurru*, one pi, nine qa of barley, tithe of the *šandabakku* official which Iqīša, son of Ša Nabû-šū, delivered to the Ebabbar. Month of Abu, twenty-fourth day, accession year of Nergal-šarra-uṣur, ⸢king⸣ of Babylon. The barley is [...].

93

BM 75285

1) 1 GÍN KÙ.BABBAR *a-na pi-ḫi-e*
2) *šá* GIŠ.MÁ.MEŠ *a-na*
3) ^{I}*ta-qiš* SUM-*in*
4) ⸢*xxx*⸣ *a-na*
5) 2 *na-ap-ṭu*
6) *a-na* DUG *qa-bu-tú*
7) *a-na* ^{Id}UTU-TIN-*iṭ*
8) ITU.BÁR UD.⸢*x*⸣.KAM
9) MU.1.KAM ⸢^{d}U+GUR⸣-LUGAL-ŠEŠ
10) LUGAL TIN.TIR.KI

Translation

(Document concerning) one shekel of silver for calk for boats given to Taqiš. [...] for two (measures) of naphtha for a bowl for Šamaš-uballiṭ. Month of Nisanu, ... day, first year of ⸢Nergal⸣-šarra-uṣur, king of Babylon.

Commentary

6) For parallel usage of *qabutu* and *napṭu*, cf.text 41:4ff.

94

BM 75181

1) 1-*en* KUŠ *gi-il-du* [...]
2) 28 *ši di ip* [...]
3) 2-*u* KUŠ *gi-il-du*
4) 28 *ši di ip* [...]

5) *a-na* 18 *šá* ⌜*x*⌝ [...]
6) *ina* IGI ^{Id}AG [...]
7) ITU.NE UD.24.KAM
8) MU ⌜SAG⌝.NAM.LUGAL.LA
9) ⌜^{d}U+GUR⌝-LUGAL-ŠEŠ
10) LUGAL TIN.TIR.KI

Translation

(Document concerning) one hide [...] twenty-eight [...] a second hide, twenty-eighth [...] for eighteen [...] placed at the disposal of Nabû [...] Month of Abu, twenty-fourth day, accession year of ⌜Nergal⌝-šarra-uṣur, king of Babylon.

95

BM 67012

1) 38 GÚ.UN ZID.DA
2) ^{I}la-*ba-ši a-na*
3) É.BABBAR.RA *it-ta-din*
4) [ITU].ŠE UD.14.KAM
5) [MU].SAG.NAM.LUGAL.LA
6) [^{d}]U+GUR-LUGAL-ŠEŠ
7) [LUGAL] TIN.TIR.KI

Translation

Labaši has delivered (lit., given) thirty-eight talents of flour to Ebabbar. [Month] of Addaru, fourteenth day, accession [year] of Nergal-šarra-uṣur, [king] of Babylon.

96

BM 60947

1) 10 MA.NA SÍG.ḪI.A
2) *ina pap-pa-su ša* ITU.GAN
3) LÚ.MU-*ú-tu a-na*
4) SAL *e-til-li-tum*
5) SUM-*in* ITU.APIN

6) UD.9.KAM MU.3.[KAM]
7) ^{d}U+GUR-LUGAL-ŠEŠ
8) LUGAL TIN.TIR.KI
9) 5 MA.NA ^{I}*lib-luṭ*
10) 2 MA.[NA] ^{Id}*bu-ne-ne*-LUGAL-ŠEŠ
11) 2 MA.NA ⌜4⌝ GÍN SÍG ^{Id}UTU-KÁD DUMU-*šú*
12) *šá* ^{Id}UTU-KI-*ia* LÚ.⌜NAGAR⌝

Translation

(Document concerning) ten minas of wool, from the allowance for the month of Kislimu (for) the cook delivered (lit., given) to the lady Etillitum. Month of Araḫsamnu, ninth day, third year of Nergal-šarra-uṣur, king of Babylon. Five minas (are) for Libluṭ, two mi[nas] (are for) Bunene-šarra-uṣur, (and) two minas, ⌜four⌝ shekels of wool (are for) Šamaš-kāṣir, son of Šamaš-ittija, the ⌜carpenter.⌝

97

BM 60231

1) 3 (BÁN) *saḫ-*⌜*li-e*⌝
2) *a-na* 1 (PI) 4 (BÁN) ŠE.BAR *i-na*
3) *ma-la-a-tum*
4) *šá* ITU.BÁR MU.⌜2⌝.KAM
5) ^{I}NUMUN-TIN.TIR.[KI]
6) *ma-ḫir* ITU.⌜BÁR⌝
7) UD.26.KAM
8) MU.SAG.NAM.[LUGAL.LA]
9) ^{Id}U+GUR-⌜LUGAL-ŠEŠ⌝
10) LUGAL ⌜TIN.TIR.KI⌝

Translation

(Document concerning) eighteen qa of ⌜cress seeds,⌝ for one pi, twenty-four qa of barley from the offering for the month of Nisanu, [second] year, (which) Zēr-Bābili has received. Month of ⌜Nisanu(?)⌝ twenty-sixth day, acce[ssion] year of Nergal-⌜šarra-uṣur,⌝ king of ⌜Babylon.⌝

98

BM 60762

1) 15 GUR ZÚ.LUM.MA *šá* ^{Id}UTU-ZALÁG-*ir*
2) A-*šú šá* ^{I}*di-ḫu-um ina muḫ-ḫi* ^{I}*kal-bi-ia*
3) ⌈A-*šú šá*⌉ ^{Id}UTU-MU *ina* ITU.DU$_6$ ZÚ.LUM.MA
4) *ina muḫ-ḫi* 1 GUR 1 PI *i-nam-*[*din*]
5) LÚ *mu-kin-nu* ^{Id}EN-MU ⌈A-*šú šá*⌉
6) ^{Id}⌈AG⌉ ⌈*xxxx*⌉
7) ^{Id}[...]
8) *u* LÚ.ŠID ^{Id}AG-NUMUN-TUK-*ši* A-*šú šá*
9) ^{Id}AG-PAP A ^{I}*da-bi-bi sip-par* KI
10) ITU.GUD UD.27.KAM MU.⌈1.⌉KAM
11) ^{d}U+GUR-LUGAL-ŠEŠ LUGAL TIN.[TIR.KI]

Translation

(Document concerning) fifteen *kurru* of dates, property of Šamaš-inammir, son of Diḫummu, charged against Kalbija, ⌈son of⌉ Šamaš-iddina. He will deli[ver] the dates (with an additional) one pi charged against every *kurru* in the month of Tašritu. Witnesses (are) Bēl-iddina, ⌈son of⌉ ⌈Nabû⌉ [...] and the scribe, Nabû-zēra-ušabši, son of Nabû-nāṣir, descendant of Dabibi. Sippar, month of Ajaru, twenty-seventh day, ⌈first⌉ year of Nergal-šarra-uṣur, king of Bab[ylon].

99

BM 75431

1) 10 *ma-ši-ḫi šá* ZÚ.LUM.MA
2) *ma-ak-ka-su ina* SAT.TUK
3) *šá* ITU.KIN *ša* LÚ.MU-*ú-*[*tu*]
4) *a-na* ^{Id}AG-NUMUN-DU A-*šú*
5) *šá* ^{Id}AMAR.UD-MU-⌈DÙ⌉ [...]
6) u ^{I}NUMUN-*ia* A-*šú šá* ^{I}⌈*xxx*⌉ [...]
7) A ^{I}*na-ba-*[*a-a*] [...]
8) 3 [...]
9) ITU. [...]
10) MU.[SAG].⌈NAM⌉.LUGAL.LA
11) ^{Id}U+GUR-LUGAL-ŠEŠ

12) LUGAL TIN.TIR.KI

Translation

(Document concerning) ten measures of choice-quality dates from the regular offering of the month of Ululu belonging to the cooks(?)[...] to Nabû-zēra-ukīn. son of Marduk-šuma-⌜ibni,⌝ [...] and Zērija, son of [...] Nabāja [...] three [...] Month of [...], ac[ces]sion year of ⌜Nergal⌝-šarra-uṣur, king of Babylon.

100

BM 74938

1) ⌜20⌝ DUG *dan-na šá* KAŠ.DU$_{10}$.GA ⌜*a-na*⌝ ⌜x MA.NA⌝ KÙ.BABBAR
2) *šá* ^{Id}EN-GI A-*šú šá* ^{Id}AG-GÁL-*ši* A ^{Id}IM-*šam-me-e*
3) 1/2 MA.NA KÙ.BABBAR *šá* ^{Id}AMAR.UD-MU-DÙ A-*šú šá* ^{Id}EN-⌜ŠEŠ.⌝MEŠ-MU
4) A ^{Id}IM-*šam-me-e šá it-ti a-ḫa-meš*
5) *a-na* KASKAL^{II} *iš-ku-nu ina* IGI ^{Id}UTU-NUMUN-⌜DÙ⌝
6) A-*šú šá* ^{Id}EN-ŠEŠ.MEŠ-MU ^{I}ÈR-^{d}EN A-*šú*
7) *šá* ^{Id}EN-GI *mim-ma ma-la ina* UGU
8) *e-pu-uš-' a-ḫa-ta-šú-nu*
9) [MU].AN.NA 8 GÍN ⌜KÙ.BABBAR⌝ *i-*⌜*di*⌝ ⌜*šá* É⌝
10) [...] *ri-šú-nu* ⌜x⌝ ITU ^{Id}AMAR.UD-MU-DÙ
11) *i-nam-din-nu*
12) [LÚ] *mu-kin-ni* ^{Id}EN-ŠEŠ.MEŠ-MU A-⌜*šú*⌝ *šá*
13) ^{Id}AG-ŠEŠ.MEŠ-*šul-lim* A LÚ.ŠID ^{d}UTU
14) ^{Id}EN-ŠEŠ.MEŠ-MU A-*šú šá* ^{Id}AG-*ú-bul-liṭ*
15) LÚ.ŠID ^{I}ÈR-^{d}EN A-*šú šá* ^{Id}EN-GI
16) A ^{Id}IM-*šam-me-e* UD.KIB.NUN.KI ITU.GUD
17) ⌜UD.⌝18.KAM MU.1.KAM ^{d}U+GUR-LUGAL-ŠEŠ
18) LUGAL TIN.TIR.⌜KI⌝ *ul-tu* UD.20.KAM *ša* ITU.GUD
19) É *ina pa-ni-sú-nu*

Translation

(Document concerning) ⌜twenty⌝ containers of fine beer for ⌜minas⌝ of silver, property of Bēl-ušallim, son of Nabû-ušabši, descendant of Adad-šamê, and one-half mina of silver, property of Marduk-šuma-ibni, son of Bēl-⌜aḫḫē⌝-iddina, descendant of Adad-šamê, which they deposited with one another for a business venture (and) placed at the disposal of Šamaš-zēra-ibni, son of Bēl-aḫḫē-iddina and Arad-Bēl, the son of Bēl-ušallim (i.e., their relatives). They share and share alike whatever they earn (i.e., in the business venture). They will deliver (lit., give) ⸢monthly⸣ eight shekels ⸢of silver⸣ as ⸢rent of the house⸣ [...] to Marduk-šuma-ibni. Witnesses (are) Bēl-aḫḫē-iddina, son of Nabû-aḫḫē-šullim, descendant of Šangû Šamaš, Bēl-aḫḫē-iddina, son of Nabû-uballiṭ, and the scribe, Arad-Bēl, son of Bēl-ušallim, descendant of Adad-šamê. Sippar, month of Ajaru, eighteenth ⸢day,⸣ first year of Nergal-šarra-uṣur, king of Babylon. From the twentieth day of the month of Ajaru the house (will be) at their disposal.

101

BM 79363

1) ⸢x⸣ GÍN KÙ.BABBAR *šá* ^{Id}AMAR.UD-MU-ŠEŠ
2) ⸢A-*šú šá*⸣ ^{Id}AMAR.UD-DÙ-NUMUN A ^{I}*mu-kal-lim*
3) [...] [^{I}*la*]-*a-ba-ši* A-*šú šá* ^{I}TIN
4) [...] ^{I}A-*a* UD.10.KAM *šá* ITU.ŠE
5) [...] *ši*
6) [...] ⸢*x*⸣ *i* ITU.ŠE
7) [...] ⸢*xx*⸣ *i-nam-*[*din*]
8) [...][^{Id}AMAR.UD]-MU-ŠEŠ *e-ṭi-ir*
9) LÚ *mu-kin-nu* ^{I}*nad-na-a* A-*šú šá*
10) ^{I}NUNUZ-' A ^{I}*mu-kal-lim*
11) ^{Id}30-*ki-di-ri-'*
12) LÚ.SAG.LUGAL
13) *u* LÚ.ŠID ^{Id}EN-*na-din*-DUMU.UŠ A-*šú šá*
14) ^{I}⸢*kal-ba*⸣-*a* A ^{I}*mu-kal-lim*
15) TIN.TIR.KI ITU.ZÍZ UD.25.KAM
16) ⸢MU.3.⸣KAM ^{d}U+GUR-LUGAL-ŠEŠ
17) LUGAL TIN.TIR.KI

Translation

(Document concerning) ... shekels of silver, property of Marduk-šuma-uṣur, ⸢son of⸣ Marduk-bāni-zēri, descendant of Mukallim (and charged against?) [La]baši, son of Balāṭu [...] Aplâ. On the tenth day of the month of Addaru [...] month of Addaru he will del[iver] [the silver(?)] [Marduk]-šuma-uṣur has been paid [...] Witnesses (are) Nadnâ, son of Pir', descendant of Mukallim, Sin-kidiri', the royal official, and the scribe, Bēl-nādin-apli, son of [Kalbâ] descendant of Mukallim. Babylon, month of Šabaṭu, twenty-fifth day, ⌈third year⌉ of Nergal-šarra-uṣur, king of Babylon.

Commentary

14) The restoration of the personal name is based on the parallel in 32:12.

102

BM 74907

1) ⌈*x*⌉ MA.NA AN.BAR
2) KI.LÁ 10 ⌈*xx*⌉ *ta*
3) *kul-ba-a-ta*
4) [Id]AMAR.UD-SUR LÚ.SIMUG
5) *a-na* É.BABBAR.RA
6) *it-ta-din*
7) ITU.AB UD.16.KAM
8) MU.2.KAM
9) [d]U+GUR-LUGAL-ŠEŠ
10) LUGAL TIN.TIR.KI
11) *kul-ba-a-ṭa*
12) *ina* IGI [Id]EN-ŠEŠ.MEŠ-TIN
13) ⌈*xx*⌉ *da a ka*
14) [...] ⌈*xx*⌉ *tum*

Translation

Marduk-ēṭir, the smith, has given ... minas of iron, the weight of ten ... jars, to Ebabbar. Month of Ṭebetu, sixteenth day, second year of Nergal-šarra-uṣur, king of Babylon. The jars are at the disposal of Bēl-aḫḫē-bulliṭ [...].

103

BM 74926

1) KÙ.BABBAR ⌈*šá*⌉ [...] *a qa am na-šá* [...]

2) ITU.⌜GUD⌝ ⌜UD.x.⌝KAM MU.2.KAM ^{d}U+GUR-LUGAL-ŠEŠ LUGAL E.KI
3) 15 MA.NA KÙ.BABBAR *ḫa-a-ṭu*
4) 5 1/2 MA.NA 5 GÍN KI.LÁ 1-*it maš-šam-tum*
5) 5 *ka-sa-a-tu* 1-*en na-aḫ-ba-ṣi*
6) 3 1/2 MA.NA KI.LÁ 1-*it maš-sam-tum*
7) 2 *ka-sa-a-tu 1-it mu-*kas_5*-si-tum*
8) 6 MA.NA KI.LÁ 4 *ka-sa-a-tum*
9) 1-*en* ⌜*x*⌝ *ni ni* GAL.LA
10) [...] ⌜MA⌝`NA ⌜17⌝ GÍN KÙ.BABBAR KI.LÁ ⌜*x*⌝ *ka-sa-a-tum*
11) [...] *aḫ-pu-ú* 1-*it šá ḫi-il-ti*
12) [...] ⌜MA.NA⌝ 50 GÍN KI.LÁ 1-*it maš-šam-tum*
13) 1 MA.NA KI.LÁ *ú-di-e gan-gu-nu-tu*
14) *ḫa*-[*a*]-*tu* ⌜*x*⌝ *a* ⌜*x*⌝
15) PAP 44 MA.NA 3 GÍN [KÙ.BABBAR]

Translation

(Document concerning) silver ⌜which⌝ [...]. Month of ⌜Ajaru⌝, ... ⌜day,⌝ second year of Nergal-šarra-uṣur, king of Babylon. Fifteen minas (is) the stock of silver, five and one-half minas, five shekels (is) the weight of one utensil, five cups (and) one vessel; three and one-half minas (is) the weight of one utensil, two cups (and) one bowl (?); six minas (is) the weight of four cups (and) one large [...] minas, ⌜seventeen⌝ shekels of silver (is) the weight of [...] cups, [...]..., one utensil, [...] ⌜minas,⌝ fifty shekels, the weight of one utensil; one mina, the weight of a utensil(?) ... -- total of forty-four minas, three shekels [of silver].

Commentary

4,6,12) The word *maššamtu* (perhaps a bowl) is similar in rendering to *maššanu* (a wooden utensil) to be found in text 28:20-21.There, however, it is preceded by a GIŠ determinative.

5) For *naḫbaṣi* (*eine Ohlmühle*) see von Soden, AHw 714a.In our present context, however, the object is not made of stone, but instead of metal.

104

BM 75193

1) ⌜1⌝ (PI) 3 (BÁN) 2 SÌLA ŠE.BAR *kis-sat*

2) 3 ME 90 *iṣ-ṣur šá* É.MUŠEN.DÙ
3) *ina lìb-bi* 1 (PI) 1 (BÁN) *kis-sat* 60 ⌜*xx*⌝
4) ⌜25⌝ [...] *iṣ-ṣur* 5 ⌜NINDA⌝.HI.A
5) 1 (PI) 1 (BÁN) ŠE.BAR *kis-sat* 2 ME 11 ⌜SILÁ⌝ MEŠ
6) *ki-i* 2(BÁN) SILÁ 2 NINDA.ḪI.A
7) ⌜*xx*⌝ *kis-sat* UDU.NITÁ
8) 2 (BÁN) *a-na* GUD
9) 3 (BÁN) 1 SÌLA *a-na* É.EN.NUN-*ti*
10) 1 (BÁN) ^{I}*ri-mut*
11) 4 (PI) *saḫ-li*(!) (*text:me*)-*e*
12) PAP 1 GUR 3 (BÁN) ⌜ŠE.BAR⌝
13) TA É ^{d}*gu-la*
14) ITU.KIN UD.2.KAM MU.SAG.NAM.LUGAL.LA
15) [^{Id}U]+⌜GUR⌝-LUGAL-⌜ŠEŠ⌝
16) [LUGAL] TIN.TIR.KI

Translation

(Document concerning) ⌜one⌝ pi, twenty qa of barley, fodder for three hundred ninety birds from the fowl run. From this amount, one pi, six qa are fodder for sixty [...] ⌜twenty-five⌝ [...] birds, five ⌜loaves of bread⌝, one pi, six qa of barley (is) fodder for two hundred eleven ⌜female lambs⌝ instead of twelve qa (for) the lambs, two loaves of bread, [...] fodder for a ewe, twelve qa (are) for an ox, nineteen qa (are) for the prison, six qa (are for) Rīmūt, (and an additional) four pi of cress seeds(?)--- total of one *kurru*, eighteen qa of ⌜barley,⌝ (which) were brought from the temple of Gula. Month of Ululu, second day, accession year of [Nergal]-šarra-⌜uṣur,⌝ [king] of Babylon.

73 (BM 54179)

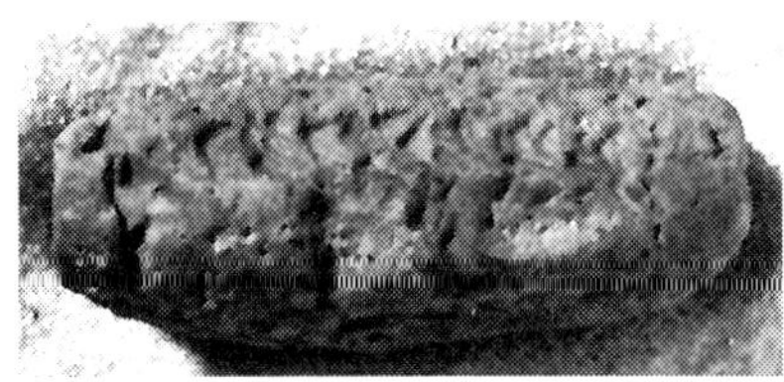

74 (BM 54180)

75 (BM 75968) obv.

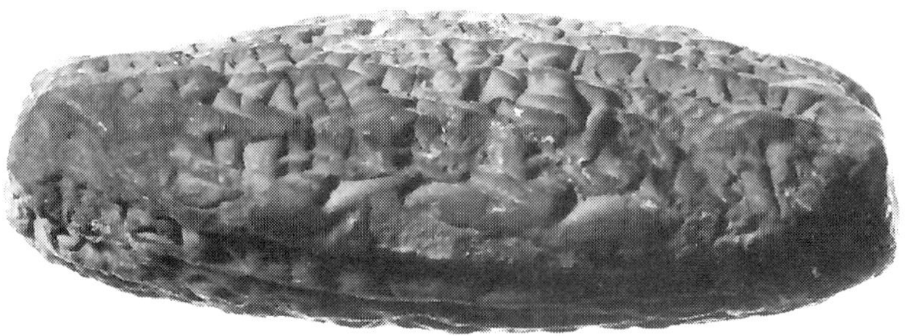

75 (BM 75968) rev.

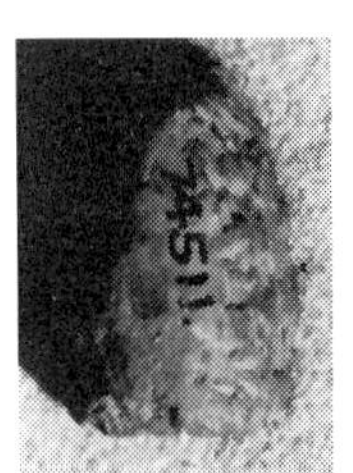

76 (BM 74511)

77 (BM 74495)

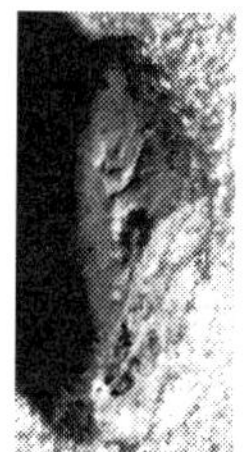

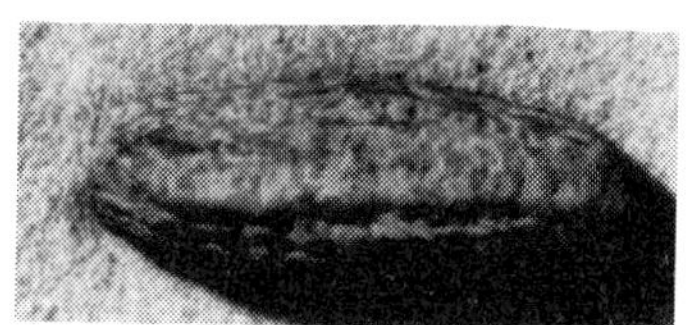

78 (BM 77626)

79 (BM 77637)

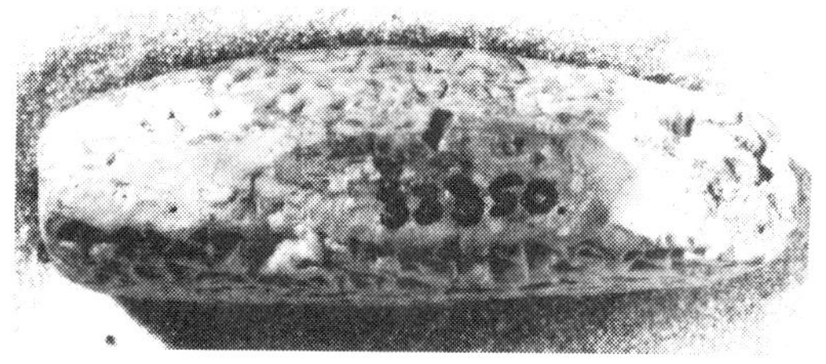

85 (BM 33350)

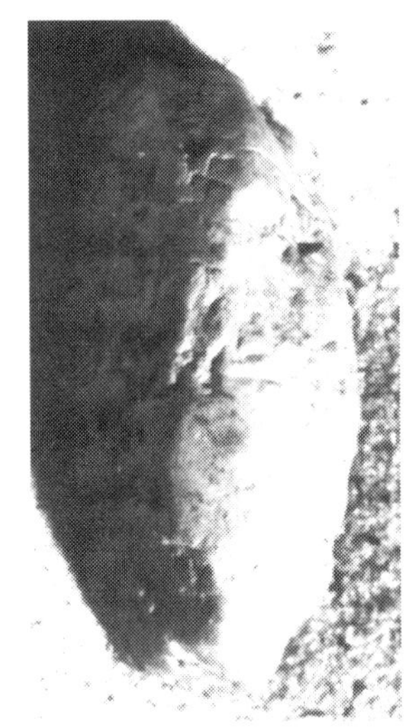

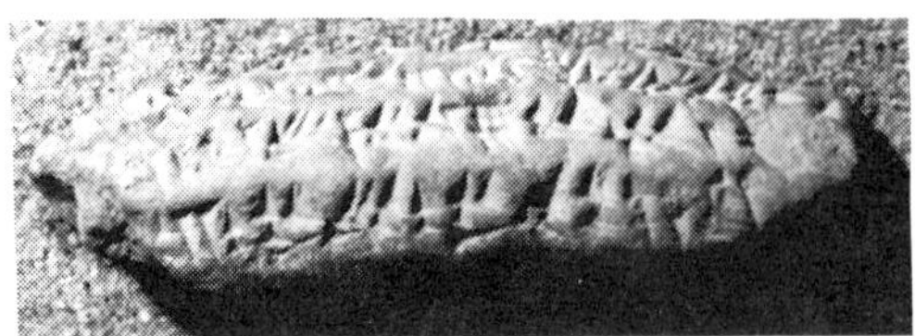

86 (BM 32602)

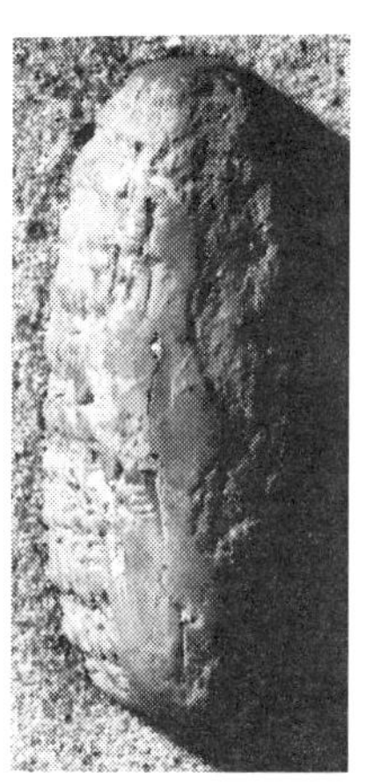

87 (BM 75509)

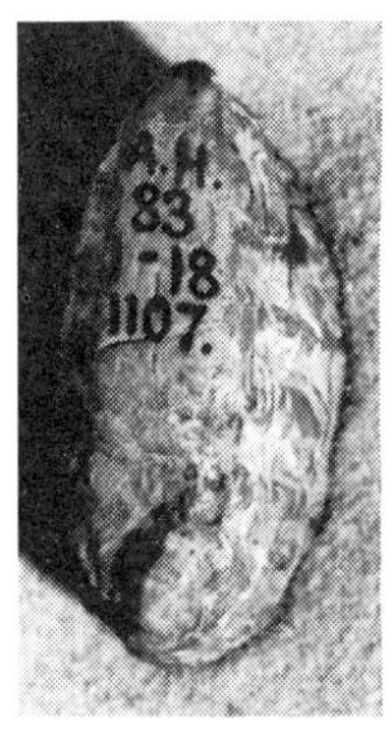

88 (BM 75757)

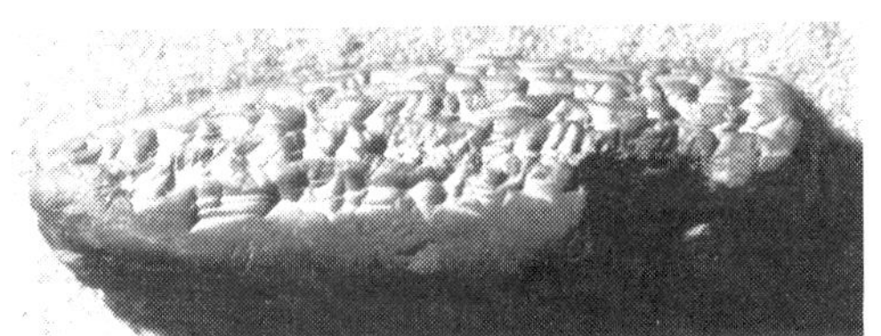

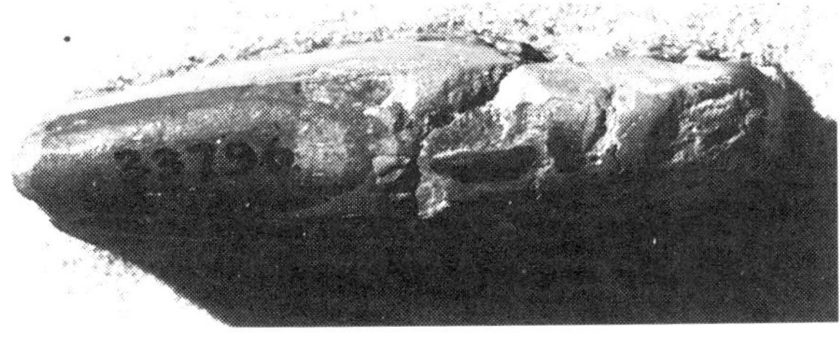

89 (BM 33796)

90 (BM 79569) obv.

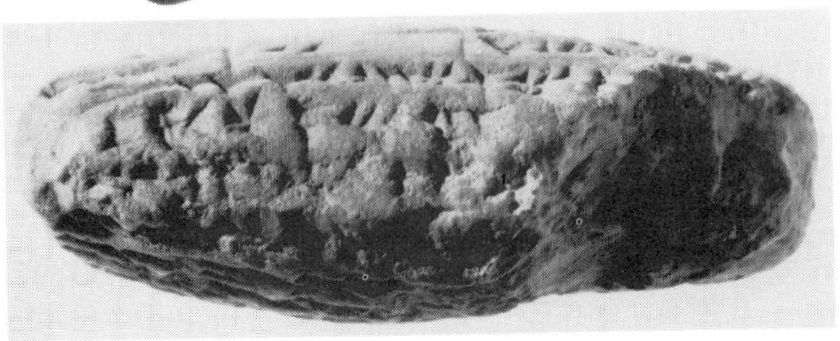

90 (BM 79569) rev.

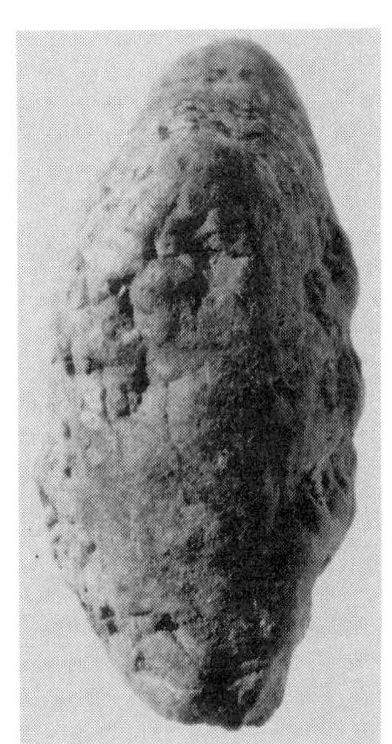

91 (BM 75489)

92 (BM 74953)

93 (BM 75285)

95 (BM 67012)

94 (BM 75181)

Photographs of Texts:
96 (BM 60 947) - 97 (BM 60 231) - 98 (BM 60 762)

99 (BM 75431)

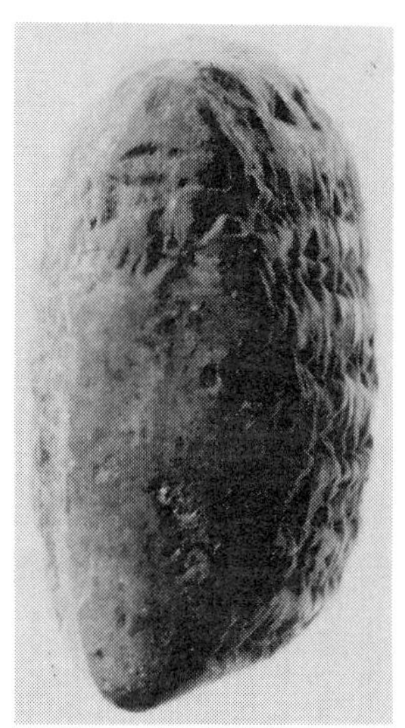

100 (BM 74938)

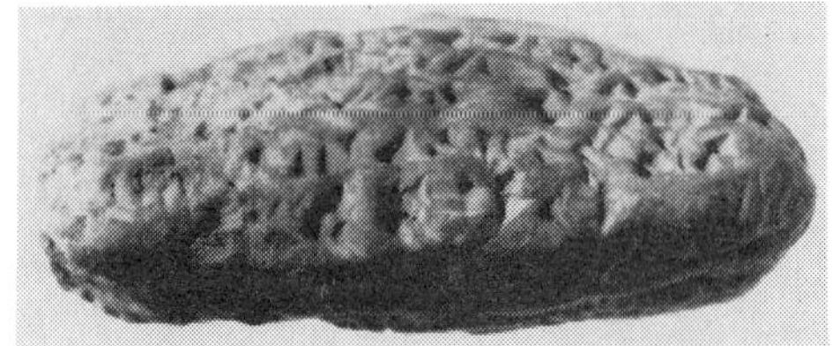

101 (BM 79363)

102 (BM 74907)

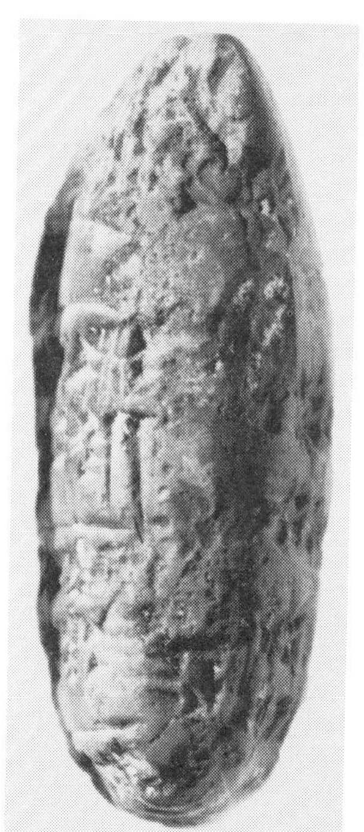

103 (BM 74926) obv.

103 (BM 74926) rev.

104 (BM 75193) obv.

104 (BM 75193) rev.

Ugarit-Verlag Münster

Ricarda-Huch-Straße 6, D-48161 Münster

Abhandlungen zur Literatur Alt-Syrien-Palästinas (ALASP)

Herausgeber: Manfried DIETRICH - Oswald LORETZ

Bd. 1 Manfried DIETRICH -Oswald LORETZ, *Die Keilalphabete. Die phönizisch-kanaanäischen und altarabischen Alphabete in Ugarit.* 1988 (ISBN 3-927120-00-6), 376 S., DM 89,--.

Bd. 2 Josef TROPPER, *Der ugaritische Kausativstamm und die Kausativbildungen des Semitischen. Eine morphologisch-semantische Untersuchung zum Š-Stamm und zu den umstrittenen nichtsibilantischen Kausativstämmen des Ugaritischen.* 1990 (ISBN 3-927120-06-5), 252 S., DM 68,--.

Bd. 3 Manfried DIETRICH - Oswald LORETZ, *Mantik in Ugarit. Keilalphabetische Texte der Opferschau - Omensammlungen - Nekromantie.* Mit Beiträgen von Hilmar W. Duerbeck - Jan-Waalke Meyer - Waltraut C. Seitter. 1990 (ISBN 3-927120-05-7), 320 S., DM 94,--.

Bd. 4 Manfried DIETRICH - Oswald LORETZ, *König Idrimi von Alalaḫ.*

Bd. 5 Fred RENFROE, *Arabic-Ugaritic Lexical Studies.* 1992 (ISBN 3-927120-09-X). 212 S., DM 74,--.

Bd. 6 Josef TROPPER, *Die Inschriften von Zincirli. Neue Edition und vergleichende Grammatik des phönizischen, samʾalischen und aramäischen Textkorpus.* 1993 (ISBN 3-927120-14-6). XII + 364 S., DM 105,--.

Bd. 7 *UGARIT - ein ostmediterranes Kulturzentrum im Alten Orient. Ergebnisse und Perspektiven der Forschung.* Vorträge gehalten während des Europäischen Kolloquiums am 11.-12. Februar 1993, hrsg. von Manfried DIETRICH und Oswald LORETZ. 1994 (ISBN 3-927120-17-0)(im Druck).

Ugaritisch-Biblische Literatur (UBL)

Herausgeber: Oswald LORETZ

Bd. 1 Oswald LORETZ, *Der Prolog des Jesaja-Buches (1,1-2,5). Ugaritologische und kolometrische Studien zum Jesaja-Buch* I. 1984 (ISBN 3-88733-054-4), 171 S., DM 49,80.

Bd. 2 Oswald LORETZ, *Psalm 29. Kanaanäische El- und Baaltraditionen in jüdischer Sicht.* 1984 (ISBN 3-88733-055-2), 168 S., DM 49,80 - Neuauflage UBL 7.

Bd. 3 Oswald LORETZ, *Leberschau, Sündenbock, Asasel in Ugarit und Israel. Leberschau und Jahwestatue in Psalm 27, Psalm 74.* 1985 (ISBN 3-88733-061-7), 136 S., DM 44,80.

Bd. 4 Oswald LORETZ, *Regenritual und Jahwetag im Joelbuch. Kanaanäischer Hintergrund, Kolometrie, Aufbau und Symbolik eines Prophetenbuches.* 1986 (ISBN 3-88733-068-4), 189 S., DM 59,80.

Bd. 5 Oswald LORETZ - Ingo KOTTSIEPER, *Colometry in Ugaritic and Biblical Poetry. Introduction, Illustrations and Topical Bibliography.* 1987 (ISBN 3-88733-074-9), 166 pp., DM 49,80.

Bd. 6 Oswald LORETZ, *Die Königspsalmen. Die altorientalisch-kanaanäische Königstradition in jüdischer Sicht.* Teil I. *Ps. 20; 21; 72; 101 und 144.* Mit einem Beitrag von Ingo Kottsieper zu *Papyrus Amherst.* 1988 (ISBN 3-927120-01-4), 261 S., DM 78,--.

Bd. 7 Oswald LORETZ, *Ugarit-Texte und Thronbesteigungspsalmen. Die Metamorphose des Regenspenders Baal-Jahwe (Ps. 24,7-10; 29; 47; 93; 95-100 sowie Ps. 77,17-20; 114)* -Erweiterte Auflage von UBL 2. 1984-. 1988 (ISBN 3-927120-04-9), 550 S., DM 90,--.

Bd. 8 Marjo C.A. KORPEL, *A Rift in the Clouds. Ugaritic and Hebrew Descriptions of the Divine*. 1990 (ISBN 3-927120-07-3), 736 S., DM 105,--.

Bd. 9 Manfried DIETRICH - Oswald LORETZ, *"Yahwe und seine Aschera". Anthropomorphes Kultbild in Mesopotamien, Ugarit, Israel - Das biblische Bilderverbot*. 1992 (ISBN 3-927120-08-1), 220 S., DM 74,--.

Bd. 10 Marvin H. POPE, *Probative Pontificating in Ugaritic and Biblical Literature - Collected Essays*. Ed. by Mark S. SMITH. 1994 (ISBN 3-927120-15-4), xvi + 406 S., DM 106,--.

Altertumskunde des Vorderen Orients (AVO)

Archäologische Studien zur Kultur und Geschichte des Alten Orients

Herausgeber: Manfried DIETRICH - Oswald LORETZ

Mitwirkende: Nadja Cholidis - Maria Krafeld-Daugherty - Ellen Rehm

Bd. 1 Nadja CHOLIDIS, *Möbel in Ton - Untersuchungen zur archäologischen und religionsgeschichtlichen Bedeutung der Terrakottamodelle von Tischen, Stühlen und Betten aus dem Alten Orient*. 1992 (ISBN 3-927120-10-3), XII + 323 S. + 46 Taf., DM 116,--.

Bd. 2 Ellen REHM, *Der Schmuck der Achämeniden*. 1992 (ISBN 3-927120-11-1), X + 358 S. + 107 Taf., DM 122,--

Bd. 3 Maria KRAFELD-DAUGHERTY, *Wohnen im Alten Orient - Eine Untersuchung zur Verwendung von Räumen in altorientalischen Wohnhäusern*. 1994 (ISBN 3-927120-16-2), x + 404 S. + 41 Tafeln (im Druck).

Bd. 4 *Beschreiben und Deuten in der Archäologie des Alten Orients. Festschrift für Ruth MAYER-OPIFICIUS mit Beiträgen von Freunden und Schülern.* Hrsg. von Manfried DIETRICH und Oswald LORETZ. 1994 (ISBN 3-927120-18-9), XI + 345 S. mit 256 Abb., DM 116,--.

Eikon

Beiträge zur antiken Bildersprache

Herausgeber: Klaus STÄHLER

Bd. 1 Klaus STÄHLER, *Griechische Geschichtsbilder klassischer Zeit*. 1992 (ISBN 3-927120-12-X), X + 120 S. + 8 Taf., DM 39,80.

Bd. 2 Klaus STÄHLER, *Form und Funktion: Kunstwerke als politisches Ausdrucksmittel*. 1994 (ISBN 3-927120-13-8), X + 115 S. mit 143 Abb. (im Druck)

Bei einem Abonnement der Reihen liegen die angegebenen Preise um ca. 15% tiefer.

Auslieferung durch -
Distributed by:
Cornelsen Verlagsgesellschaft
Postfach 8729
D-33609 Bielefeld

Distributor to North America:
Eisenbrauns, Inc.
Publishers and Booksellers
POB 275
Winona Lake, Ind. 46590
U.S.A.